RESISTANCE

NECHAMA TEC

RESISTANCE

*Jews and Christians Who
Defied the Nazi Terror*

OXFORD
UNIVERSITY PRESS

OXFORD
UNIVERSITY PRESS

Oxford University Press is a department of the University of Oxford.
It furthers the University's objective of excellence in research, scholarship,
and education by publishing worldwide.

Oxford   New York
Auckland   Cape Town   Dar es Salaam   Hong Kong   Karachi
Kuala Lumpur   Madrid   Melbourne   Mexico City   Nairobi
New Delhi   Shanghai   Taipei   Toronto

With offices in
Argentina   Austria   Brazil   Chile   Czech Republic   France   Greece
Guatemala   Hungary   Italy   Japan   Poland   Portugal   Singapore
South Korea   Switzerland   Thailand   Turkey   Ukraine   Vietnam

Oxford is a registered trademark of Oxford University Press
in the UK and certain other countries.

Published in the United States of America by
Oxford University Press
198 Madison Avenue, New York, NY 10016

© Nechama Tec 2013

Library of Congress Cataloging-in-Publication Data
Tec, Nechama, author.
Resistance:Jews and Christians who defied the Nazi terror/Nechama Tec.
pages ; cm
Includes bibliographical references and index.
ISBN 978-0-19-973541-9
1. World War, 1939–1945—Jewish resistance—Poland. 2. World War,
1939–1945—Underground movements—Poland. 3. Holocaust, Jewish
(1939–1945)—Poland. 4. Poland—History—Occupation, 1939–1945. I. Title.
D810.J4T426 2013
940.53'438—dc23
2012041864

1 3 5 7 9 8 6 4 2
Printed in the United States of America
on acid-free paper

To my husband, Dr. Leon Tec, who encouraged me to write and never to stop.

Contents

Introduction: At the Edge of Nowhere 1

CHAPTER 1   Learning How to Oppose 16

CHAPTER 2   The Ghettos 47

CHAPTER 3   The Forests 84

CHAPTER 4   The Concentration Camps 122

CHAPTER 5   The Couriers 158

CHAPTER 6   The Special Case of Jan Karski 181

Conclusion: "Not Alone" 191

Acknowledgments 197
Notes 199
Works Cited 215
Index 231

Introduction

At the Edge of Nowhere

I came to the study of resistance indirectly, through my long involvement with Holocaust research and teaching. As a frequent lecturer on the subject of German policies of Jewish annihilation, I have always been eager to take audience questions. The more challenging the queries, the more I welcome them. And precisely because I look forward to questions and the discussions they stimulate, I became puzzled that certain queries made me feel uncomfortable and even resentful. Invariably the questions were variations of the following: *Why didn't the Jews strike back at their oppressors? Why did the Jews submit so passively to the German assaults upon their dignity and their lives? Why did the Jews refuse to fight?* Woven into the fabric of these queries was the cliché that Jews went like sheep to their slaughter. At bottom, the questions involved Jewish resistance during World War II, in which scholarly interest grew during the 1960s and has continued to this day. However, nearly a half-century of exploration of this topic has still let stand, unchallenged, a myth.

It crossed my mind that these troubling questions might have been fueled by ignorance. Yet, rather than make an effort to fill the implicit gaps in knowledge behind them, I dismissed the questions as rhetorical. Those who posed them did not seem to expect answers. Each contained unsubstantiated claims but also implicit assumptions. One was that the opportunities to resist were present, but that Jews simply failed to take advantage of them, and since the

Jews took no advantage of such opportunities, they themselves were partly to blame for what happened to them. In a roundabout way then, assumptions about Jewish passivity led to the conclusion that Jews had become collaborators in their own destruction. This idea effectively absolves the perpetrators of the responsibilities for the crimes they had committed against the Jewish people.

Similar kinds of "blame the victim" accusations have been leveled against a variety of others. Usually, however, they appear within the context of discussions about racism, sexism, slavery, and, of course, anti-Semitism.

Throughout history a wide range of accusations—sometimes concealed innocently as complaints—have been directed at the Jews. If only they would stop dressing in conspicuous ways, no one would bother them. If only they were not so greedy, manipulative, and loud, they would be fine. If only Jews were not communists, capitalists, and religious fanatics. The list seems endless, particularly when presented by anti-Semites. History shows how pernicious this mindset was and the tragic consequences it had.

My interest in Jewish resistance during the Holocaust grew out of these persistent queries. Discussions about Jewish resistance are burdened by their close association to queries such as these, presented as facts, but in reality driven by unsubstantiated assumptions. Similar to them are assertions about Jewish complicity. They continue to surface in current debates. As I delved into these issues, I became convinced that neither these assumptions, nor their implications, could be settled during a question-and-answer session. They needed to be clarified through systematic, comparative examinations of historical facts. This project sets out to do just that. In addition, it explores some of the contextual sources connected to queries, assumptions, accusations, and counteraccusations. The results could be of value to Holocaust scholars, but they are also intended to address those questions from the audience about Jewish and non-Jewish resistance, in particular.

At the end of the war, conspicuously absent was any attention to Jewish resistance. Similarly, Jews as a category of victims did not even appear in the many postwar court deliberations. In 1945–46, at the International Military Tribunal the Jews were not discussed as a distinct entity. Also, at the subsequent Nuremberg Trials (1947–48), they were not considered as a special category of victims. Jews appeared only in individual documents and only when specific charges were made against the German occupation.

By the 1950s and beyond, historians who had examined the destruction of European Jewry concentrated on the perpetrators rather than the victims. Later on, when attention was paid to these victims, they were identified simply as Jews. There was little if any discussion about the different fates of Jews, nor any particulars—age, sex, or nationality. This inattention should not come as a surprise, given that the enormity of the German crimes overshadowed their victims. Perhaps, too, it should not come as a surprise that early historians of that period were primarily interested in learning about the forces that caused such unprecedented destruction. Only after the basic outlines of the processes of Jewish annihilation had been explored did scholars begin to notice the less visible parts to the puzzle, namely, the different categories and subcategories of victims.

And that included Jews who tried to resist the annihilation. Under the German occupation, continuous oppression and targeted abuses of diverse local populations was met by three distinct reactions: submission, resistance, and collaboration. Each of these responses varied with time, place, and specific populations. Submission was the most common reaction. Resistance was the exception. Severe German retaliations limited resistance activities of the conquered majorities. However, the threat of retaliation did not affect the majorities' resentments toward their occupiers. Passive or not, they saw the mere existence of organized opposition among them as a validation of that resentment.

As for collaboration with the occupiers, it was more common than most people were willing to admit. Denials about collaboration grew with Germany's approaching defeat. But not all conquered groups had real options to become collaborators. Exceptions applied to groups destined for destruction—the Jews and the Gypsies. It took a while for some to realize that, unlike their neighbors, they might only be collaborators fleetingly. The more victorious the Third Reich was, the more willing some among the occupied peoples were to serve their German masters, who used them against those whom they perceived as special "threats" to the Third Reich. Hence, anti-Semitic countries, such as Latvia, Lithuania, and, in part, Poland, provided fertile ground for active collaboration with Nazi policies. As German defeat loomed on the horizon later in the war, many of the collaborators attempted to switch sides. Similarly, when confronted with severe reprisals from Jewish and non-Jewish undergrounds, collaborators were more likely to retreat from their pro-German duties. Nevertheless, collaborators were recruited from all groups, even Jews, however short-lived the advantages for Jewish collaborators, a fact which many of them did not understand.[1]

Rather than collaboration or submission, the subject of this book is resistance, best defined as a set of activities motivated by the desire to thwart, limit, undermine, or end the exercise of oppression over the oppressed. Toward the end of 1943, as German defeat grew ever more likely, opposition to the Nazi occupation became a more attractive option for local populations. But by 1943, most Jews in Eastern Europe had already been murdered or forced into concentration camps. Those who wanted to stand up to the Germans had little time. Till the very end, the Germans continued to vigorously pursue their policies of annihilation. The fact that Jewish and other groups had different resistance chronologies does not necessarily invalidate comparisons between them and other national resistance groups.

The emergence of resistance is contingent on the presence of several conditions. One of these central conditions is oppression itself; without oppression there would be no reason to resist. For it stands to reason that the more oppressed people are, the greater is their need to resist. Yet, at the same time, the more oppressed people become, the less capable of resistance they are. Thus, there seems to be a paradoxical relationship between the oppressor and the victims. German oppression was specifically designed to strip Jews of their resources and to undermine their ability to resist.

The second condition is cooperation, which is key to facilitating resistance. It is indeed the key to resistance itself. I have written in the past about resilience, the ability some had under horrific conditions not to yield to despair and passivity—those who could find some inner core of self-reliance to maintain their sense of themselves. But resistance is more than not submitting—it is active and requires taking action, and that means cooperation with others. Resilience is individual in orientation; resistance assumes others. Under German occupation, the emerging Jewish leaders searched in vain for cooperative parties. The Allies, for example, took virtually no interest in the plight of Jews. This indifference translated into a disregard for all known pleas, including those for arms and ammunition. Throughout the war, Jews experienced chronic shortages of the means to resist, their needs far more dire than other resistance groups.

Topography also affected the emergence and success of resistance efforts. Mountains and/or forests increased the opportunities for opposition; flat lands diminished the odds of success. By and large Eastern Europe had much more terrain suitable for this purpose than Western Europe. In part, the relative inaccessibility of woodlands and mountains made them alternatively useful as sustaining ground for rebellion and as havens for some of the persecuted.

No matter how favorable the conditions, resistance required time to mature, for it took time for cooperation and setting to result in the establishment of a strategic base of operation. Such a base, by providing adequate space, promotes mobility. Guerrillas need to vanish and blend into the local population. Making that possible, a strategic base helps compensate for the relatively small numbers of rebels and for their inadequate supply of arms. Few, if any, Jewish resisters were so situated. Confinement in ghettos automatically deprived them of the ability to cooperate. Only underground couriers, most of whom were women, maintained exchanges of information between these ghettos. And these couriers, like other Jewish resisters, could count on the supportive attitudes of local populations. Apart from a handful of Christians who risked their lives to save Jews, local collaborators undermined the chances of success.

In addition to established bases of operation, effective leadership and a steady supply of arms were two additional preconditions for success. Several national underground organizations maintained direct contact with their political leaders who had left the country and established governments in exile. These leaders supplied their undergrounds with both tactical advice and arms. In some cases, arms reached a national underground through the Allies.

Here again, Eastern European Jews were at a huge disadvantage. Jewish leaders who left Eastern Europe in 1939 failed to organize a unified front. Moreover, many Jewish leaders had already been murdered during the first stage of the German occupation. Of the remaining prewar leaders, some were recruited by the occupation authorities into the German-mandated Jewish Councils, the Judenrat. With continuously changing Council membership, powerless and often ambiguous toward resistance, only a few of these Judenrat leaders wholeheartedly supported the Jewish underground. The existing leadership gap was filled in part by the young heads of the local branches of the various youth organizations. Most of these underground commanders were idealistic and eager to protect and fight for the Jewish people. However, they were also inexperienced.

Interest in resistance under the German occupation during World War II continues to grow. To gather evidence about the subject, researchers have been exploring the complexities imbedded in the very idea of what it means to resist.

As I mentioned earlier, I was drawn to the issue by unexamined assertions about Jewish passivity and concurrent assumptions about Jewish responsibility. A closer view at the origin and history of why Jews supposedly did not resist promises a better understanding of this mythology.

The phrase "like sheep to the slaughter" first appeared in a 1942 New Year's Manifesto published in the Vilna ghetto. It was an official proclamation, collectively created by the leadership of several ghetto youth movements. This document boldly stated that the Germans were engaged in the systematic annihilation of European Jewry. It further emphasized that in view of this murderous goal, the only option open to the Jews was resistance. In short, the New Year's Manifesto contained two interdependent parts. First, it flatly stated that it could no longer be ignored that the Germans aimed at the total destruction of European Jewry. In this regard, it was the first unequivocal statement of what was happening. Second, in light of this understanding, it urged Jews not to follow German orders. Specifically, the Vilna ghetto inmates were implored not to assemble for deportations.[2] The writer of this final version of the document, Aba Kovner, a 23-year-old poet and one of the Hashomer Hatzair leaders, was calling for resistance. The original document was a plea for Jews to unite in opposition and therefore in resistance.

In fact, three weeks after the issuing of this proclamation, several of the Vilna youth movements united in establishing the Vilna Partisan Organization (FPO).[3] In various Jewish quarters, the assertion that the Germans were engaged in exterminating Jews met with some disbelief. Even certain members of the Jewish underground movement in Vilna and in other ghettos had a hard time accepting that this in fact was happening. Kovner himself assessed the collectively created proclamation, "as a battle cry to people confronted with death." The historian Dina Porat, now Chief Historian at Yad Vashem, who has researched these issues, concluded that at the time Kovner had relied "on intuition." The moment had called for a strong statement and he had opted for "an uncompromising formulation, daring to speak about the destruction of all European

Jews."[4] Yet this anguished call to stand up to their enemy turned into an accusation against the Jewish people. When and how did this happen?

It took years for this January 1942 proclamation to morph into a general statement of Jews' complicity in their own destruction. Bruno Bettelheim was an early promoter of such views. Bettelheim's connection to the Third Reich originated in his 1938 arrest in Vienna. Charged with political transgressions, Bettelheim, who was Jewish, was incarcerated in two concentration camps, Dachau and Buchenwald. In 1939, a year later, an American benefactor sent him a US immigration visa. In short order, his release from the concentration camp and a trip to America followed. In the United States, Bettelheim became a well-established psychoanalyst. His wartime experiences and professional work became closely intertwined.

In 1943, in a long article, Bettelheim allegedly documents his life in the German concentration camps. Claiming for himself the role of an objective observer, he emphasized the slavelike docility of concentration camp inmates. His article does not differentiate the prisoners by country of origin or religion. During the period of his incarceration, 1938–39, all concentration camp inmates were held on charges stemming from alleged political and/or criminal transgressions.[5] Only from 1942 on were Jews brought to the expanding concentration camps solely because they were Jews and with the goal of extermination.

In the early 1960s, two more Bettelheim publications appeared, featuring extensive discussions of Jewish behavior during the Holocaust. Figuring prominently in these works are assertions that Jews' passivity had contributed significantly to their doom. In making his case, Bettelheim points to the case of Anne Frank, her family, and the Jews who had shared their hiding place in Holland. He argues that "the Franks could have provided themselves with a gun or two, had they wished. They could have shot down at least one or two of the 'green police' who came for them. There was no surplus of such police. The loss of an SS with every Jew arrested would have noticeably hindered the functioning of the police state. The fate of the Franks would not have been any different because they all died anyway except for Anne's father, (but)…they could have sold their lives dearly instead of walking to their death."[6]

Bettelheim continues in a similar vein, disapproving of the Franks' selection of their hiding place, referring to it as "a trap without an outlet." In effect, he blames the hidden Jews for failing to build an emergency escape passage, through which at least some of them could "have tried to escape while one or two of the men blocked and defended one of the small entrances with a homemade barricade."[7]

Such objections underscore how little Bettelheim understood about the insurmountable obstacles Jews had to overcome when trying to find shelter in the Christian world. Guns were unattainable. Virtually every Jew who attempted to purchase weapons failed, and many who tried were murdered in the attempt. Moreover, Jews who wanted to hide among Christians could not find shelter. The Franks and those who joined them were a select minority. Suggestions about their finding more suitable hiding places assume there were options, which there were not. Actually, finding any hiding place was virtually a miracle. But, despite these serious misconceptions, as a former victim of the Nazis, as a successful psychoanalyst, as a talented writer, as someone who had presented himself as a Holocaust survivor, Bettelheim was listened to.[8]

Support for Bettelheim's interpretations came from Hannah Arendt's 1963 book, *Eichmann in Jerusalem*. Concentrating on the wartime Jewish Councils, Arendt concludes that the Germans "created Jewish Councils who almost without exception, cooperated in one way or another with the Nazis."[9] She continues that "to a Jew, this role of Jewish leaders in the destruction of their own people is undoubtedly the darkest chapter of the whole dark story [the Holocaust]. It had been known about before, but it has now been exposed, for the first time, in all its pathetic and sordid detail by Raoul Hilberg [in *The Destruction of the European Jews*]." Without citing specific page references, Arendt offers vivid descriptions of a wide range of humiliating, extremely cruel anti-Jewish measures, which culminated in Jewish deportations to various concentration camps. She goes on, focusing upon the complicity of the Jewish Councils, claiming that, "In the matter of cooperation, [with the Germans] there was no distinction between the highly assimilated Jewish communities of central and western Europe and the Yiddish speaking masses of the East....In the Nazi-inspired, but not Nazi-dictated manifestoes they issued, we still can sense how they enjoyed their new power."[10]

Hilberg's manuscript, the above-mentioned *The Destruction of the European Jews*, served as a source for her interpretation of the wartime activities of the wartime Jewish Councils. Hilberg himself objected to Arendt's interpretation of his research. As a co-editor of the Czerniakow wartime diary, the head of the Judenrat in Warsaw,

Hilberg's views about the Jewish Councils, at times critical, were far more nuanced and complex.[11]

But Arendt was persistent. For additional "confirmation" of her views, Arendt turned to the prominent Jewish Dutch historian, Louis de Jong. Supposedly, from her exposure to de Jong, she had concluded that the Judenrat in wartime Holland, "quickly became an instrument of the Nazis." We as readers, however, are never told where this statement came from. Nor did my familiarity with quite a number of de Jong's publications direct me to any of these sources. Arendt continues writing that out of the 103,000 Dutch Jews who were deported to Auschwitz, with the cooperation of the Jewish Council, only 519 returned. Next, still presumably relying on de Jong, she notes that of the Dutch Jews who lived illegally in the forbidden Aryan world, 40 to 50 percent of them managed to survive the war. Finally, in a strange twist of logic, she blames the Jewish Council of Holland—for both the death of the Dutch Jews in Auschwitz and for the fact that not more of them had escaped into the Aryan world, where more could have eluded being murdered.[12]

Hilberg's seminal contribution to the Holocaust literature, published first in 1961, retains its prominent position to this day. The author has revised his book twice, most recently in 2003. Each new edition has benefited from the infusion of additional historical evidence. Hilberg has consistently emphasized that his work concentrates on the perpetrators, the structures, and processes they employed as they pursued the annihilation of European Jewry. In the recently revised version, as in the two earlier ones, Hilberg states that "[p]reventive attacks, armed resistance and revenge were most completely absent from Jewish exilic history...for the Diaspora Jews; acts of armed opposition had become isolated and episodic. Force was not to be a Jewish strategy again until Jewish life was reconstituted in a Jewish state...during the catastrophe of 1933–45; the instances of opposition were small and few. Above all, whenever and whichever they occurred, they were actions of last (never first) resort."[13]

Hilberg assumes an absence of Jewish resistance and attributes it to the long tradition of Jewish passivity. Introducing himself as an expert researcher on the perpetrators of the Holocaust, he nevertheless frequently returns to the topic of Jewish resistance. But Hilberg's descriptions of Jewish uprisings are consistently brief. Critical facts are missing from these accounts. It must be a daunting task to describe events which had required months of preparations and fit them into a single paragraph of a sentence or two. Such brief treatments of complex topics cannot do justice to their historical significance. In fact, Hilberg's comments about Jewish resistance show consistent patterns of omissions about central facts and circumstances.

No matter how complex or perilous Jewish resistance efforts were, Hilberg never discusses the obstacles which Jews had to overcome, nor the great sacrifices they were ready to make and made. Similarly, he never bothers to describe the ingenious strategies that were continuously devised by the Jews in order to survive. Hilberg's special emphasis is illustrated by his statement that, "[m]easured in German casualties, Jewish armed opposition shrinks into insignificance." [14] Hilberg's concluding remarks about Jewish underground operations consistently repeat how inconsequential Jewish resistance was because so few Germans were killed. In a variety of ways, over and over again, he stresses that Jewish resistance failed to diminish Germany's overall military power.

He is right. The Jews were never in a position to undermine or diminish the effectiveness of the German Army. Still, those Jews who stood up to their oppressors were realistic both about their limited aims and the expected consequences of their opposition. They were aware of German superior power just as they were aware of their own powerlessness. Through their opposition, nonetheless, these resisters tried to achieve a certain measure of autonomy, such as by choosing their ways of dying. What they wanted was to die fighting. Through disobedience, they resisted the Germans' brutality.

Is it appropriate to evaluate Jewish or any other kinds of resistance only in terms of how much concrete damage it had inflicted upon its enemy? Perhaps it should also be examined in terms of the moral effects it might have had upon the resisters themselves, upon the majority of the victims, most of whom could not be directly involved with any underground movements?

Some light might be thrown upon these and other questions by describing an encounter that happened in Warsaw during the 25th commemoration of the Warsaw ghetto uprising. It was an encounter between two men, a journalist who covered this event and Yitzhak Zuckerman, the second in command of the Warsaw ghetto uprising. The journalist asked Zuckerman what kinds of strategic lessons have been learned from the Warsaw ghetto uprising. Zuckerman replied, "I don't think there is any need to analyze the uprising in military terms. This was a war of less than a thousand people against a mighty army and no one doubted how it was likely to turn out.... If there is a school to study the *human spirit*, there it should be a major subject. The really important things were inherent in the force shown by Jewish youths, after years of degradation, to rise up against their destroyers and determine what death they would choose: Treblinka or Uprising. I don't know if there is a standard to measure that." [15]

Bettelheim, Arendt, and Hilberg came to their respective views from diverse directions, bringing with them a variety of experiences, perceptions, and conclusions. And yet, rather surprisingly, with some qualifications, their overall interpretations about Jewish resistance and Jewish Councils reveal only limited differences. Bettelheim and Arendt conclude that the Jews were passive, and in a real sense they had given up their opportunities to stand up to the Germans. Through their refusal to resist they had cooperated in the destruction of the Jewish people.

Both Bettelheim and Arendt present their arguments as if these were based on facts.[16] In reality, Bettelheim's discussions rely on hypothetical images and value judgments, not on facts. Arendt's discussions also grew out of a particular context. Some were closely related to her journalistic assignment—covering the Eichmann trial in Jerusalem. Relying on personal views rather than on factual materials, Arendt introduced the concept of the "banality of evil," [17] through which she asserts that human beings are capable of assuming roles of both victims and murderers.

Arendt's assumption met with strong oppositions from Primo Levi. As a former underground fighter, an Auschwitz prisoner, a survivor, and a respected thinker and writer, Levi argued that in the banality of evil Arendt was confusing the roles of victims and murderers. He wrote: "I do not know and it does not much interest me to know, whether in my depths there lurks a murderer, but I do know that I was a guiltless victim and I was not a murderer. I know that the murderers existed, not only in Germany, and still exist, retired or on active duty, and that to confuse them with their victims is a moral disease or an aesthetic affectation, or a sinister sign of complicity, above all in the precious service rendered intentionally or not to the negators of truth." [18]

Hilberg's conclusions are more ambiguous. When it comes to the idea about Jewish wartime passivity, as expressed through an absence of Jewish resistance, the differences between Bettelheim, Arendt, and Hilberg are minimal. Nevertheless, their respective arguments vary. While Bettelheim and Arendt simply assume that there are facts behind their assertions, Hilberg is concerned about checking the veracity of his conclusion. Relevant here is the fact that Hilberg's views come from his particular definition of Jewish resistance. As we have seen, for him the existence of resistance, particularly Jewish resistance, is contingent on its effectiveness in reducing the strength of the powerful oppressors, the Germans. This means that he focuses purely and narrowly on armed resistance. Resistance exists only if it achieved its intended goals—a diminished or defeated enemy.

Facts do not necessarily speak for themselves. Researchers give to their facts voices and view them through particular lenses. In social science, in particular, facts are easily undermined by the researchers' value judgments. Needless to say, this is more likely to happen when, for a variety of reasons, researchers are more devoted to their own value judgments than to empirical evidence.

Not surprisingly, inevitably, the concept of Jewish passivity, and by extension complicity in the systematic destruction of European Jewry, eventually did come under attack. Prominent among these attacks was Nathan Eck's lengthy 1967 article.[19] Such objections led to a mixture of history, polemics, and myths in much of what has been written about Jewish passivity and its accompanying accusations.[20]

One of the results was the emergence of new definitions of what resistance or underground opposition meant. By itself the term "underground movement" suggests an organized entity. In fact, most publications on the topic refer to collective resistance forms. These in turn are further differentiated into armed and unarmed, spiritual and non-spiritual, urban and rural, as well as many other dichotomies. When observed directly, all underground activities were dynamic rather than static, appearing under many guises. They were fluid. Moreover, resisters could simultaneously engage in a variety of acts, suggesting that the many varieties of resistance were not necessarily mutually exclusive. The multiplicity of forms, and their transformations and flexibility, underscore the complexity of the subject, and even hint at contradictions.

Frequently "resistance" conjures up images of actual combat. In reality armed confrontations between oppressors and their victims are rare. Under the German occupation most opposition involved hit and run tactics by resisters. For example, urban national resistance to the Germans frequently focused on the collection and dissemination of information, on forging documents, and on the accumulation of arms. The few actual armed uprisings occurred late, like the 1944 revolt in Paris, when the Allies were already at the gate. Another example is the August 1944 Warsaw uprising, which ended with the destruction of the city and an estimated death toll of over two hundred thousand Poles. In fact, a consistent policy of most leaders of national underground movements was to prevent premature uprisings. Correctly, these leaders assessed early uprisings as suicidal gestures.[21]

Given the German goal of Jewish annihilation, some scholars have argued that any Jewish effort to stay alive, and any and all efforts to undermine the Nazi goals, qualified as a form of resistance. Others, however, believe that this definition is too broad and that it would cloud our understanding of the subject. From another perspective, Jewish day-to-day survival efforts are an order of activity very different from derailing trains or participating in an armed uprising. Attempting to live represented resisting death, not resisting an oppressor. Some of these objections seem valid; others less so. A compromise is possible.

Collective humanitarian activities on behalf of others, such as those in the ghetto, required extraordinary moral strength. Such efforts contributed to the perpetuation of Jewish life, while denying Nazi policies of annihilation. Organized and selfless attempts to protect others do constitute resistance of a kind, even if they do not result in concrete rewards. They affirm moral values. A more realistic and inclusive definition of resistances should include a range of prohibited armed and unarmed activities, such as: humane acts on behalf of others, the collection of prohibited historical evidence, and the rescuing of the persecuted.

Review of the Holocaust literature on resistance provides insights into how some assumptions about Jewish resistance evolved and endured. Philip Friedman, for one, questioned the view of Jewish Councils as contributors to Jewish destruction. A Polish Jew and historian, Friedman left a lasting impact on Holocaust research. In his relatively short career, Friedman covered a wide range of topics, including Jewish resistance, Jewish Councils, gentiles who rescued Jews, ghettos, and many more. His research concentrates on the victims rather than on the perpetrators. He had a keen awareness about the complexity of wartime history and an equally keen sense about its moral dilemmas. Friedman's research echoes a position taken by the prominent wartime historian Emanuel Ringelblum, who insisted that all of Jewish history—the admirable and the less admirable—must be recorded. Indeed, Friedman stayed close to the empirical evidence, consistently warning against rush conclusions. His research about the Jewish Councils carefully distinguished different kinds of Judenrat groups. His findings show how varied these Councils were, ranging from the heroic to the collaborationist, therefore questioning any conclusions about Jewish complicity in their wartime destruction.[22]

In 1977 came Isaiah Trunk's pathbreaking research about the Judenrat,[23] a book that retains its place as the definitive study on the subject. Trunk's results show how diverse the reactions of the Judenrat groups and individual Judenrat members were. His systematic survey of the roles played by the wartime Councils covers a wide range of behaviors, including full support for underground ghetto movements, heroic, collective and individual opposition to German orders, individual and collective suicides to protest calamitous orders, as well as reactions that verge on collaboration with the enemy.

Trunk's research offers no simplistic, uniform conclusions. All along, he emphasizes the complexity of the subject, inviting readers to venture their own interpretations of the data. His volume also explores the unprecedented historical changes that were an inherent part of the Holocaust. His exhaustive research undermines persistent assertions about Jewish passivity and complicity.

Focusing on Eastern Europe, Ruben Ainsztein specifically set out to refute accusations about Jewish passivity. He proceeded by documenting Jewish participation in a wide range of underground operations. Ainsztein's book *Jewish Resistance in Nazi-Occupied Eastern Europe* sought to rehabilitate the Jewish honor by showing how widely and often heroically the Jews participated in anti-German struggles.[24] His book was followed by *They Fought Back*, which is a collection of articles by different individuals, each describing how Jews struggled in a variety of European countries and in a variety of wartime settings.[25]

Over the years, Israeli Holocaust historians have contributed important research about Jewish resistance under the German occupation.[26] Outstanding among these historians is Israel Gutman, whose publications on the Warsaw Ghetto and Warsaw Ghetto revolt are enduring classics.[27] As a holocaust survivor, a Warsaw

Ghetto uprising underground fighter, and through his personal connections to the underground movement in Auschwitz, Gutman provides a unique, first-hand perspective of the meaning and implications of Jewish resistance during the Holocaust.

The debates surrounding the issue of resistance have often led to conflicting and contradictory conclusions. Sometimes these discussions fail to produce clear-cut answers to the many emotionally charged questions they raise. And yet, out of these attempts to clarify and to instruct, two polar positions have emerged. One concentrates on Jewish passivity and complicity. The second portrays the Jews as active, courageous, and heroic resisters. Imbedded in each are some similarities. Those who accuse the Jews of passivity and those who insist on portraying them as heroic, collectively view resistance mainly as armed struggles. Most Holocaust scholars fail to embrace fully either extreme. Some try to reconcile these views, warning about the weaknesses of each, promoting a more moderate and balanced approach. Among the latter is Lucjan Dobroszycki, a survivor of the Lodz Ghetto and of Auschwitz. Dobroszycki offered an original approach to the study of resistance by posing questions: "Has anyone seen an army without arms? An army scattered over 200 isolated ghettos? An army of infants, old people, the sick? Armies whose soldiers are denied even the right to surrender?"[28] This book seeks to answer this question with a resounding yes. Unprecedented oppression led to equally unprecedented forms of resistance, and what they shared was a belief that no one was alone and that, with the help of others, resilience could turn into resistance—acting not just on behalf of oneself to survive, but on behalf of an entire community of people. Resistance requires cooperation, a sense of belonging to something greater than oneself.

CHAPTER ONE

Learning How to Oppose

To tell the story of resistance, we need to tell the stories of individuals, Jews and Gentiles. I have decided to start with the very young—those for whom opposition came perhaps most naturally. What follows are brief portraits of three teenagers—two of them Gentile and the third Jewish—and how they coped with their wartime experiences. They were different yet similar. They dealt with their confrontation with a common enemy in ways that overlap and yet remain distinctive.

Born in 1922, in the small town of Krzemienice, Zygmunt Rytel attended the local elementary school, and later on the public high school, which was quite prestigious. As a Catholic and a good student, Zygmunt was automatically enrolled into this high school in 1936. Some of his Jewish friends were not as fortunate. Because it was a nationally funded school, the percentage of Jewish students enrolled in a particular year could not exceed the percentage of Polish Jews, who made up 10 percent of the Polish population.

Estimates of Krzemienice's prewar proportion of Jews are close to 50 percent. Given the Jewish emphasis on higher education, competition for entrance into this high school was fierce. Inevitably, Jewish students who enrolled into this select school were the brightest the community had.

I met Zygmunt in a 1978 meeting in Warsaw. During our conversation, he emphasized that in Krzemienice many of his friends had been Jewish. He also told me that he was a member of the Polish Socialist Party (Polska Partia Socjalistyczna, or PPS).

Throughout the war years, he devoted himself to saving the most persecuted. What kind of a person was Zygmunt Rytel? What values pushed him toward the protection of the most oppressed? His wartime protection of Jews led to a Yad Vashem—the museum and research center in Israel devoted to the Holocaust—recognition as a Righteous among the Nations of the World.[1] Before the public ceremony, Zygmunt learned that evidence had established that he had saved the lives of at least one hundred Jews.[2]

"I am an individualist," he said to me. "I like to live in a way that does not make me dependent on others. I also stand up for things I believe in, and often pay for it. But, this is the only way I can respect myself."[3]

During the war, as he himself says, Zygmunt's activities were closely intertwined with who he was and how he saw himself. With high school education behind him, he enrolled in an engineering program. But he soon gave up the idea of becoming an engineer and, following the invasion and occupation of Poland by the Germans, turned instead to writing and to journalism—to reporting and documenting history as it evolved. Zygmunt was deeply concerned about the multiplying threats that grew out of the German occupation. His assessments of the political situation were gloomy and confirmed his sense that there was a need to stand up for those who were its victims. His affiliation with the PPS bolstered his social and political obligations.[4] Initially, Zygmunt's activities concentrated on the protection of the so-called Polish elites—the intellectuals, artists, academics—because they were, in fact, the most threatened. The concentration camp Auschwitz was built in 1940 and its initial inmates were Polish leaders and intellectuals.[5] Outspoken and direct, Zygmunt explained, "I was not helping more Jews than Poles. On the contrary, around 1940 I had concentrated on aiding the Polish elites. At that time they were targeted by the Germans for destruction."

Zygmunt was himself subjected to hardships, as well. Barely eighteen, he became an Auschwitz prisoner. The eight months he spent in Auschwitz made a deep impression on him. As a former inmate, Zygmunt was convinced that Auschwitz prisoners cannot bear to look at the sufferings of others. Zygmunt's sensitivity to the distress of others was tested at the start of the war, when a German officer murdered his teenage brother in 1939. Serving as a Polish soldier, this brother was slightly injured. His injury caught the attention of a German officer, who, without checking the extent of the young man's injuries, took out his gun and summarily shot him. This event only strengthened Zygmunt's determination to protect all those who suffered. He explains:

> I take a strict position toward myself, and towards others. Particularly toward those who could but failed to help....I see them as some kind of lower type beings....By 1943, it was clear that the worst off were the Jews. Because I wanted to save those who were in greatest danger, I concentrated on rescuing Jews. Had I not done this, I would have lost all my self-respect...I would look at myself as a zero, a nobody, and would feel disgusted with myself.

I was curious to know whether Zygmunt had been afraid while standing up for the oppressed. First, he seemed to hesitate. Then he explained, "I do not like the so-called courageous people who say that they are not afraid. People, who lack the sense of danger, endanger themselves and others....Of course I was afraid, but I tried not to show it."

Asked how he related to the Jews he was protecting, he responded, "There were some Jews with whom I became close friends. Some of them I liked; some I did not. Some I even felt repulsed by. But none of this affected my actions. I helped all. Those I liked and those I disliked."

How did those who benefited from Zygmunt's protection react to him? The unhesitating answer was that there was a difference in the reaction of the "poor" and the "rich." Those survivors who had limited resources were eager to maintain contacts with their rescuers and their family. The opposite was true for survivors who were financially well off. The latter group was aloof and disinterested in having continuous contacts with their wartime protectors.

By 1944, Zygmunt's involvement with the Polish socialist underground and his protection of Nazi victims brought him to Warsaw, to the part of the city called Zoliborz, an area known for its generous aid to the persecuted and its opposition to the German occupation. In Zoliborz the Socialist Party offered Rytel a one-room apartment. Since the socialist underground had recently lost its best document forger, Rytel was asked to take over this job. This young journalist-reporter tried to match the accomplishments of his predecessor. First, for safety, Zygmunt prepared for himself four documents, each with a different name. Soon a range of orders began to reach his living quarters, which were transformed into a semi-factory, producing all kinds of certificates, records, and documents. The more orders that reached Zygmunt's place, the more skillful he became. Naturally, as his reputation as a forger grew, the more strenuously the Socialist Party tried to keep the location of his apartment secret.

While Zygmunt was willing to help move Jews to safe places, he could not bring them to his apartment, which was filled with incriminating evidence. However, Zygmunt knew that in Zoliborz he would most likely find temporary lodgings for those who were on the run, and that later on he would be able to replace these limited quarters with more permanent shelters. About his varied illegal activities he told me, with persuasive conviction, "If I were acting alone I would not have saved a soul! Only a group of people could succeed, not a single individual!" Zygmunt was affirming the importance of cooperation. Experience had taught him that solutions to problems grew out of cooperative efforts, which in turn grew out of his underground affiliation.

FIGURE 1.1 Zygmunt Rytel in 1966. During the war, Zygmunt, a member of the Polish Socialist Party, devoted himself to saving those who were most persecuted. (Courtesy Yad Vashem)

Zygmunt's underground involvements expanded in diverse directions. He joined Żegota, also known as the Council for the Aid to Jews. Żegota was particularly involved in aiding Jews who tried to survive by passing as non-Jews and hiding in the forbidden Christian world—the so-called "Aryan side." After October 15, 1941, all unauthorized Jewish presence on the Aryan side was punishable by death. The same punishment applied to any Pole, and his or her family, who was caught helping Jews stay in the Christian world.[6]

The Socialist Party was actively supporting Żegota. Zygmunt, for example, distributed funds to Jews who were in hiding and or passing as Christians in the Aryan world. Some of these funds came from the Polish government-in-exile in London; some came from several organizations in the remaining free world. The money helped Jews in a whole range of circumstances. Often threats from denouncers required changes of living quarters, as well as new documents.[7]

Zygmunt was also busy transporting Jews from one town to another, keeping them one step ahead of the authorities. These moves involved risks, yet he undertook them without much second thought. "Whether one worked for the underground or not, life was endangered anyway. One could be caught every day for no reason at all, or for a serious reason. My mother was arrested in 1942 while working on an illegal newspaper. All people I knew did work in the underground, in one capacity or another. Whether you transgressed or not, you could be picked up."

With time, Zygmunt learned how to make films. At first film-making seemed frivolous and useless to him. But when his superiors explained the value of movies as historical documents, he changed his mind. In the end he was very good at it.

Zygmunt acknowledged to me how hard it was to keep entire Jewish families for prolonged periods of time. Inevitably those who harbored in their homes Jews for extensive periods of time experienced a variety of inner and outer conflicts. Using himself as an example, Zygmunt tried to explain some of the differences between long- and short-term protections of Jews. "I was constantly on the run; among my duties was the transportation of illegal individuals, Jewish and non-Jewish. I was constantly active, constantly switching from one activity to another. I had constant changes fighting actively. In a sense, I was fighting. Those who had kept Jews in their homes for prolonged periods of time were fighting passively.

To fight passively is harder. I don't know if I had the strength, especially as a youth, to keep someone in my place for a year or longer. Those who kept Jews for a long time turned their lives into a process of waiting for something that had to come from the outside."

As he acknowledged, however, it was his youth that helped him through it:

As a young person, I might have even found the dangers of underground activities exciting...I might have experienced illegal pastimes as a part of an adolescent game, as some kind of an adventure. We should neither hide nor deny that we were engaging in activities that were dangerous and daring, something which gave us satisfaction....As young people we were participating in doing something against those who were strong and powerful. We were acting in opposition to those who were in authority. This in itself might have satisfied the young. Also while acting in opposition to authority we were engaged in highly valued acts, we were at once opposing the enemy and saving the oppressed. Similarly, when during the war we studied illegally we had an easier time learning because for us, at that time, learning was a forbidden pastime. To the extent that the young people welcomed the illegal part of studying, they probably learned better.

Zygmunt argued nonetheless that the "very young" did not have "the moral strength to keep people in their apartment for long stretches of time." It was, instead, older people, those who had "passed through many difficult experiences [and] were hardened psychologically" who had the strength to do that. "Older people are more patient. They did not require constant changes in their underground activities."

I asked why Hitler concentrated on murdering Jews, and Zygmunt was surprised by the question. "The extermination of the Jews was the best business for the Germans. Murdering the Jews was based on economics. I cannot understand why people do not want to take a pencil and calculate the profits that came to the Germans."

When I asked about the sources of anti-Semitism, always a very touchy subject in Poland, Zygmunt had a ready answer. Groups which differ from those in their environment will evoke negative feelings from the majority. But anti-Semitism was a political and economic activity, stimulated by leaders. It didn't stop with the end of the war. The Polish government persecuted the Jewish elite in 1968, when most of the prominent Jews immigrated to Denmark. Denmark was delighted to accept this highly intelligent group of Jewish professionals.

For most of Zygmunt's life, he was faithful to the PPS. Only during the Warsaw uprising did he cooperate with the Home Army (Armia Krajowa, or AK). Eventually, however, he joined the Gwardia Ludowa (GL), which was the leftist pro-Soviet party. In the facts and details of Rytel's life, he had much in common with Antoni Zieleniewski, though it is a curious fact of history that they never met.

Antoni Zieleniewski was born in 1913 in the small town of Kolo, located in the heart of Poland close to the River Warta. Up to 1939, this town's inhabitants had been split into practically equal parts; one Jewish, the other Polish. Zieleniewski was Polish. I met Antoni in 1978, hoping to learn from him about prewar and war-time history. What made him a particularly interesting subject was the archival evidence, which identified him as someone who had been a part of the Polish underground and who had risked his life to save Jews.

We met at the Jewish Historical Institute in Warsaw, and after a brief chat I plunged into the subject at hand, asking him how Jews had affected his life. Antoni delivered his replies in a measured voice. He told me that many of his schoolmates were Jewish. "One of them was an especially valued friend, Lolek Leczynski. Our friendship began in the elementary school, continued in high school and beyond. We always studied together. Our mothers were both widows and they, too, were close friends. They might have encouraged our friendship, but we were not aware of this." After Antoni and Lolek graduated from high school, they enrolled at the Warsaw University. Both decided to study law. "Lolek was an outstanding student. I looked up to him. Together we expected the University to fulfill all our dreams. Initially, we simply ignored that being Jewish or being Polish might have had serious implications for our hunger to learn. Somehow our friendship made us insensitive to the mounting prejudices around us."

Quite naturally, the two law students leaned toward leftist political ideologies and eventually joined the PPS. For quite some time, they were content with life around them. Only gradually did the political changes demand their attention. The atmosphere at the university began to change, and by 1937 Jewish students were being attacked—"viciously," remembers Antoni—by non-Jewish students.

As if by "chance" these Polish–Jewish encounters ended with severe beatings of the lone Jew. Five to six Polish students would surround a single man whom they identified as a Jewish student. As a rule, these Polish attackers were members of the extreme political nationalist right, *Endecja*. Mixed with their nationalism was an equally powerful anti-Semitism. When five or six attackers are poised against a single victim, the outcomes are predictable. Inevitably, these assaults caused severe injuries. A swift departure of these "heroic" Polish attackers inevitably followed. Some of the Jewish victims never recovered. Whenever such unprovoked, one-sided attacks were taking place, the Polish police was nowhere to be found. Nor did any of the occasional passersby dare to interfere.

Antoni went on to tell me that the Jewish students tried to diminish their presence at the university.

Warsaw University had some built-in provisions, which indirectly allowed the students to limit their appearances on campus. Students who were officially enrolled at the university received an index card, which served as their identification. When a professor signed an index card, it gave its owner an opportunity to be tested at a newly specified time and place. This meant that a signed index card would exempt a student from attending this professor's lectures. In turn, such students had an obligation to cover the material, which was presented by the professor during his lectures. It was easy to obtain a signature on the index card that automatically entitled a student to change the time and place for his exam. To be sure, not all students were equally able to take advantage of such opportunities. The professor could decline a signature. They rarely did. Lolek had a reputation of a highly intelligent student. He was known as one of the few who were distinguished by the Jewish community of Kolo with a special fellowship that covered all his university expenses.

Lolek's and Antoni's friendship endured. Antoni was glad to collect the professors' signatures for Lolek's index card, which reduced his need to appear at the university. For quite some time, protected from attacks by the roaming Polish Endeks, Lolek continued to pass his exams with flying colors. Although the friendship and partnership of these two youths worked well, eventually, what they had tried to avoid did happen. One evening in 1937, the two friends parted at the university grounds. After the end of his exams, Lolek was to come to Antoni's apartment, which the latter shared with another Polish student.

Antoni picked up the story:

> I returned to my room looking forward to Lolek's visit. Suddenly, earlier than I had expected, Lolek burst into our place. He threw himself on my bed. What I saw shook me up. There was no need for explanations. Badly disfigured, Lolek obviously had been the victim of a severe onslaught. Several of his teeth were missing; a finger of his hand was broken. The upper part of his entire body was covered with blood...Keep in mind that this had happened in 1937. I can still hear Lolek's angry, distorted voice saying that he had completed all exams! And that never ever again will he come back to this hellish place.

He kept his promise. While Lolek never returned to the Warsaw University grounds, he had to remain in Kolo for a while. The two friends continued their active involvement with the PPS. Of the two, Lolek was much more politically active. His leftist views grew more extreme than Antoni's.

In 1939, Antoni was mobilized into the Polish army, where he automatically assumed the rank of an officer. Lolek was not asked to join the army, very likely because of his strong leftist leanings and his Jewish background. Officially, both Lolek and Antoni qualified for an officer's rank.

The PPS encouraged Lolek to go east. They offered help. Lolek eventually ended up at Moscow University, where he became a prominent professor. Antoni said that they never met again.[8] However, their commitment to the socialist ideology and their devotion to the study of law bonded Lolek and Antoni, and after Lolek's absence his influence upon Antoni's life lingered on.

It would have been put to a brutal test by the events that followed in Poland. By the fall of 1940, the Germans were consolidating their hold over the newly acquired territories, pouring into them a proliferation of rules. Failure to comply with any of these so-called "laws" resulted in severe punishments. Faced with unending assaults, and unable to cope with such ruthless force, the army and Polish civilians were overwhelmed. Many people took to the roads. Enemy planes bombed some of them. Some, discouraged, turned back. Precise figures for those who escaped are not available, but I am interested in finding out who these runaways were and what happened to them. A secondary question is how Germans and Poles coped with their respective circumstances, and whether reactions to oppression affected Jewish and non-Jewish resistance.

History shows that the Polish political leaders who were a part of the mass migration quickly recognized what the German offensive would mean. Initially, a group of these political leaders escaped to France where they established a Polish government-in-exile. When the Germans threatened France's independence, this government moved to London, where it reassembled.

What the Poles failed to accomplish through direct military means against the Germans, therefore, they set out to achieve from a distance, with the aid of the newly created Polish government-in-exile. An important step in this process was the realization that scattered members of the Polish army, especially Polish officers, could serve as links between German-occupied Poland and the government in London.

In no time, a protective Polish underground surrounded former officers. They were informed about the lurking dangers. They were automatically supplied with new documents. Early on, the Germans had ordered all Polish officers to register with the appropriate authorities. Recent experiences had proven that official registration would automatically translate into execution. Whatever help was received saved their lives and simultaneously increased the ranks of the already existent Polish underground. About 20,000 former Polish officers are estimated to have successfully concealed their officer status. All former members of the Polish army, including the unidentifiable officers, contributed in a variety of ways to the development and continuity of the Polish underground.

Soon this underground movement had crystallized into two major ruling bodies. One of them consisted of the coalition of the four largest political parties: the Peasant, the Socialist, the Christian Labor, and the National Party. The second part, the official military organization, was recognized by the government as a military unit, enjoying equal rights with the Polish army first in France and subsequently in England.[9]

In all the countries under German occupation, men were usually more vigorously persecuted than women. Men were seen as more threatening and potentially more rebellious than women.[10] Since Jewish men rather than women were perceived as the chief enemies of the Third Reich, most of the anti-Jewish terror was directed against them.[11] Nevertheless, the Jews, in general, were singled out for the most ruthless treatment.[12]

The 1939 anti-Polish campaign included five German security police (Schutzstaffel, or SS) and security service (Sicherheitsdienst, or SD) task forces—the Einsatzgruppen—operating behind the front lines. Their main task was to secure and "pacify" the occupied area. In so doing they, along with some German army units, routinely murdered Jewish civilians. The majority of the victims were men; women and children were a small minority.[13]

Time and the emergent political, military, and economic circumstances would occasionally alter the ever-expanding course of Jewish destruction. In the absence of other evidence, most historians agree that the plan for Jewish annihilation—the "Final Solution"—crystallized after the start of the Russian-German war in June 1941. As the Germans moved east, they searched for more efficient methods of destruction. The capture of Russian-held territories coincided with the mass murder of Jews.[14]

Within the context of future Germanization of Poland, Goebbels quoted Hitler as saying that the Poles were "more animal than human beings" and that "the filth of the Poles is unimaginable." Poles were at the very bottom of the racial ranking system, only slightly above the Jews. Hitler had therefore consistently opposed any close connections between the Poles and the Germans. He felt that the Poles should be pushed into their beleaguered state, namely the General Government, the part of Poland designated for German rule but identified formally as a separate region of the Third Reich.

The Einsatzgruppen were used in Poland for the first time. Their cruelty had moved the conduct of the war and Poland to an unprecedented level of criminality.[15] Initially, the German army objected to excessive oppression toward the Polish population; with time, however, their objections evaporated. Eventually, the order to liquidate the Polish aristocracy, clergy, and intelligentsia claimed an estimated 60,000 victims.[16] German concentration upon the destruction of Polish elites affected the entire Polish underground, including Antoni and other officers of the Polish army.

The Nazis defined all Jews as fitting into a racial category distinguishable by specific physical, social, and psychological characteristics. Yet, undermining this myth was the fact that in the newly occupied territories of Eastern Europe, the conquerors often had difficulty separating Jews from the rest of the population. An official decree requiring Jews to wear a Star of David helped, but it took some time before it went into effect. Therefore, at the start, the Germans relied on collaborators to identify the Jews and their property. To gain the cooperation of the local populations, the Germans bombarded the newly conquered territories with virulent anti-Semitic propaganda. Not only did this propaganda describe the Jews as subhuman vermin to be exterminated, but it also blamed them for every conceivable ill, including the war. These ideas fell on fertile ground, and anti-Semitic mobs sprang up, encouraged by this official attitude.[17]

The chronicler Chaim Kaplan described Warsaw in an entry of October 1939: "Every public place shows hatred and loathing against Jews. Isolated incidents of violence against Jews have grown too numerous to count. Eyewitnesses tell horrifying stories, and they are not exaggerations." Half a year later, the situation had worsened: "Gangs of tough Polish youths (you won't find one adult among them), armed with clubs, sticks and all kinds of harmful weapons, make pogroms against the Jews. They break into stores and empty their goods into their own pockets. The Jews they encounter on the way are beaten and wounded. The Jewish quarter has been abandoned to toughs and killers who were organized for this purpose by some invisible hand."[18]

The Germans followed each territorial conquest with a viciousness that was specifically designed to debase and humiliate. Numerous photographs show gleeful German soldiers looking on and laughing while their comrades cut off the beards of Orthodox Jews. Often such encounters involved brutal beatings, with the victims forced to kneel, pray, dance, and sing.[19] From the beginning of the war, the Germans viewed their military victories as opportunities to destroy those segments of local populations they defined as barriers to the creation of the ideal Aryan world. The Jews, the Slavs, and Poland's other minorities fit this description.

But time did not favor the Germans. In the summer of 1943, the Germans were losing ground, both at the front and in the occupied territories. The Polish underground was increasing its opposition, blowing up trains and bridges and killing high-ranking Germans.

Unable to track down those who were responsible, the Germans were becoming more ruthless and more arbitrary in their retaliations against the civilian population. Raids, deportations, and killings occurred more frequently and less predictably. In the past, they had stayed away from the poorer section of town, but with time, they were beginning to move their operations into such areas as well.[20] As the Third Reich continued to incur more substantial losses, the Germans became more vigilant, suspicious, and hostile. What the Germans lost by increased casualties, they tried to make up by greater cruelty.

Actively involved in a range of underground operations, threatened by the increased German persecutions, Antoni escaped to Podlesie in Eastern Poland. Here, in a village so remote that it did not even have a police station, he found a job as a secretary to the mayor of the village. Although the pay was modest, the duties were undemanding. This village was surrounded by several equally small villages. More advanced than these surrounding villages, it attracted local peasants, who liked to discuss their problems with the mayor, a native peasant. He was a decent, well-liked man who had a reputation for brains.

The summer of 1943 was a time during which the Germans were viciously persecuting local populations for all transgressions, large and small. Eager to avenge their failure to win the war, the German authorities were busy overseeing public hangings of Poles and Jews. Antoni picks up the story,

> On a hot day, during the lunch hour, a delegation of local peasants paid a visit to the mayor's office. The mayor was away on business. This delegation brought with them an official report, which they insisted, on reading loudly, in front of all those who were present. The report stated that in a nearby village, Skarzyn, they came upon a group of Jews who lived in a dugout shelter, close to the forest, under a specific pear tree. As law-abiding citizens, they came to report a legal transgression. The law required that such a report should be telephoned to the local police. All those who listened knew that this story would end with the execution of the hidden Jews.

He was initially horrified and puzzled, then realized that this delegation had purposefully selected a time when the mayor was away. The public way in which this report was presented was aimed at protecting the mayor from an unpleasant task. The accusers wanted Antoni, a stranger, to do the dirty work and not the mayor, who was one of them. Antoni reflected on the problem. "I could not denounce the Jews, who after all were not guilty of anything.... It crossed my mind to run away." But Antoni realized that he had nowhere to go. His duties were to call the police, though he knew they would shoot the Jews. "I was vacillating, unsure, groping." Finally he assured the group that he had accepted their report and would notify the police. The group left, apparently satisfied. "When they were gone, I decided to consult with a friend of mine, Wojcik, a local peasant, a decent good-natured person. I sent for him. He came and responded to the news with deep sadness. After all, he argued, they survived till now. What a shame to give them into the hands of the German murders."

Wojcik came up with a solution, Antoni remembered. He told his friend to send someone trustworthy to the Jews and warn them to get out, and then give them instructions about a new hiding place deeper in the forest. They should wait there until someone contacted them.

> That very evening we called the police and shared the report with them. We went to the hideout with the police. There, we were confronted by an empty place. A new report had to be written, which meant that the original report was false. When next day the mayor returned, he seemed very happy with the situation. This mayor was a decent, smart man. He must have guessed what happened. He seemed to be in high spirits, probably because he had avoided committing a horrible crime.

Antoni and Wojcik formed a bond over their successful plan. Eventually, they became the protectors and ultimately the rescuers of the "missing Jews." The group included four women and three men, their ages ranging from twenty to thirty. They had been in hiding together for about a year. Occasionally, in the evening, one of these men would approach a trusted farmer to purchase some food from him. Antoni was vaguely aware of these transactions. By chance, here and there, he would meet one of them in a farmer's hut. He preferred not to ask about them. Secrecy went hand in hand with safety.

As Antoni and Wojcik became the official food suppliers for these hidden Jews, I asked him if they were reimbursed. Antoni was taken aback by my question. "I could never accept payment for food from people who were forced to live under such dire circumstances. I simply could not do that!"

Antoni explained that the Germans had ordered the local peasants to supply the authorities with produce, and especially with luxury items such as meats, cheeses, eggs, and cream. The farmers resented these demands. They tried to sabotage orders by making sure that a substantial portion of their deliveries would miss their destination. Some of these goods stayed on the farms and were consumed by the farmers and their families. Some found their way to other Poles, usually those whom the owners liked. Antoni and Wojcik looked for safe ways to supply the seven Jews with flour and whatever else these suppliers could spare. Food found its way into the Jewish hideout in the nearby forest. Deliveries happened at night.

How did these self-appointed rescuers view what they were doing? When I raised this question, Antoni gave me a range of responses. He felt that his continuous involvements with risky AK operations helped him identify with the way the Jews felt. "The Nazis were trying to get me, so I knew what it meant to be persecuted. It was my duty to help, so I did." He, too, was living in danger. To be sure, the village had welcomed him by offering him the position of the mayor's secretary. On the other hand, he was still an outsider.

The report about the Jews' hiding place pointed to the distinction the local people made between their mayor, whom they wanted to protect, and Antoni, who for them was the outsider. To those who presented the report, the Jews were even more outsiders, and as such had no right to live. Antoni refrained from telling me in detail the kinds of activities he pursued on behalf of the AK. I knew that with the Soviet takeover of this part of Poland, the Home Army had been made illegal. Even in 1978, with Poland still under Soviet domination, Antoni was cautious about revealing AK's secrets. As an AK member and former officer of the Polish army, Antoni was involved in illegal activities throughout the war. He was aware that the Germans were on the lookout for members of the Home Army.

Antoni was visibly uncomfortable when I asked him whether the Jews he had rescued were grateful enough. He said that he had expected no gratitude. Then he said that the Jews were very grateful, but that while the war was on they had no opportunities to show their gratitude. It would have been very dangerous to have much contact between the hidden Jews and their protectors.

In fact, it was only after the war was behind them—and the Soviets had taken over this part of Poland—that the Jews learned that Antoni and Wojcik had been their rescuers. Antoni insisted that they were grateful. After the German retreat, he said, "I was invited to their home. For quite a while, I did not even tell them that I was involved in helping them. To be sure they knew in part, the next day, what had happened when they had to relocate. But there was no time to explain the details." In a way, gratitude was a luxury that no one could afford.

I asked Antoni if he ever regretted his involvement with the rescue of Jewish lives. His answer was insistent. "I never regretted this! I did what I should have done. I could not have lived with myself had I not done everything in my power." When touching on the protection of wartime Jews, he felt constrained about talking openly until quite late. Not until 1975 did he talk about the war years. "Up until then, most of the people who denounced the Jews were still alive," he told me. "As long as the people were still alive, I did not want to talk about it to hurt them. I did not want to be a witness. Besides, I was afraid to respond to questions about my AK involvement." But word about his activities began to spread at his workplace, and things became uncomfortable for him. "This is what prompted me to admit publicly that I saved Jews during the war. Bringing this into the open helped stop all negative whisperings about my wartime conduct."

When I raised the subject of Polish anti-Semitism, Antoni replied that it was merely a part of life. The Poles felt inferior to the Jews, many of whom had become successful in business and in institutions of higher learning. "I am a Pole, but I have to admit that Jews are more capable than Poles. Maybe not all of them but many are. When Jews perform more demanding tasks, then they are better at it than Poles, who seized upon anti-Semitism as a way 'to eliminate competition.'"

Without asking whether he shared that feeling, I asked Antoni how he felt about his rescue efforts during the war. "Today I would have done exactly the same thing. For sure I could not act in any other way. Besides, I was not alone. There were quite a number of people who helped Jews. I knew an old bachelor, a Pole, who kept four people in a cellar. There were many more Poles who risked their lives to save Jews in a variety of ways and never spoke about it. On the other hand, I also know that some Poles were following German orders and were harming Jews."

What both Zygmunt and Antoni underplayed in our conversations was the danger they had put themselves in by helping Jews. There was no direct benefit for them to do it, and they consistently put their own lives on the line. The Germans were merciless in the treatment of Poles who took in the Jewish cause. They had to fight a two-front battle—against the Germans, of course, but also against a good number of their fellow Poles, who simply could not understand why there was any moral imperative in assisting Jews.

Now we turn to a young Jew and his experience with resisting the Nazis. Ephraim (Frank) Bleichman was seventeen when the Germans occupied his small town, Kamionka, home to about a hundred Jewish families. The closest big city, Lublin, was some twelve miles away. Ephraim was the second-eldest son of eight children in a Jewish Orthodox family. Except for Ephraim's older brother, the rest of his siblings were considerably younger. As with most other Jewish parents in Kamionka, the Bleichmans were deeply religious. Also, like most Jews of their generation, they viewed the German occupation as a temporary setback, something which in due time would be redressed by God. Despite the continuously expanding brutality, their trust in God's wisdom persisted.

The younger generation was less complacent. Their confrontations with the new reality did not increase their trust in God. Quite the contrary, the youth of Kamionka were restless. Searching in vain for solutions, they soon became frustrated. They believed in self-reliance but were at a loss as to how to effectively channel their mounting frustrations, or what form their resistance should take.

Among the many restrictive German rules was an order to create the aforementioned Judenrat, or Jewish Councils, and a Jewish police force. These two bodies had to cooperate in carrying out the orders of the occupying forces. One of these requirements called for a steady quota of Jewish laborers for work outside their community in camps, factories, and in maintaining or building roads. Many such laborers had disappeared without a trace. Disturbing rumors about their fate soon began to circulate. One day a group of Jewish laborers returned to Kamionka in a most deplorable condition. Practically all of them were covered with bruises and wounds, inflicted either by brutal work supervisors or by horrible working conditions and probably both. These laborers were unable and seemingly unwilling to talk about their experiences—but they did not need to. Their physical and emotional state spoke more loudly than any actual stories could have. In dire need of care, most of them found solace in their family homes. Despite all this, German pressure for the delivery of more young Jewish laborers did not cease.

While the older generation of Jews continued to await God's intervention, the young became more convinced than ever that they themselves would have to come up with their own solutions. The experience of the Bleichman family in large part reflects that of most Kamionka Jews. Mr. Bleichman, Ephraim's father, had been barred from earning a living as a wood merchant. He was coerced into hard, humiliating work for which he received no payment. Ephraim was then caught by the Jewish police and sent off for compulsory labor. He began his work in a group of young Jewish laborers, on a nearby private farm. There he had to collect and pack a variety of produce into boxes, destined for German consumption. The labor was accompanied by incessant beatings and cursing by their Gentile supervisors. Requests to visit the outhouse were met with vigorous punching and crude swearing and name-calling, as if no Jew were entitled to such a privilege.

With each passing minute, Ephraim was more determined to make this first day of compulsory labor his last. Indeed, beginning the next day, Ephraim disappeared. The Judenrat and the Jewish police searched for him eagerly. Familiar with his surroundings, he received help from many friends, both Jewish and Gentile, who conspired successfully to hide him from the police.

With increasing food shortages, Ephraim became preoccupied with easing his family's hunger. He considered contacting some of his Gentile friends to see if he could purchase food from them and resell it at a profit. He was confident that he could do that because of his appearance: he did not look Jewish and was completely fluent in Polish. One day, he mounted his bicycle, ripped the compulsory Star of David band from his arm, and disappeared into the countryside, which was off-limits to Jews. Avoiding busy roads, he visited his Gentile friends who welcomed him warmly. They were happy to sell him their produce, milk, bread, flour, vegetables, and much more. Their prices were fair. They even helped him attach his purchases to the bike and volunteered important safety tips on how to avoid encounters.

When this new entrepreneur reached the Jewish territory, he divided his purchases into two parts. One part he sold to some of his fellow Jews at a profit. The rest he kept for his family. Satisfied with the outcome of this first venture, he repeated these transactions with some regularity. Although his parents welcomed the extra food, they were concerned for their son's safety. Ephraim tried to alleviate their worries by minimizing the dangers, even denying there were any. In turn, knowing how stubborn their son was, his relatives eventually stopped objecting. News about Ephraim's illegal transactions reached the Judenrat. The police increased their efforts to arrest this flagrant renegade. Knowing that Jewish functionaries were out to capture him, Ephraim became more innovative. A cat and mouse game ensued, with Ephraim taking refuge in one safe haven after another, with his Jewish and Gentile friends and a variety of family members, close and distant.

By 1942 rumors reached the Jews of Kamionka that they, like so many Jews in the region, would be soon transferred into a specially created Jewish ghetto. They heard about small Jewish communities that were being moved into larger ghettos. For the Bleichmans these rumors took on special meaning. Ephraim's parents knew how deeply their son valued his freedom and that he would never voluntarily relocate to a ghetto. Deportation to a ghetto would cause a family split. This expectation remained a painful possibility; it was too painful even to talk about.

The summer of 1942 brought the official news that all Kamionka Jews would be transferred to another community where, with other Jews, they would work and live in peace. This was soon followed by an announcement specifying the time and place of assembly for relocation. The Kamionka Jews were told to bring only a limited number of belongings, to make the move easy. Noncompliance carried with it the death penalty. At the designated time and place the Bleichman family showed up as ordered. The majority of the Kamionka Jews obeyed, but some of the younger unmarried men, including Ephraim, and a few young women did not. "From the beginning I knew that I wouldn't let them kill me," he told me, "and that I would not submit."[21]

By placing Jews into ghettos, the Germans were taking a logical step in the fulfillment of their policy of annihilation. All Jews were destined to die. But the process of destruction could not happen instantly. In retrospect, we can identify a number of distinct stages or steps in this process of extermination. The first involved identification. This was followed by the expropriation of all property, continued with the removal of Jews from gainful employment, and culminated with isolation in the ghettos. Once separated from the rest of the population the Jews were led to their deaths, either through mass executions or forced transfers to concentration camps. Complex, often overlapping, these stages were a steady process of humiliation and designed systematically to degrade any possibility of resistance.

Ephraim recalled these painful times and the equally painful decisions to which they gave rise. "My parents knew that I would be leaving, that I could not take the humiliations; but I just didn't have the heart to tell them that I was not joining them. I left without saying goodbye. But, I knew that they had expected it." Ephraim's instinct was to seek out those who felt as he did. The first evening of his escape, a group went to a nearby estate where some of their Jewish friends still worked and spent the night there. "In the morning, we came upon others who had also refused to go to the Jewish assembly place.... There was a group of about thirty or so of these youths." He explained that they chose two boys who looked most Aryan and asked them to spy for them and bring back the latest news. "Upon their return, we heard that there had been a deportation...and they had taken all the assembled Jews, made everybody run very fast. Whoever couldn't run was shot.... The rest had been brought to the Lubartow ghetto."

This news was met with a painful silence. Ephraim sat beside his friend Jankl. Earlier, they had agreed to stick together. Ephraim offered to take Jankl to Klos, a Polish peasant who a while back had told Ephraim that should he need help he should come to him. Ephraim shared this information, explaining that he was not sure just how firm this offer might be.

The group began to debate their options. Soon it was realized that among them were some former Jewish policemen. Several of them suggested that there might be a need for policemen in the Lubartow ghetto; others concurred. Jankl turned to Ephraim and asked him how he felt about going into a ghetto. "It is easier to go into a ghetto than out of it," Ephraim replied. Then a few of these youths began to scatter, some singly, others in small groups. Still others just sat there, silent. Ephraim signaled to Jankl that it was time for them to leave. The two moved away, heading in the direction of Klos's home. Suddenly, Jankl stopped abruptly, explaining that he had decided to join the others who were going into the

Lubartow ghetto. This was the last time the two of them ever saw each other.

"To be left all alone, with hardly any money, and without a definite promise of aid was not easy," Ephraim said. As he continued toward the home of Klos, he wondered whether he had made a mistake, if perhaps the others knew better. "I had all kinds of thoughts. Was I wrong? Then, I began to talk to myself, 'What are you afraid of? You are a free person. Be free!' But inside me I was unsure."

Rather than go to Klos's house, Ephraim decided to wait until night and hid in the fields. Finally, later, he went to the hut. "They received me as if I were their son. I was amazed. They hugged me. I could not talk. I was numb. They were all so wonderful, the whole family. They sat me down and sat around me. Klos said: 'Don't be afraid; the Russian front is approaching.' They talked to me, but I was speechless. The wife invited me to just sit. They were very fine people. They said, 'Wait, and see what happens tomorrow.'"

Ephraim was afraid that his being in the peasants' house would condemn these good people and told them that he would sleep in the barn. "They looked at each other, husband and wife, and they agreed. The wife gave me pillows and blankets and I went to the barn. They followed later. They put me in the upper part there. I was completely a broken man. They tried to console me, to comfort me, and stayed with me. I pretended that I was falling asleep, because I wanted them to sleep. I was imposing on them and I felt sorry for them. When they left, I couldn't sleep all night. I walked all over that barn. I was so very, very restless."

In the morning Klos went to investigate the situation. Ephraim recalled that when Klos returned he told him that the Kamionka Jews who had arrived in the Lubartow ghetto were kept together and would be shipped off to an unknown destination. Most of the young Jews who, like Ephraim, had left had also been picked up. "This was the summer of 1942. At that moment, I realized fully that I would never see my parents again. Klos tried to comfort me with better news. He had visited his two brothers-in-law, in this area, and they promised that in case of danger they too were prepared to take me in. I was stunned."

Ephraim told them that he could not wait in the barn. "I just couldn't absorb it....So, I went into this peasant's house and said that I needed to know more details about my family, and that I would return. He said, 'Go with God.'"

Ephraim went to another Polish friend, a widow. She also received him warmly and was willing to help. Basically, she reconfirmed what his other friends had said. This only deepened Ephraim's sadness and increased his restlessness. On leaving this widow's place, Ephraim met a Jewish boy he knew. The boy told him that he was on an errand for his parents who were hiding in the nearby forest. The boy readily told Ephraim where they were. "I went to tell Klos that I had to be away for a few more days. He asked me to be very careful, because many people were looking for Jews. He also gave me warm things to wear, food and bread."

Familiar with the area, Ephraim wanted to find the Jews that this boy told him about. Eventually, he learned that there were about a hundred of them living there, in bunkers they had built in the forest. They came from several little towns around them. They welcomed him and offered him a place in a bunker. He felt less lonely, and grateful for people with whom he could so easily talk. "It was strange for me, the first night in the forest, because I wasn't used to it: the little animals, the birds…I was fearful of anything that moved. After a few days I settled in."

Nevertheless, Ephraim recalls thinking about his fate and about the family that was ready to take him in. "I asked myself how long would this very decent, peasant family have kept me. Perhaps, after a while, they would have become tired of me." In the forest, however, he felt free. "All of us cooperated. Jewish women would take turns going to the nearby villages to buy food. Some of them were confronted by anti-Semitic name-calling. They managed to escape. We all knew that our situation was shaky. To spread the danger we decided to divide into several bunkers. We were close to the forest, Bratnik."

Among the one hundred or so fugitives, there were about twenty young men. Ephraim was the youngest. His group decided to organize. They elected as Commander Yankel Klener, because he had served in the Polish army. They had two guns, each in deplorable condition, and they lacked ammunition. Still, when peasants were confronted with these "weapons," they were likely to part with their provisions.

One day two of their group went to fetch water. They returned very agitated with the news that the Germans were attacking the other bunkers and would no doubt come for them next. Ephraim recalls that there were twelve of them. "We decided to run away. I urged them to follow me, because I knew the area very well."

They went for about a mile, until they came to a road that led to another forest. "As we reached that road, we saw three Germans with machine guns, looking in the opposite direction. We realized that they had surrounded the forest. They were coming from the other side, so we fell to the ground. Grenades fell all around us; soon they were shooting at us. We ran close to the ground, perhaps for an hour. When we returned at night, the place was silent."

Had it not been for the separate bunker, Ephraim knew, they would all be dead. He and the others suspected that Polish collaborators had brought the Germans. "A day earlier, we had seen Poles walking around with pails, as if collecting mushrooms. They had probably been spying on us."

Not sure what to do next, the young men kept away from the bunkers and stayed on the move, buying food wherever they could. As they continued to roam around, they came upon a variety of people. Some identified themselves as Jewish partisans, some as Russian partisans. Most of them had very few weapons. In one of these groups, someone told them about a Polish peasant who had some hidden arms. At night two from their group, Ephraim and another tall and rather impressive-looking man, each equipped with a defective gun, demanded weapons from this peasant. They told him they had been sent from the Soviet Union to organize a partisan unit. This peasant had some communist connections. He supplied them with several guns. More significantly, he directed them to others who had a variety of guns and ammunition. "I personally didn't know how to hold a gun, let alone how to use it. But the minute we had weapons, we became much braver."

After winter came, conditions in the forest grew difficult. They were attacked by a small group. "We concluded that three Polish collaborators were at the head of this group. Earlier, they had been seen walking around in the forest, as if lost, looking for a way out. Now, they started to shoot at us. When they realized that we were armed they lost their courage and we caught two of them, we tied them up, stuffed rags into their mouths and retreated, taking them with us. At first the rest of their group was following us. But, soon when we began to shoot back, they were less heroic, not as eager to be near us."

That night they interrogated the men they had captured and learned that their goal had been to find Jews. "They were also fighting those who were helping Jews. In addition, they were informing on Poles who were illegally selling their produce, cows, chickens, and so on. They were well organized, and they gave us important information. We were so excited, we couldn't sleep."

That same night Ephraim and the others went to find more of the collaborators that the captured men had told them about. "We shot them right there, that very night." He recalled how strange it was to see these men who had denounced them "kneel in front of us and beg for mercy. We realized that they were much more frightened than we were. We didn't care so much about life; we had lost everything; they had their families to lose still, so they were afraid."

Life in the forest improved. The network of informers had been destroyed and the few collaborators who were still left had more difficulty. "Without collaborators, Germans could not easily identify Jews. They stopped searching specifically for Jews and for Poles who protected them."

Still, threats to the forest Jews could and did continue to come from various directions. From 1939 to 1941, because of the Soviet–German friendship treaty, the communists had to put their open criticism of the Third Reich on hold. The June 22, 1941, outbreak of the Soviet–German war transformed this situation. Immediately after the start of the war, entire Red Army divisions collapsed. Thousands of Soviet soldiers escaped into the surrounding wooded areas to avoid being caught by the Germans, whose treatment of prisoners was merciless. Estimates of Russian causalities in German captivity run into the millions. German brutality directed toward these former Soviet soldiers served as a strong incentive for escape into the forest and for the subsequent formation of partisan groups.

The Soviet government was quick to recognize the benefits that could accrue from these former soldiers. Stalin knew that these men could help them fight the enemy from within the German-occupied areas. As early as July 1941, the Central Committee of the Soviet Communist Party urged the formation of an anti-German partisan movement. With headquarters in Moscow, one of the first steps of this organization was the creation of a school for saboteurs. The central staff of the Partisan Movement was established in the spring of 1942. Marshal Clement Efremovich Voroshilov became Commander in Chief and Pantileimon Ponomarenko, first secretary of the Communist Party in Western Belorussia, was appointed Chief of Staff.[22]

Thousands of former Soviet soldiers scattered into the forests, some belonging to the USSR and others to parts of prewar Poland. Endless and inaccessible, these woods cover much of Belorussia, now known as Belarus. Here and there men who scattered into a variety of wooded areas organized into many small splinter groups. Initially, avoiding confrontations with superior enemies, and all other forest dwellers, these early partisans limited their activities to finding food and shelter. Only rarely would they attack Germans and then only if presented with easy targets. The main inducement in such cases was the capture of weapons.

By 1942, young Gentile men were joining these partisan groups. Some hoped to avoid forced removal to Germany as slave laborers. Haphazard military attacks mounted by these early partisans had led to exaggerated ideas about their power; rumors of partisans' heroism multiplied. To Jews who were in desperate need of options, these rumors were a respite from German brutality. Partly as a result of these rumors, in the summer of 1942, Jewish ghetto runaways began to attach themselves to the various forest groups. With the exception of a few armed young men, most Jewish fugitives were unarmed civilians, older people, women, and children.

Significantly, too, in prewar Poland, more than 75 percent of Jews had lived in towns and cities. Adjustment to forest life was therefore challenging. Inevitably, many of these unarmed civilians became easy targets for robbery, extortion, and murder. Occasionally, the young men among them, if able-bodied, would join one of the Soviet groups. For Jews, German terror still loomed everywhere. It was this terror that had propelled them into the woods in the first place.

At the early stages of the German–Soviet war, a weakened and humiliated Russia was short of allies who might ease its military burdens. The Jews were also in need of allies. The precarious situation of the Jewish population, in and of itself, made them receptive to any gesture of help. Usually they refrained from making unreasonable demands from their prospective allies. To some of the local communists, the Jews looked like appropriate partners for forging anti-German opposition.

With a large portion of the Red Army in disarray, and some of it scattered throughout Eastern Europe, the Soviet Union could hardly offer concrete aid. Furthermore, not all forests in Eastern Europe were hospitable to guerrilla warfare. Nor were all forests equally hospitable as protection to other fugitives who reached them.

The situation in most forests was fluid and Moscow's control over Soviet partisans was limited. Initially, the Russian partisans looked to Moscow for guidance. They were likely to see themselves as vulnerable and were conciliatory toward those from whom they sought cooperation. However, the more vulnerable the Russian partisans felt, the more likely they were to cooperate with ethnically diverse partisan groups, including the Jews. Russian tolerance extended even to women, whom they were also more likely to treat as partners. Mutual cooperation went hand in hand with mutual tolerance. However, with time, as Soviet partisans became better organized and felt stronger, they insisted on breaking up ethnically and religiously based detachments. They were also more likely to bar women from becoming leaders and fighters.

The 1943 German defeat at Stalingrad marked a turning point in the conduct of the Soviet–German war. These changes increased Stalin's concerted efforts to expand the efficacy of the Soviet partisan movement. More men from the USSR were parachuted into a variety of forests. Others came in planes that landed at secretly constructed airstrips, close to the woods. But winning the war, although a priority, was only one of Stalin's objectives. Beyond the defeat of Germany, the USSR had a range of political agendas. Some of them were tied to Poland's destiny. Once Stalin became certain of the outcome of the war, he began to pressure his allies, the United States and England, for recognition of the Polish–Russian borders as specified in the Ribbentrop-Molotov Agreement. This called for the return of Polish lands occupied by the Soviets in the fall of 1939 to the USSR.

Stalin's aspirations, however, went further. He also wanted a Moscow-sponsored government for all of postwar Poland. Toward this end, Stalin set out to bureaucratize and politicize the Russian partisan movement, sowing the seeds of future Communist Party rule. Eastern Europe, with its extensive forests and thousands of forest dwellers, became a crucial element of this plan. As the Soviets consolidated their control over the partisans, they established two separate power centers: one military, the other political.

Gradually these efforts helped transform many Polish forests into centers of the Soviet partisan movement. The Soviet partisan organizers gained more control, not only over their own men but also over entire forest areas. Occasionally this control spilled into adjacent towns and villages. Toward the end of 1943, it was not unusual for local authorities to avoid some partisan enclaves. Such territorial takeovers were uneven, frequently punctuated by exceptions and changes.

In part, the Soviets had succeeded in establishing a firmer grip over some partisans, but they never gained full control over them. For the duration of the war, in some areas the USSR had to compromise by bowing to local demands. Almost up to the end of the war, determined to dominate much of Eastern Europe, the Soviets continued to tolerate a variety of subgroups with distinct, at times even mutually hostile, aims. Most of their partisan units remained an ethnic mixture of Russians, Belorusians, Ukrainians, Jews, Poles, and Lithuanians. Most of these groups had culturally and politically implicit and explicit agendas.[23]

This was particularly the case in Poland. As early as 1940, the Polish government-in-exile in London had established an underground made up of four political movements: the Socialists, the Nationalist Movement, the Polish Peasant Party, and the Christian Labor Movement. Excluded completely were the communists and the extreme right National Armed Forces (Narodowe Siły Zbrojne, or NSZ). At the head of this wartime government was the Chief Delegate, whose duty it was to coordinate the activities of the four major political parties. The military arm of the government-in-exile was the Home Army, or AK. The AK was in charge of the internal struggles in occupied Poland and was roughly divided into a propaganda section and a section that dealt with Poland's daily struggles, sabotage, and a wide range of activities, which collectively aimed at undermining the German occupational control. The Polish government in London offered some technical continuity to the political and military aspects of life.

From the start of the war two basic principles guided the Polish government-in-exile: first, as a collectivity, the Poles swore never to collaborate with the German occupiers. Second, the administration of the underground had to coordinate its activities with the government-in-exile in London.

Out of the four political parties represented in the Polish underground, the Nationalist Movement was most influential, particularly when it came to anti-Semitism. Sometime around 1942, a variety of Polish partisan groups began to operate in the Eastern European forests. The particular influence of the Nationalist Movement Party was reflected in AK's anti-Semitic policies and actions toward Jewish partisans.[24]

Ephraim soon became aware of this situation and the potential threat it created for Jews in the forest. He remembered that "the AK thought that they would take care of us Jews, but when they realized that we were fighting back, they changed their tactics." The main tactic was to set traps and ambushes. "We learned how to defend ourselves by employing the same tactics. For us it was a matter of life and death...we learned how to fight, how to oppose. It was either to kill them or they would kill us." Opposition brought more than survival. "When we retaliated against them, again and again, they became friendly and seemed to be backing down a bit."

Ephraim remembers one confrontation with AK, at which they decided to talk rather than to fight. "One of the AK said to us, 'What is this? You are robbing our people? Killing them!' And I said: 'After all, we are partisans. Look, if I come to you and ask for food, and you meet my requests with a gun, I will try to shoot you back. I'm a partisan, and I must be helped...' Still it took the AK a while to learn that we wouldn't tolerate their persecution or abuse."

Once, during the winter, one of the Jewish partisans set off on an errand in a sleigh. He was disarmed and shot, and his sleigh was confiscated. The Jewish partisans investigated the case. Their investigation identified a few AK men who had committed the robbery and the murder. When the Jews assured themselves that they had identified the guilty parties, they tracked them down and executed them. The message was clear. The AK realized that the Jews would fight back decisively. In turn, the AK became more fearful and cautious. They even warned their people to leave the Jews alone to avoid bloodshed. At one point the AK called for a conference with the Jewish partisans. The two parties reached an agreement to leave each other alone and not fight.

"From day to day, it got better," Ephraim concluded. "The hostility between us was reduced; they were afraid of our strength. It got so that we could stay in villages for a few weeks without being harassed. Eventually, the Germans were afraid to enter some of these villages. At that point we were so intermingled with the AK, that if they would denounce us and the Germans would come, there would be a battle, and the AK would die and we would die. Our fates were entangled. They somehow saw that they had no choice but to cooperate with us."

By 1943, different Polish partisan groups invaded the forests. The AK was only one of those groups that had operated in the

Eastern European forests. These other partisans, unlike the AK, formed different alliances. Initially one of these groups was the Polish Workers' Party (Polska Partia Robotnicza, or PPR), a communist group. Unlike the AK, which was tied to the Polish government in London, the PPR cooperated with the Soviet Union.

The PPR and the AK were hostile. In Ephraim's area of operations, Southeastern Poland, the PPR partisans were interchangeably referred to as Gwardia Ludowa, or GL. These groups were friendlier to the Jewish partisans than the AK. In part this was probably due to the fact that, early on, the PPR was small and lacked partisan skills. They were in need of allies. The Jewish partisans were also in need of allies and ready to cooperate. Ephraim describes the PPR's transition from a weak to a powerful fighting force: "They actually learned from us...we had no choice, we had to fight. Otherwise we would have been killed." In this area the PPR was closely connected to the GL, which was equally connected to the USSR. The Jewish partisans in this area cooperated with these Polish pro-communist partisans who were grateful to the Jews for getting rid of German collaborators.

Ephraim always remained in the same kind of a group. Various Jewish partisans cooperated with each other; all were eager to move against the enemy, particularly the German murderers whom they had previously seen as all-powerful giants. With time, however, these former giants, when caught, would plead for mercy. The nature of such encounters only encouraged the Jewish partisans to resist. These changes occurred gradually, almost imperceptibly. With time the Jews understood that these Germans were more afraid of them than they were afraid of the Germans. As Ephraim had argued, they had more to lose than the Jews: "They had their homes, their families. The Jews had nothing."

As the Jewish partisans continued to cooperate with the PPR, both groups benefited from the association. At some point the PPR wanted the Jewish partisans to become an official part of the organization, to integrate fully. But the Jews refused this offer, explaining that they wanted to be responsible for their own people and wanted to remain a separate unit. Ephraim explained, "We wanted to show them that as Jews we could fight and accomplish much and we did not want to be pushed around."

The PPR organized different anti-German moves, which the Jews were asked to join. In addition, the GL was ordered—no doubt by the somewhat-better organized Soviet partisans—to cooperate with the Jewish partisans. About Jewish participation with these pro-communist groups, Ephraim says that the PPR was forced to share with them because the Jews had fought so well and were well-established. Polish peasants even turned to the partisans for help. "For instance," remembered Ephraim, "when they were expected to hand over a certain amount of their produce to the Germans, we would help by giving them a receipt saying that the partisans had taken their products,...this way, the local peasants would deliver to the Germans fewer products keeping more for themselves....At other times a head of a village would ask us to come, make believe that we were attacking them, and that we took from them some produce. After that they would kill a cow or other animals, and blame it on us."

With time GL became an Armia Ludowa (AL), a fighting unit. Toward the end of 1943 the AL was better organized, and the Jewish units had to abide by its orders. At first the Jewish partisans did not trust them. They were afraid that they might surround them and disarm them. To assure their own safety, when going on an anti-German mission, the Jewish partisans usually asked for some AL fighters to join them. With four or five AL fighters among them, the Jews could more easily assume that it was a legitimate move and not a trap.

By the end of 1943 mutual trust had been established through several successful cooperative anti-German moves. At that point the Jews realized more fully that members of the AL were not as anti-Semitic as the AK. Moreover, through the intervention of the AL, the Jewish partisans received arms from the Soviet parachutists. Other important mutually helpful exchanges were also set in motion. In the end the Jews felt that they were treated like equals and continued to offer to the AL important information about local conditions. Eventually the AL trusted Jews more than they did local Poles, and preferred to use the Jews rather than their own special guides. The AL and the Soviet army were occupying different parts of the country. When the Soviets conquered the Lublin area in 1944, they selected Ephraim as their special guide.

In addition, the local population had gradually come to recognize that the Jews were not bandits exploiting innocent people. Indeed, when the Jewish partisans had to punish an informer, they would go to his house, and if he was not there, they would wait. They would not kill an innocent person instead. As a rule, Jewish partisans did not punish anyone unless they were convinced that the particular person had committed a crime, especially against Jews. The local population recognized the fact that Jews were only attacking those who were guilty of particular crimes. With this realization came more friendly relations between the Jews and the Gentiles. The local population began to respect the Jewish sense of fairness.

The more contacts the local Poles and the Jewish partisan had, the more they appreciated each other. Cooperation between Poles and Jews created special bonds between them. They became more appreciative of their differences, as well as their similarities. Understandings developed between the local population and the Jewish partisans and facilitated the Jewish fight for life.

In the end it helped them to learn to oppose. Ephraim told me again and again: "I never dreamt that I would be able to fight those murderers, that I would be able to oppose them. I never imagined that the Germans might run away from me, be afraid of me. I never thought of that." To a large extent it was cooperation with others, with people who were very different from them, that made this possible.

For Ephraim, the war ended on July 23, 1944—the day he began to search for his family, a search that went on for years. Here and there his efforts uncovered clues and fleeting hopes that someone might have survived. But these always ended in disappointment. Not one of Ephraim's close relatives had survived.

Recently, I was impressed while reading Ephraim's *Rather Die Fighting: A Memoir of World War II*, in which he offers an invaluable addition to the Holocaust literature: testament to the ways Jews first learned how to be resilient and self-reliant—and then, through cooperation with others, how to resist.

CHAPTER TWO

The Ghettos

In August 1939, the twenty-first World Zionist Congress convened in Geneva, Switzerland. Emanuel Ringelblum (figure 2.1), a member of the Polish political party Poalei Zion Left, attended as an observer. When the official segments of this international gathering began to wind down, the proceedings were overcome by anxious ruminations about the impending war; the German occupation of Poland, of course, was imminent at the time of the Congress. While most of the departing participants were focused on reaching safe havens, Ringelblum, in this regard a minority, planned to return to Warsaw.

In Warsaw, Ringelblum became immersed in relief activities with refugees who started pouring into the capital on the eve of the German invasion on September 1, 1939. Swept up by the growing demands around him, he continued to refuse to follow the example of some friends who were preparing their departures. He felt morally bound to stay, promoting the welfare of the Jewish refugees who arrived from every direction.[1] Each day brought new developments. Nonetheless, in the fall of 1939, neither Ringelblum nor anyone else had the foresight to predict the Holocaust. No one imagined the scale or speed of the German destruction of European Jewry, which started with identification, expropriation, and removal from gainful employment, and ended with isolation and annihilation. These stages were complex and overlapping, but part of an inexorable process of degradation that would lead eventually to death in the concentration camps.

FIGURE 2.1 Emanuel Ringelblum. (Courtesy Yad Vashem)

Artur Eisenbach, Ringelblum's friend and brother-in-law, had urged him to leave Poland.[2] Eisenbach and Ringelblum were both historians and shared connections and insights. Later, separated by the war, Eisenbach was convinced that German assaults against the Jewish people brought the finest out of Ringelblum, whose commitment to humanity and to the Jewish people became more firmly intertwined with his uncompromising feelings of resentment toward fascism. To Eisenbach and others, Ringelblum became a symbol of dedication and self-sacrifice.[3]

From Eisenbach we learn that on the evenings of September 6 and 7, 1939, not even a week after the German invasion, friends and family gathered in the Ringelblum apartment with one overwhelming objective: to persuade their hosts to depart Warsaw, which they themselves had decided to do immediately. Their destination was the Soviet-occupied part of Poland. Many Jews—an estimated 250,000 to 300,000—fled into parts of Poland that were then Soviet territories (according to the terms of the German-Soviet pact). The arguments of Eisenbach and other friends fell on deaf ears, however. Ringelblum and his family were staying. No matter how perilous the situation became, and no matter how often those close to him urged him to move away from the German-occupied territories, Ringelblum insisted that it was his duty to remain in Poland, extending aid to as many as he could. The German occupation eventually created situations in which their needs surpassed Ringelblum's abilities to respond. Still, for the rest of his life, he never gave up trying.

Significantly, Ringelblum's outstanding work as a welfare organizer would eventually feed into his determination to collect large amounts of evidence about life and death under the German occupation of Poland. From 1940 on, this hard-working historian and activist attracted a dedicated group of writers, teachers, scholars, and social activists, all of whom were devoted to the documentation of the evolving tragedy of Polish Jewry.[4] Historian David Engel notes that "of all the people of occupied Europe, only the Jews in the Polish ghettos seemed to have assigned supreme values to activities directed toward the distant future."[5] As a keen observer of the events in Warsaw leading to the establishment of the ghetto and after, Ringelblum wanted to study and learn from all of the individuals and groups that were a part of this unique period. Whatever groups or activities Ringelblum and his coworkers observed, they tried to broach their historical implications and significance. In the view of Ringelblum and his associates, no topic was unworthy of thorough, careful exploration. The wealth of knowledge that grew out of their labors is a unique and invaluable archive, and collectively referred to as "Oneg Shabbat," or "the pleasure of the Sabbath."[6]

On September 21, 1939, Reinhard Heydrich, head of the Reich Security Main Office, ordered that a "Council of Jewish Elders" be established in every Jewish community and that "as far as possible" it consist of leading figures and rabbis. This council was to be made "entirely responsible, within the meaning of the word, for the exact and prompt fulfillment of all instructions which have been or will be given."[7] In other words, these Jewish Councils, or Judenrats, were special administrative bodies designed to transmit German orders.[8] At first, they tried to recruit prewar communal leaders to serve, but many had escaped, while others refused to become involved with the German authorities in any way. The history of the Judenrat is clouded by a number of unresolved debates.[9] The character and functions of these councils were perpetually in a state of flux. At the slightest sign of independence, the Germans would execute a part or even an entire Judenrat, then immediately replace it with a new one.

With one notable exception, aside from a few women who performed clerical jobs, all these newly appointed councils consisted of men.[10] One exception was Wieliczka, a small town near Krakow. Here the initial German takeover was marked by the immediate execution of most Jewish men. Their murder traumatized the community and the remaining male survivors refused to become a part of a Judenrat. The Germans insisted, threatening reprisals. When no men responded and the threats grew, women volunteered to take their places, one of them as chair. Women had traditionally filled gaps created by the absence of men. The Wieliczka Judenrat changed in 1941 when two male refugees from Krakow took over.[11]

By October 1939—six weeks into the occupation—German authorities had issued special decrees making work by Jewish men mandatory. These decrees called for random and sometimes violent captures of men, many of whom were unfit for hard labor. Whenever the Germans seized rabbis, prominent intellectuals, or successful businessmen, they would assign them to the most degrading and debilitating jobs, like cleaning toilets or doing road work. These roundups made clear that men rather than women were in particular danger.[12] It has been estimated that two-thirds of those who fled to the Soviet-occupied territories were men.[13] For those Jewish men who stayed on in German-occupied Poland, assaults continued. In addition to street violence, many were forced to clear rubble, fill anti-tank ditches, shovel snow, and perform other kinds of hard labor.

A close observer of historical shifts, Ringelblum describes how these events were reflected in the lives of Jewish women under the German occupation. He notes that:

> [W]omen maintain the home. The men stay home. The woman keeps pace with things that must be done. The woman is ready to follow the Germans who have power, asking for and complaining about the circumstances she doesn't approve of. Women join long lines which promise some rare and valued acquisitions. The elegant lady who used to spend hours in coffee shops has disappeared. Now, Jewish women visit official offices, trying to make sense out of current circumstances. Women's elegant hats have

also disappeared. They have been replaced by simple head scarves. When Jews must pay a visit to officials in power, daughters and mothers step in. If this is not possible, these women remain standing and waiting in the hallways. When there is an opportunity to remove heavy packages from stores and living quarters, this is done by a husband or brother. But this too is often accomplished under the watchful eyes of the wife on the opposite side of the street. Busy with many chores, women still find time to attach themselves to long lines which promise the sale of coal. Accordingly, on the city streets, one encounters many more women than men. Many Polish men have been caught for compulsory labor in Germany.[14]

Less punitive, yet still degrading, were Warsaw's long bread lines, created by food shortages. Vladka Meed (figure 2.2) was the

FIGURE 2.2 Vladka Meed poses in Theater Square (Plac Teatralny). Vladka moved into the newly created Warsaw ghetto with her entire family in 1940. (U.S. Holocaust Memorial Museum, courtesy of Benjamin Miedzyrzecki Meed)

daughter of a haberdashery store owner. During World War I, her father had positive experiences with the German military, so when Vladka's family joined their neighbors in their shelter, her father assured them that they had nothing to fear from the Germans, that they were cultured and unlikely to harm civilians. Vladka knew that her father was more interested in reading books than in attending to his haberdashery business. In fact, she admired him for it. When the German bombs demolished parts of their store, he consoled his family; substantial quantities of materials had been salvaged and they would be fine. When the Germans occupied Warsaw, he took it in stride, not anticipating any special hardships.

The first morning of the occupation of Warsaw, Vladka's father, Shlomo, joined a group of Poles in a bread line. It took him a few minutes to comprehend that they were screaming at him, insisting that as a Jew, he had no right to the bread. Their shouting attracted the attention of a German soldier, who pulled Shlomo out of the line and began beating him mercilessly. The experience made clear that the Germans had changed since his World War I experiences.

Ringelblum observed that from the moment Polish anti-Semites helped the Germans drive Jews away from the food lines, the "street" was where they joined forces, "for this was where both victors and collaborators found their Jewish prey."[15]

Ghettos were set up as temporary Jewish quarters, a first step to Jewish annihilation. Before the actual construction of these ghettos, Jews lacked clear-cut information about their character and purpose, and what contradictory information they heard heightened their apprehensions. Here and there among the grim reports was a hopeful note. Some claimed that future Jewish quarters would be autonomous communities with free access to the surroundings. But, on the whole, these rumors failed to calm the people.[16]

Responding to the mounting tensions, Adam Czerniakow (figure 2.3), the newly appointed head of the Warsaw Judenrat, petitioned the German authorities to halt construction of the ghetto.[17] The Germans responded by establishing two ghettos, one in Warsaw and the second in Lodz. This was followed by a phase of intensified construction of ghettos, which eventually numbered an estimated 400.[18] Their common traits outweighed by far their differences. All ghettos were located in the most dilapidated parts of urban centers, lacking running water and electricity. Several families were assigned to one room, and the accumulation of filth led to all kinds

FIGURE 2.3 Adam Czerniakow, Jewish Council chairman, works in his office in the Warsaw ghetto. (U.S. Holocaust Memorial Museum, courtesy of Zydowski Instytut Historyczny imienia Emanuela Ringelbluma)

of epidemics. Death could and did come from a variety of sources: starvation, sporadic violence, disease, and, indirectly, from forced deportations to concentration camps. Ghetto inmates were cut off from the world around them and, thus deprived of information, made decisions based on limited and subjective observations and experiences. The Judenrats, for example, were viewed by the ghetto population with suspicion. Sometimes these suspicions evolved into accusations of betrayal. In part these stemmed from the direct contact that Judenrat members had with the Germans. Probably, too, the relative advantages that the Judenrat members and their families seemed to have and the growing deprivations of the rest of the ghetto population fueled resentment. In some instances, actual corruption by some Judenrat members might have contributed to these accusations.[19]

However, the Judenrat was by no means the sole focus of conflicts and dissension within the ghetto. The German occupation had made the ghetto into a community in which most traditional social orders were shattered and in which the new ones were, as historian Philip Friedman noted, kept in flux. "Social distinctions in the ghetto and survival depended on shrewdness, audacity, indifference to the plight of others, physical strength, manual dexterity, and external factors such as direct access to German authorities."[20]

The heterogeneity that was characteristic of the ghetto populations contributed to the conflicts among inmates. Large portions of ghetto inhabitants had come from the surrounding, generally smaller, communities. Also among the new arrivals were Jews who had converted to Catholicism and were known for their virulent anti-Semitism, and gypsies who shared with the Jews only a range of mutual suspicions. New arrivals also included Jews from Western Europe who looked upon Eastern European Jewry with contempt.[21] In addition, the periodic removals of ghetto inmates to concentration camps, or for mass shootings, continually modified the composition of the ghetto populations and contributed to general instability.

This, of course, was the point. The German authorities knew that cohesive ghetto populations could try to unite against them. They also recognized that diversity of the populations, and the resulting distrust and hostility, prevented cooperative action. In the end, the Germans were hugely successful in the achievement of their goals. Nonetheless, Jewish underground opposition emerged in the ghettos, as did plans to escape into the Christian world. Some Jews, like Ephraim Bleichman, escaped to the forest, where they hoped to elude the Germans. The odds were stacked against escape, however. The Nazis had seen to it that ghettos were partly "led" by former Jewish leaders who were powerless, resigned, and ineffective. In general, the ghettos were ravaged by hunger, disease, and terror; they were sealed off communities, isolated from the world, and left to their own meager resources.

Merely being transferred into a ghetto involved a series of personal hardships. One teenage boy, Yitskhok Rudashevski, whom the Germans murdered after the liquidation of the Vilna ghetto, left behind his diary in which he described what a ghetto transfer entailed:

> The streets are turbulent. A ghetto is being created for Vilna Jews....The Lithuanians drive us on, they do not let us rest. I think of nothing: not what I am losing, not what I have just lost, not what is in store for me. I do not see the streets before me, the people passing by. I only feel that I am terribly weary, I feel that an insult, a hurt is burning inside me. Here is the ghetto gate.

I feel that I have been robbed; my freedom is being robbed from me. My home and the familiar Vilna streets I love so much are gone. I have been cut off from all that is dear and precious to me. People crowd at the gate....We settle down in our place. Besides the four of us there are eleven persons in the room. The room is a dirty and a stuffy one. It is crowded. The first ghetto night [w]e lie three together on two doors. I do not sleep. In my ears resounds the lamentation of this day. I hear the restless breathing of people with whom I have been suddenly thrown together; people who just like me have suddenly been uprooted from their homes.[22]

Confined to crowded spaces, removed from gainful employment, forced into jobs that offered only meager food rations, Jewish men became despondent and unable to protect their families. Women's roles, although obviously affected by the war, were not subject to the same dramatic changes as the men's. In the uncertain environment of the ghetto, the ability to survive physically, to evade notice, and to keep their families fed—these mattered the most. Each required special efforts and called for special skills. Women's traditional roles as caregivers, housekeepers, and cooks remained essential. Deprivation and hunger made those who could procure and skillfully handle food particularly valuable. Women were well suited for fulfilling these roles. Thus, in the ghetto, unobtrusively yet consistently, women contributed significantly to survival.

This was especially true for women with families. Their contributions ranged from tangible help, such as the smuggling of food, to keeping up the spirit and the morale of those around them. Of the survivors I met with, especially those whose parents survived with them, most mentioned fathers who were broken by German oppression. At the same time, they described strong mothers who refused to capitulate and who kept the family going, often helping others whom they saw as more needy. Some of these women stepped into spaces created by the loss of their husbands. Others took over the roles of husbands, who were too despondent to act on behalf of their families.

Vladka Meed moved into the newly created Warsaw ghetto with her entire family. Initially reluctant to admit that men and women behaved differently, she soon changed her mind.

I have a feeling that women could withstand the difficult conditions more easily than men. The women were more practical, more of an organizer, and able to take over what had to be done in those days. The men had a profession, an occupation, a business. But when these things were taken away then they were lost, they had nothing to cling to. More often than not the women were at home. They were among those who knew how to deal with the home and its needs and they worried about the entire family. It is also true that in many ghettos, most of those who were buying and selling were women. This was probably wise. If a German passed by he would more likely notice a man than a woman....I am not so sure that I am right, but the devotion, the ability to sacrifice for others, were more strongly developed in the ghetto in the women than in the men...when a mother was hungry she could cope with this situation better than a man.

Again and again, Vladka talked about her father in the Warsaw ghetto, describing him as helpless, depressed, and malnourished. He eventually contracted pneumonia and died. She contrasts his passivity to her mother, who "was able to keep our house clean only with water and a strong will," and in the process fighting disease, particularly typhoid fever. She was a woman of considerable willpower:

When my brother was almost thirteen, our mother, though starving—there was a swelling under her eyes from hunger—would save a slice of bread for the rabbi who came to teach my brother for his bar mitzvah. The bread she hid under her pillow. She had no money to buy extra bread, but in exchange for the bread the rabbi would give bar mitzvah lessons to my brother. A simple, uneducated woman, this mother refused to sell her husband's books for food.

The reason? She thought that sometime in the future "her children would learn from these books." It seems significant that this woman, who in the past had been annoyed by her husband's devoting too much attention to his books, should now refuse to sell some of them even though his family was hungry. By refusing to part with her husband's books, she was showing her family's respect for the memory of their father and her husband.

Vladka's assessment is also reflected in Sara Zyskind's experience. In the Lodz ghetto, this teenager watched her mother supplement the family's income by selling hot coffee to ghetto inmates who, early in the morning, had to pass close to their dwelling. At first this daughter was embarrassed by her mother's efforts. With time her attitude shifted to admiration. "It never occurred to this intelligent and gentle woman to turn up her nose at the lowest tasks, as long as she was able to help her family. Although selling coffee was not a profitable venture, it made it possible for us to buy an additional ration of bread for father, acquired at the black market, and buy an adequate supply of coal. Now our room was heated, greatly lessening the fear of the winter." After a short time her mother died, leaving Sara and her father in a more deplorable situation.[23]

German directives were continuously pouring in. Severe punishment, usually death, followed disobedience to any of them. On October 15, 1941, a new law mandated the death sentence for any Jew caught outside of the ghetto and involved in "illegal" activities. A violation of this law led not only to the death of the Jew but also to the death of anyone who might have been somehow involved in this transgression.[24] German authorities were serious about enforcements of this law. The laws and consequences of breaking them were widely publicized and discussed. Indeed, most German laws were propelled by the principle of collective responsibility.

Within these continuously evolving environments, most ghetto inmates were confronted by growing oppression. Despite the horrendous circumstances, some Jews engaged in mutual aid activities. Some devoted themselves to the establishment of soup kitchens; others to the building of orphanages; still others to the collection of money and goods for the sick and the helpless. In the ghettos, a large number of women, the young and the not-so-young, tried to take advantage of whatever opportunities they could find to make things better.

Still, few ghetto inmates could permanently escape the oppressive measures that the authorities imposed upon the Jews. Vladka Meed could not escape from the effects of chronic hunger. "In the ghetto I thought about myself mainly in relation to food. I did not want to be hungry. But I was always hungry." One day, she was so swollen from hunger that she could not work. "Maybe this saved me, because one day I could not put on my shoes and could not go to work. And just that day there was a selection and all those who came to my working place were taken away."

The Germans contributed to the tensions between diverse ghetto inmates by issuing documents that gave the right to live to one inmate—at the expense of another. In the Vilna ghetto, Mark Dworzecki describes how he and his friend appealed for a life-saving pass: "Both of us sat in the dark office corridor...waiting for the judgment upon us. We talked to each other...at the same time we knew that a life voucher for one of us meant a death warrant for the other." In the end he got the voucher and not his friend. "I was ashamed to raise my eyes but nonetheless I took the document."[25]

Work assignments and appropriate documents did not necessarily translate into adequate food rations. Officially, in occupied Poland, ghetto inmates were entitled to fewer than 400 calories per day.[26] Added to the effects of chronic hunger were severe problems caused by cramped living quarters. The absence of electricity, running water, and adequate toilet facilities led to hygiene problems and epidemics. Overcrowded hospitals lacked basic equipment and medications. The Jewish hospital staff was required to report all patients with chronic and contagious diseases. When identified to the authorities, such patients were immediately killed.[27] Ghetto prohibitions extended to school attendance, to private instruction, and to religious observances. All these were a part of the established processes of humiliation and degradation.

Faced with these and other expanding assaults on freedom, dignity, and survival, many Judenrat leaders and others refused to submit. Collectively and individually they organized a variety of fund-raising events: lectures, theatrical performances, and contests. The leadership imposed taxes on the few ghetto inhabitants who still had money. With these funds they created soup kitchens and bought medications.

In some of the ghettos, young people of various political groups offered lessons to children and lectured to adult audiences, though this was illegal. One of them was the enterprising Vladka Meed. One of her most vivid recollections is of a lecture she gave about Boncze Szveig, a character in a novel by the Jewish writer Peretz. This lecture was just one of the many cultural evenings, an important part of the Warsaw ghetto life. In her case, it took place in a large room filled with older listeners. The windows were securely covered. A special watchman stood next to the gate of the building, in a secluded corner of the house. Vladka was younger than anyone in her attentive audience, but people were accustomed to these youthful and passionate lecturers. The air was filled with a tension that held until the very end of the presentation, which was followed by questions. Animated, eager to learn, to explore, audience and lecturer were locked in an intense and heated exchange of ideas. This and other similar cultural events had the power to transport the participants away from the ghetto poverty, from hunger, from the devastation, and to inhabit briefly a more meaningful and dignified world. What happened in this and similar rooms was real, and perhaps even more real than that which inevitably greeted each Jew outside of the room.

In large ghettos in particular, certain morale-building activities also took place. Among them were special committees devoted to the establishment of theatrical presentations, libraries, and a variety of other educational pursuits. Illegal schools seemed to have flourished in the ghettos of Estonia, Poland, Lithuania, and Latvia.

Yitskhok Rudashevsky, the teenage boy in the Vilna ghetto, underscored the value of these efforts: "Finally I have lived to see the day," he wrote in his diary. "Today we go to school. The day passed quite differently. Lessons, subjects both of the sixth classes were combined. There is a happy spirit in class. Finally the club too was opened. My own life is shaping in quite a different way. We waste less time. The day is divided and flies by very quickly…yes, that is how it should be in the ghetto, the day should fly by, and we should not waste time." This hopeful assessment was followed shortly by the author's death.[28]

Although the Germans had utilized Jewish labor from the start of the occupation, more systematic economic exploitation followed the establishment of ghettos. Eventually, compulsory employment applied to Jewish women as well. Those whose husbands could not support them were glad to work, even for inadequate rewards. Large-sized ghettos had two kinds of workers: a municipal labor system and employment by private enterprises. The municipal labor system was more extensive and it was arranged via the Judenrat, who were under pressure to deliver Jewish workers to the Germans. The Judenrat received starvation wages for inmates' jobs. The occupational authorities closely supervised all labor transactions, including those involving private enterprises, most of which were owned by German firms that had the freedom to exploit low payment for Jewish workers, which translated into enormous profits. The Jews themselves were motivated to work hard. Some equated their economic contributions with personal survival.[29]

Everyone—Jews and the occupational authorities—knew that ultimately survival depended on access to adequate food. By controlling the ghetto food deliveries, the Germans had the power to turn the wartime ghettos into death traps. In Poland alone, an estimated 20 percent of the ghetto populations died of hunger. But for the Germans this figure was not high enough.[30] Around 1942 and beyond, the occupational authorities were determined to do away with "useless" ghetto Jews. This translated into the murder of the old, the sick, children, and even the unborn.

Eager to speed up the process of Jewish annihilation, some Germans by 1942 must have guessed that time was not on their side. After the initial, spectacular German victories at the eastern front, the Soviets stiffened their opposition. Hitler's army continued to incur losses. With these changes German victory was becoming less certain. As prospects of military conquests continued to dwindle, the Third Reich began to concentrate on winning a different war: the war against the Jews.[31]

With time, this war against the Jews heightened awareness about Jewish women, especially their function as vehicles for the perpetuation of the Jewish race. Among the weapons directed against the Jews were more extreme labor demands and laws that prohibited the birth of children.[32] Children represent the future. In the ghettos women, propelled by their own special ties to children, by tradition and by views about the future, continued to gravitate to activities related to children. But precisely because ghetto children promised a Jewish future, the Germans targeted them for annihilation. Because Jewish children did not contribute to the wartime economy through labor, they were not even temporarily exempt from annihilation. The severity of German opposition to Jewish children and procreation varied with time and place. Humiliation, starvation, and the accompanying oppressions themselves reduced the chances of successful births. When pregnancies did happen, to avert punishments, Jews often relied on abortions.

Dobka Freund-Waldhorn was caught in a web of conflicting orders and wishes: prohibitions against Jewish motherhood and the desire to give birth to a baby. Dobka came from a wealthy Orthodox family of nine children. Her father in particular saw her as a rebel. He even saw her 1939 marriage to Julek Frohlich as a form of resistance to his authority. Handsome, intelligent, from a respectable family, Julek was deemed unsuitable because he was not Orthodox. The war and the opposition to Dobka's marriage pushed the young couple to Vilna and from there into the Vilna ghetto.

When Dobka was transferred from the Vilna ghetto to a nearby estate, she realized that she was pregnant. By then Jewish women were prohibited from giving birth. Dobka's husband and a Polish doctor at the estate pleaded with her to discontinue her pregnancy. She refused. She wanted Julek's child.

When she was seven months pregnant, as a concession to her husband, Dobka went to the ghetto hospital to learn first-hand about her options. Although sympathetic, the doctor in the ghetto hospital urged her to give birth and "to dispose" of the baby. Unless she followed his advice, he said, both she and the baby would die. The doctor admitted Dobka into the ghetto hospital and tried to induce delivery. "I stayed in the hospital for a long time, maybe a month. They gave me medication to have the water move, but there was no birth. They increased the dosage. They did all kinds of things, but the child refused to be born. Eventually, I got a fever, high fever. I think that it was already the eighth month. Only then it happened. She was alive. They showed me the little girl. She was so beautiful. She looked just like my husband, and we were so much in love! Then, they took her away." Later her husband came to the hospital. "He knelt next to my bed....He took my hands into his, and he cried...terribly, terribly. 'You will see, we will have children, there will be children.'"

With Julek Frohlich, there were no more children. He died in the concentration camp Klooga. After the war, Dobka remarried and gave birth to two sons.

> After the birth of my second son, with my second husband, I dreamt that my first husband, Julek, came to me. He looked very neglected, [had] not shaved. "Where were you?" I asked, "so many years? I have a husband and children." He answered, "Yes, but you will come back to me." In the dream I thought how could I go back to him? But to him I said: "I will come back to you." I woke up and found my pillow soaking wet from my tears.[33]

Like many women in the ghettos, Ringelblum was particularly sensitive to the suffering of Jewish children. He anguished over their fate. He noted that "the Hitlerite beast wants to devour that which is most precious, that which arouses most compassion, most tenderness and sympathy, namely, innocent children." The suffering was ever-present: "Mortifying and incredible are the street children who beg for alms, reminding us of their homelessness...each evening at the corner of Leszna and Karmelicka Streets, the children are there, their faces flooded with bitter tears. After these encounters, sleep eludes me for most of the night. The few pennies I offer them fail to ease my conscience."[34]

In his writings, he shared a story others had told him. It was about a six-year-old boy lying on a Warsaw ghetto street, trying to reach for a slice of bread someone must have thrown to him from a balcony. Next morning, the boy was found dead; close to him was his untouched slice of bread.[35]

Efforts to protect Jewish children were part of a life-or-death struggle. It was also an uneven struggle, one with many child victims and few survivors.[36] Still, all ghettos had organizations devoted to helping children. As mentioned, even as ghetto congestion and deprivation continued to mount, paradoxically they were matched by a proliferation of welfare activities, including a wide range of health services, and educational and cultural pursuits.[37]

Within the ghetto, the Judenrat was entrusted with the implementation of German orders and with helping the refugees to settle in. In Warsaw as in most other places, the councils gradually expanded their operations to oversee the employment of the ghetto inmates, organize public kitchens, instigate educational and cultural activities, and much more. A significant part of the welfare organizations was sponsored by the American Jewish Joint Distribution Committee, known as the JDC. The "Joint" retained many of its prewar leaders.

Similarly important in the Warsaw ghetto were the House Committees. By 1943, practically each building had such a unit, bringing the total to about 2,000. As with most other ghetto organizations, House Committees also diversified their functions over time. They likewise created public soup kitchens, offered health care, collected and distributed clothing to the poor, and attended to the educational and cultural needs of children and others.[38]

Some of these ghetto organizations functioned as covers for underground activities. Collectively and individually, occasionally overlapping and competing with each other, they became symbols of survival and, in their way, of resistance. And again, very often, they were run by women. Emanuel Ringelblum, as the head of the Oneg Shabbat archives, commissioned Cecylia Slapak to conduct a survey about the fate of Jewish women during the war. Findings from this research point to two groups—those whose primary goal was to protect themselves and their families from the German oppression, and those whose response to life-threatening disaster was to engage in activities that reached beyond mere self-preservation and the preservation of their immediate families. Whether as private individuals or as employees of welfare organizations, they devoted themselves to helping a wider circle of people. Slapak reported that this second group was able to identify with the suffering of strangers and with the Jewish community at large.[39]

One example of this second type was a professional librarian identified in Slapak's survey as "Mrs. B." In the Warsaw ghetto, Mrs. B's job had to do with sorting old clothes. Nonetheless, she also found time to devote herself to building a children's lending library. She began by collecting books and contacting potential volunteers. Despite seemingly insurmountable obstacles, she persevered. Eventually, Mrs. B's dream came true and she was appointed Director of the Children's Lending Library.

In a wartime interview with Slapak, she shared her feelings about this accomplishment: "My library job has a wonderful psychological effect on me. It gives me life. I believe in the importance of this kind of work for the present and for the future. Before, when I used to sort clothes under much better physical conditions, and I also had then more strength, I frequently felt exhausted and sick. With my library work, although what I do is physically more taxing, and the surroundings are less agreeable...and even though I am now undernourished, I feel healthy and invigorated. I feel fulfilled. My feeling of self-fulfillment must be strengthening my immune system."[40]

Independent of Slapak's research, by 1942 Ringelblum had arrived at similar conclusions: that the men, "exhausted by strenuous labor," let women take control of some of the House Committees. "For our expanding welfare operations, we need new people. It is fortunate that we can rely on these new sources of strength."[41] Ringelblum paid special tribute to two activists whose work on House Committees expanded into other community needs—Eliahu Kahn, who established the first House Committee that aimed at easing the suffering of the needy and at the promotion of educational and cultural activities in the ghetto; and a "Mrs. Mokrska" from Lodz.

Mrs. Mokrska had a gift for finding women who were ready to sacrifice. Many of her coworkers became patrons of boarding schools, of refugee centers, and of public kitchens. The tireless and resourceful Mrs. Mokrska seemed to be everywhere. During the height of the ghetto deportations in 1942, she had located a work-shop which accepted laborers free of charge. At that point, people were convinced that employment would shield them from deportations. In reality, work was either a temporary respite or none at all. In the end, Mrs. Mokrska herself fell victim to deportation.[42]

Not surprisingly the oppressed, starved ghetto inmates welcomed the expanding welfare activities of the committees and organizations. From the perspective of the German occupiers, on the other hand, their efforts undermined the Third Reich's objectives. Given its determination to pursue their anti-Jewish policies, Germany was eagerly trying to demolish these interfering forces. In fact, by itself, the creation of ghettos was an effective system of oppression which had come close to accomplishing the annihilation of the Jewish people. By May 1942, Emanuel Ringelblum pointed to an overall demoralization taking place in the Warsaw ghetto due to the sharp contrasts he observed: a growing number of beggars were on the verge of death while visible were overdressed, elegant young women.

Ringelblum found the contrasts deplorable but turned his focus to issues involving the effectiveness of ghetto welfare organizations. He listened to those who had considered the value of the soup kitchens. They recognized that those who had depended *only* on the soup and bread which came from these kitchens had died more rapidly than others, with starvation as the major cause of their deaths. For Ringelblum these findings raised morally painful questions. Should more food be allotted to a select few who would live longer? Should one offer better quality of food to fewer people? If so, who should these people be? Who has the right to act upon these kinds of alternatives?

The Germans who had the power to decide how much food should be allotted to the ghetto inmates were, of course, indifferent to the morality of these decisions. Predictably, the German Heinz Auerswald, who had insisted on expanding his influence over the ghetto, had no problem acting upon some of these "dilemmas." In fact, he was eager to shrink the amount of food allotted to the ghetto inmates. He looked upon the new ghetto arrivals as merely wilted leaves. Auerswald had insisted that food should be allotted only to working people. He introduced the rule that a Jewish ghetto inmate could purchase soup only three times a week. He also insisted that the price for the soup should be raised by about 20 percent per portion.[43]

On June 10 and 11, 1942, the German authorities decided to stop the smuggling of food into the Warsaw ghetto. On those two evenings some Jewish smugglers were removed from their homes and executed. Such killings continued. One German whom the Jews nicknamed "Frankenstein," disguised himself as a Jew and ran around the ghetto covered with a sack. Inside this sack, he held a gun with which he shot at whomever he could reach. The smugglers were not ready to give up their livelihoods. Ringelblum quotes some of them as saying that they will not give up smuggling, that they were not afraid of bullets. They refused to endure the slow, painful death from starvation. Smuggling in the ghetto continued.[44]

Ringelblum also reported how the ghetto physicians studied the implications and consequences of chronic hunger, noting that the Warsaw ghetto had served as a kind of laboratory. News came from Lodz that a recently arrived physician from Prague had discovered that eating boiled potatoes would eliminate swellings caused by starvation. Unfortunately, potatoes were not available in the Lodz ghetto. Others suggested a different remedy against swelling created by chronic starvation: the total German withdrawal from the country.[45]

By June 1942, the Germans became more serious about stopping the smuggling of goods into the Warsaw ghetto. To accomplish this, the head of the Jewish police, Yakov Lejkin—a Nazi supporter—had asked Jewish policemen to volunteer for this new undertaking. He emphasized that they were responsible for enforcing anti-smuggling rules in areas assigned to each of them.

This was a diabolical plan, which aimed at transforming Jewish policemen into a means with which to starve other groups of Jews, particularly those whose lives depended on smuggled goods. This was by no means the first time that the German authorities had forced Jews to dig graves for themselves and other Jews. This time the numbers of volunteers for such jobs were few. In the end, the Germans had to forcefully assign some Jewish policemen to these tasks: "I must admit that in the end the German oppressors found some Jews who had agreed to do the dirty work for them," noted Ringelblum ruefully.[46]

Ringelblum's wartime experiences were characterized by few rewards and many devastating disappointments. Among his close friends and longtime coworkers was Itzchak Giterman. Itzchak came to Poland as a representative of the Joint, the aforementioned American Jewish welfare organization. For years, their lives were closely intertwined. Giterman, as the Director of the Joint, continued to stay and work in Warsaw during the occupation.[47] Even after war was declared between the United States and Germany, Giterman decided to stay.[48] Ringelblum and Giterman shared a deep commitment to the welfare of the Jewish people. Both were convinced nothing would alter their deep personal friendship and stop their cooperative efforts on behalf of the needy.

Although an American Jew, Giterman still had to move into the Warsaw ghetto. By 1942, the Warsaw ghetto inmates had designed ingenious shelters and hiding places, which were intended to function as protection against deportations. Giterman was unfamiliar with the ghetto. One morning he decided to find his hiding place, which also served as his new living quarter. He came upon two friends. They stopped to exchange greetings. As they chatted, an SS man's bullet found its way to Giterman, killing him instantly.

Ringelblum was shaken by this loss. Distraught, he paid a secret visit to the illegal offices of the Oneg Shabbat records. What happened reminded him of an earlier visit to the same office, which he had shared with Giterman. At that time Giterman was busy adding the names of fallen comrades to the record. Ringelblum mused that "now the list which Giterman had worked on has his name added to the others. My hand shakes as I write the name, Itzchak Giterman. Who knows if a future historian will be correcting this list, by adding to it the name Emanuel Ringelblum? So what? We are used to death and it makes no impression on us. If anyone of us will survive, he will be looked upon as belonging to another planet. Our survival will be seen as a miracle or a mistake." He noted that Giterman's name was next to Sagan's, who had been murdered during an earlier deportation. "One could write a book about each of them and about many others who had been murdered. These tragic circumstances only underline how precarious and unpredictable life for the Jews is."[49]

Such tragic events as these were constant in the ghetto. Indeed, with transfer into the Warsaw ghetto came the loss of basic comforts, personal freedom, and property. Most ghetto inmates tried to hide their valued possessions. Even though pushed into dilapidated, overcrowded living quarters, many carved out spaces that protected their goods from inquisitive eyes.

Thus, Vladka's family, the Peltels, had hidden fabrics which they had saved from their partially bombed haberdashery. With time they would convert these into cash and food. Other ghetto inmates hid leather and other materials, as well as a range of nonperishable foods: flour, sugar, dry beans, and much, much more.

Ghetto dwellers who had managed to avoid deportations had no illusions. Convinced that they could rely only on their own resources, they became inventive. They created sanctuaries by digging below the surface, first beneath the floors and then lower still. They were separated into several layers. The final layer of these hideouts came close to the sewage system.

The other kinds of hiding places started just below the street level. From there, unobtrusively, these places spread out beyond the ghetto limits and into the forbidden Christian world. Most of these relied on Jewish-Polish cooperation, and the creation and maintenance of all of these hideouts required close ties. Anyone involved in the use of these structures was sworn into secrecy.

With the worsening of circumstances, those who had built and maintained these shelters devised extraordinary solutions. Most of them grew in size. Some of them were equipped with proper ventilations, electricity, bathrooms and kitchens. Added to these comfort features were all kinds of nonperishable foods, which could be prepared with relative ease.

The main deportations from the Warsaw ghetto to the concentration camp Treblinka began on July 22, 1942. On July 23, Adam Czerniakow, the head of the Judenrat, committed suicide by drinking cyanide. His coworkers found him in his office chair, dead. Nearby on his desk were two brief notes. One was addressed to his wife. He asked her for forgiveness for leaving her all alone, adding that he could not act in any other way. The second note explains: "They are demanding 10,000 for tomorrow, then 7,000..." The second note ends with two unreadable words.[50]

When the deportations began, the Germans and their collaborators concentrated first on collecting the beggars and other starving segments of the population—the sick, the old, and unattached children. Some who were considered too weak to travel to Treblinka were executed at the ghetto's cemetery. It is assumed that at least 20,000 inmates were murdered this way. This early focus on the infirm suggested to some that the intellectuals and the professional ghetto inmates might be spared deportation. This was not so. As the deportations continued, each policeman was required to deliver a specific number of professionals and intellectuals. Whoever failed to deliver his quota was himself subjected to deportation. Such demands and threats led to high levels of demoralization among these policemen. The deportations resulted in a growing rate of suicides among the prospective victims.[51]

During these deportations some unusual things happened. At the place of departure, the Umschlag Platz, the gifted young poet Henryka Lazowert joined her mother, even though she was not required to board the train which took them both to Treblinka. Some of the doomed refused to leave their apartments. They were killed on the spot. Many of the rabbis were shot prior to deportation. Rabbi Kanal resisted their orders. He was shot next to the loaded train.[52] Rabbi Huberband was an expert of Hebrew literature and a historian. As a member of the Oneg Shabbat archive, he contributed greatly to the writing of the evolving Holocaust history. Some of his historical contributions were lost; others were preserved as a part of the Ringelblum archives. Hidden in a workshop during the first deportation, Huberband was found and taken to his death at Treblinka.[53]

The journalist Ahron Einhorn refused to leave his quarters. Those who came to pick him up simply shot him right there in his room. Some prominent figures managed to jump out of the moving trains carrying them to Treblinka. The secretary of the Zionist party, Nathan Asch, succeeded twice in escaping. Others took different paths. The well-known psychiatrist Stefan Miller and his wife committed suicide in protest.[54] According to other reports, women in particular physically fought the policemen who pushed them onto the trains.[55]

Ringelblum writes that Czerniakow's death came too late, proving his weakness.[56] His assessment of Czerniakow's suicide is followed by a painful description of the deportations. Ringelblum notes how close some of the departing Jews came to losing their minds, driven to insanity by the violent whims of their oppressors and the capriciousness of survival.[57]

Before these deportations, the ghetto underground had persuaded the Ringelblum family to relocate to the forbidden Christian world. This move brought Ringelblum, his wife Judyta, and their son Uri to a large bunker on Grojecka Street. The owner of this place, Wladyslaw Morczak, had agreed to hide thirty-four Jews. With the Ringelblum family that number rose to up to thirty-seven.[58] At the height of the Warsaw ghetto deportations, Emanuel Ringelblum disappeared. He was last seen in the ghetto on April 18. Then news reached the underground that he was an inmate in the Trawniki camp. The Trawniki camp had contacts with the Warsaw ghetto. Eventually these contacts reached Theodor Pajewski, a member of the Polish underground. He was protected by his cover job as a train conductor. Pajewski and the Jewish courier Shoshana (Emilka) Kossover became Ringelblum's rescuers. Dressed as a train conductor, accompanied by Pajewski and Emilka, Ringelblum arrived safely back in Warsaw. For him this meant a return to the bunker on Grojecka Street, on the outskirts of Warsaw, and a reconnection with Judyta and thirteen-year-old Uri.[59] The Warsaw ghetto deportations continued.

Nachum Remba worked as a secretary in the Warsaw ghetto Judenrat. He was involved in aiding Jews selected for deportation. Remba was known for his eagerness to ease the sufferings of as many of the victims as possible. Ingrained in his memory was the day of the deportation during which the children in Janusz Korczak's orphanage and several others were deported to Treblinka. He wrote that the day the Germans decided to empty the Jewish orphanages was a very hot day. Remba tried to delay the deportation. "I had hoped that a delay might give me a chance to save some of them. And so, first I begged Dr. Korczak to come with me to the Judenrat before the start of the children's deportations," he wrote, "explaining that maybe we would succeed in saving some of the children. But he would not hear of it. Korczak was not about to leave his children, not even for one minute. They counted on his presence!"

Remba recalled standing next to the Jewish police who were assisting with the deportation of the adults. "I continued to hope that there might not be enough room for all the children. The loading was about to start. The Jewish masses were cruelly pushed, many were beaten with clubs. The Jewish policemen handled them roughly, screaming at them to move faster and faster. Each of the policemen had to deliver a number of victims." The crowd that had formed tried to delay the deportation, perhaps knowing where they would be taken.

> Then I heard the German in charge announce that the orphanages will be coming next. At the front of this precession was Korczak. No, this picture I will never forget! All of his children were clean. Each child carried a bottle of water and a brown paper bag with a slice of bread in it. Theirs' was not a walk to the wagons. Rather, it was an organized mute protest; it was a march in opposition to

these bandits! In sharp contrast to the previous, demoralized roughly pushed, severely beaten Jewish inmates, who were forced to reach their humiliating destination....These children were arranged in rows of four. At the head of the group, Korczak walked erect, his eyes looked up at the sky. At each of his sides was a child's hand, resting in each of his hands. The next part of the procession was led by Stefania Wilczynska, a teacher and Korczak's close associate. The third group of children resembled the others. They were led by Broniatowska. The fourth and last group was led by Szternfeld.

Remba noted that the children went to their death quietly, "throwing at the barbarian murderers facial expressions filled with a collective, uniform disdain. Through these mute communications the children and their educators conveyed the idea that the time will come when powerful avengers will hold them responsible for this tragedy." When they saw this, "commanded by no one, the Jewish police force stood erect; soundlessly, respectfully, they saluted this dignified procession of children and their educators. When the Germans saw Korczak approach, some of them asked: 'who is this man?'" Remba was overcome with emotion. He notes:

> I could not stand this anymore. Tears came pouring down my face. I placed my hands over my eyes. I was filled with a profound pain. Thoughts about our endless helplessness filled my entire being. It was followed by a question. How did it happen, that all we could do was to watch passively how these murderers were destroying us? At night, I kept hearing the sounds of the little children's feet, marching in unity with their teachers. I heard the rhythm of their steps moving into an unknown destination. Still today, this picture is burned into my memory. I also see ghostlike figures appear in front of me. After that, I seem to be staring at thousands of people who stand there with clenched fists, high up. In the end I see these clenched fists land on the heads of our oppressors.[60]

Nachum Remba perished in a concentration camp somewhere in the vicinity of Lublin.[61]

Even as the 1942 Warsaw ghetto deportations were in full swing, many Oneg Shabbat archivists continued to work. They were racing against time. At this stage, unable to protect the Jewish people, they concentrated on saving Jewish history. This was their act of resistance. Ringelblum and his coworkers took steps to safeguard their collected treasures. The Oneg Shabbat archives were sealed into ten large units, which consisted of metal boxes and empty milk bottles. Two parts of these units were buried in the ghetto on August 1942, at 68 Nowolipki Street. By February 1943, the rest of the archival materials were buried at 36 Swietokrzycka Street. These parts of the archives were later retrieved, one in 1946, the second in 1950. The third section seems to have been lost.[62]

When collecting historical evidence, Ringelblum was sensitive to the interdependence of facts. He was convinced that if presented in an orderly fashion, all evidence, ugly or uplifting, would be useful for those who would be reconstructing this history. Over time, Ringelblum lost his confidence that he himself would be the author of this history. But he never lost his confidence that the risks and difficulties associated with their clandestine collections and their preparations were worthwhile.

When on September 12, 1942, the deportations stopped, the ghetto population had been reduced by an estimated 300,000. Exact figures about the remaining ghetto prisoners are elusive. According to some estimates, only 10 percent of the Jewish inmates survived these deportations. Significantly, no one had any idea what the Germans aimed at doing with those who remained. What seemed clear was that for the occupiers Jews had no economic value and that their presence was attached to unknown political and propaganda measures.[63]

The general consensus among the remaining Jews was that they should have fought the Germans, preventing them from having such an easy time during the deportations. Young people in particular felt that they should have gone into the streets and set fire to the entire ghetto. There would have been victims, but not as many as 300,000. Many survivors were ashamed, and felt that this tragedy should never have come to pass. The determination to fight soon grew. At first, however, the deportations dominated all discussions. Some wanted to know why the Germans had refrained from eliminating all Jews. Others speculated that had they murdered all the Jews, the Germans would have deprived themselves of scapegoats for explanations of disasters, real or imaginary. Some noted that strangely enough the Germans failed to boast to the world that they had murdered millions of Jews. What was the reason? Similarly, some asked whether Hitler still wanted to keep his promise of freeing the world of the Jewish presence. Others determined that the cultural climate was ripe for a vigorous resistance to the final Jewish annihilation.

Ringelblum's reunion with his family in the Warsaw bunker was a miraculous gift. Once more, this historian threw himself into writing. His friends, the Bermans, managed to visit him, supplying him with historical evidence, which he wanted to re-examine, clarify, and render more accessible to future historians. Faced with more evidence, Ringelblum would come up with new questions. At one point, when he received information about the Warsaw ghetto underground known as the Jewish Military Union or Żydowski Związek Wojskowy (ŻZW) and made up mostly of former Polish army officers, he asked "Why is there no more data about ŻZW? Their traces must remain for history, even if we don't find them likeable." This comment shows how concerned Ringelblum was about being objective and using reliable evidence. It also suggests how nonjudgmental he was. He consistently reiterated his position that no matter how we feel about a part of history, it has to be recorded and preserved in a fair and value-free way as possible.[64]

Although removed from the ghetto, Ringelblum followed the historical implications of the ghetto deportations that lasted from July 22 until September 12, 1942. These deportations had overlapped with the Jewish underground preparations by political groups—made up mostly of young people—such as Hashomer Hatzair, Dror, Akiva, and the vacillating members of the Bund, who had identified strongly with the Polish socialists. Only when the Bund recognized that the Polish socialists had no intention of uniting with them did they also join the Jewish Fighting Organization, Żydowska Organizacja Bojowa, also known as ŻOB.

The ŻOB was officially established on July 28, 1942. In addition to Antek Zukerman, other leadership positions were assumed by Shmuel Breslaw, Yosef Kaplan, Zivia Lubetkin, and Jurek Wilner. The official head of this underground was Mordechai Anielewicz.[65] Earlier on, ŻOB began its operations by eliminating collaborators. The Nazis had relied on collaborators and placed them in high positions. The ŻOB had thought that by doing away with collaborators they would be strengthening their own anti-German operations. In the Warsaw ghetto, some of the converted Jews were identified as virulent anti-Semites. Jozef Szerynski was one of them. The Germans had appointed him as head of the ghetto police. The Jewish ghetto underground designated one of its valued members, Israel Kanal, to be Szerynski's assassin. But Kanal's bullet missed, only wounding Szerynski in the cheek. Szerynski was soon accused by the Germans of stealing fur coats. Before the authorities meted out the "proper" punishment, Szerynski committed suicide.[66]

Another more dangerous collaborator was Yakov Lejkin. A converted Jew, he was known as a corrupt and enthusiastic supporter of the Nazis. Lejkin was assassinated during the Warsaw ghetto deportations. His killer was never identified.[67] Next, the ghetto underground had ordered the killing of Alfred Nossig. Born in Lwow, Nossig was a journalist and a sculptor. After his assassination, some ghetto inmates had guessed ŻOB's involvement. The majority had approved of this act, yet hardly anyone spoke about it. Discretely, ŻOB continued to pursue its preparatory cleansing activities.[68]

To function more effectively this ghetto underground had to reconcile a range of differences among diverse groups. Eventually it included all major political and social streams of Jewish life. One conspicuous division, however, was with the ŻZW, who were well equipped because of their former connection to the Polish Army and therefore did not need to join the other Jewish undergrounds. Relatively less evidence is available about the ŻZW than about the ŻOB. According to some sources, the ŻZW had three hundred fighters, all of whom were well armed.

In the bunker, one of Ringelblum's writing projects was a portrait of Mordechai Anielewicz, the twenty-five-year-old former leader of the Hashomer Hatzair group, a leftist political organization (figure 2.4). Ringelblum was impressed with Mordechai's idealism and with his devotion to his young followers. Anielewicz was also aware of Hashomer Hatzair's pro-Soviet orientations and how these might extend to ŻOB and to the PPR, the Polish Workers Party. He was interested in how diverse political systems were connected to Russian politics. Anielewicz cultivated his ties to the Polish Scout Organization. He was a quiet leader, willing to learn from his followers.

Early on, as the head of the Hashomer Hatzair youth group, Anielewicz had traveled to a number of ghettos, urging other Jewish youths to join them. These trips offered opportunities for the exchange of ideas within wider circles of young people. Such travels, however, were dangerous. The Nazis imposed the death sentence upon Jews found outside of the ghetto without special authorizations. The same punishment applied to Christian Poles who knowingly helped Jews move or stay outside of a ghetto.[69]

FIGURE 2.4 Mordechai Anielewicz (standing, far right) with other members of the Zionist youth movement in Hashomer Hatzair. Anielewicz was the head of the Jewish Fighting Organization (ŻOB), and one of the leaders in the Warsaw ghetto uprising. (United States Holocaust Memorial Museum, courtesy of Leah Hammerstein Silverstein)

Despite these risks, Anielewicz and many of his colleagues continued their tours, eluding the authorities' watchful eyes. They shared an eagerness to learn about the fate of the Jewish people. These trips offered fresh insights into the deteriorating conditions under which ghetto inmates were forced to live. Significantly, too, such travels confirmed to Anielewicz and the young leaders who had crossed their paths that worse was to come. Indeed, news about future anti-Jewish measures continued to spread. Soon added to this general news were more specific reports about the murder of the Vilna ghetto inmates' deportations from a number of ghettos: Slonim, Novogrodek, Lida, Lublin, and many others. Figuring prominently were details about the Warsaw ghetto deportations. Anielewicz and his comrades concluded that all Polish Jews were destined for annihilation.

He and many of his young colleagues agreed that they had to settle a central question: What kind of a death should the Polish Jews select for themselves? Should they face death in a passive way, without engaging in resistance, or should they stand up to their oppressors?

After the end of the big Warsaw ghetto deportations, Anielewicz and other young leaders insisted that in the future the killing of Polish Jews should not be made easy for the Germans. A consensus emerged that in the future the Germans would pay a high price for their crimes.

The moment Anielewicz turned from passivity to active resistance, all preoccupation with the promotion of cultural and artistic pastimes retreated into the background. These activities no longer seemed to matter. Also put to rest were endless debates between the youthful political leaders and the older Jews. From earlier discussions with the older generation, Anielewicz had learned that the more experienced Jewish leaders were opposed to fighting the Germans because they recognized that Jews would not survive direct confrontations with the occupiers. Unlike Anielewicz and his followers, they were ready to do all that was in their power to protect and prolong their lives. The young expected the Germans to murder them all; this was an inevitable fact. For them the question was how to die an honorable death.[70] And so, the young fighters did not try to get illegal documents nor did they look for safe haven in the Christian world. Faced with annihilation, they remained idealistic. They had no wives or children. Their goal was to connect and to cooperate with others who were also ready to fight. In times of disasters one should not be concerned with committees and propositions.[71] At such times, one had to rely on instinct.

Ringelblum felt that initially Jewish youths were too disciplined, and therefore incapable of assessing clearly their circumstances. To Ringelblum, this seemed to be one of the basic reasons why, during the Warsaw ghetto deportations, so many Jews lost their lives while their Nazi oppressors did not even pay with one dead German. This truth dawned on the young only when it was too late—after most of the Warsaw Jewry had already been murdered in Treblinka.

Still, as far as the preparations for resistance were concerned, Anielewicz threw himself into this job. Together with other groups and other political parties, he reorganized the Jewish underground. All who knew Anielewicz concur that he was one of the most dedicated activists in the movement. He bore no resemblance to other leaders, who would send others into the line of fire and distance themselves from a fight.

The ghetto deportations were followed by a flood of self-accusations about Jewish passivity and complicity. Such reactions led to growing involvement with Jewish resistance. Attached to this was a growing interest, verging on an obsession, to build more sophisticated hiding places. Practically all of the remaining Jews wanted to participate, as Israel Gutman insists, "in the construction of shelters and secret places that would prolong Jewish lives."[72]

Many of the ghetto activities were dictated by darkness, which practically guaranteed an absence of Germans and their collaborators, who had avoided unfamiliar places at night. The Jews took advantage of their nightly disappearances to construct new shelters. As mentioned previously, the ghetto turned into a community built on several levels. One was above the ground. Another, the newer one, was below the ground and consisted of a complex network of tunnels and underground bunkers. Ringelblum praised the ingeniousness with which the Jews created such inaccessible, secret accommodations.[73] Shelters were also built close to the roofs. These offered opportunities to move from bunker to bunker without being detected. This secrecy meant safety to the Jewish underground, which was eagerly preparing for upcoming confrontations.

Early on the underground sent Jurek Wilner to the Aryan part of Warsaw. Here Wilner had contacted the Polish underground, the AK, and asked them for weapons and special guidance.[74] At this point, very few had weapons and no definite plans for action. Some members of the ŻOB were preparing a manifesto.

The ŻOB youths were eager to work in a variety of ghettos. This required constant adjustments to different situations. Because of their extensive travels, they knew the particular methods which the Germans were likely to use, as well as about entries and exits of ghetto hiding places. Every possible move by their enemies was carefully studied. Conspicuously absent from all these underground plans were any considerations of withdrawals. "We do not wish to save our lives," wrote Wilner. "None of us will come out of this alive. We only want to save the honor of mankind."[75]

Wilner viewed any interruption in the Warsaw deportations as a breathing space for those who were left behind. ŻOB's plans differed from the plans of the Jewish Fighting Organization in Vilna (FPO), which was preparing to escape into the forests, where they intended to fight. In this respect, the Vilna youths resembled the ŻZW, which also tried to reach the forests. In the case of ŻZW, however, a basic shortage of reliable evidence prevents historians from making clear assessments of their situation.

The first armed confrontation in the Warsaw ghetto was led by Mordechai Anielewicz. His plan was simple. He selected twelve fighters with pistols. They were instructed to join the lines of inmates who were ordered to go to the waiting freight cars, which were supposed to take them to extermination camps. It was pre-arranged that at a sign from their leader, the fighters would burst out of their places and attack the Nazis and their collaborators. This was a suicide mission. The Jews had pistols, with a limited supply of ammunition. The attackers had semi-automatic rifles with an ample supply of ammunition. Yet, the Jews had a temporary advantage of surprise, which they fully exploited. In no time the Germans recovered from their initial shock and regrouped.

Nevertheless, this first encounter was decisive for several reasons. Hundreds of Jews who stood by recognized that this chaotic situation offered an opportunity to disperse and to disappear. Most of them tried to do just that. In addition to this, also for the first time, the Germans were confronted with a real opposition and were shocked to see Germans being killed by Jews. One Jewish fighter, Hirsch Berlinski, who participated in this confrontation, noted how quickly the Jews were able to disarm several Germans, depriving them of their weapons. He also noted how a number of the SS men were killed and how others were wounded, while other Germans fled, losing their caps and weapons in the process.

The Germans retaliated by setting fire to the building that Anielewicz and his group had occupied. In the end, quite a number of the Jewish fighters reached the safety of a nearby factory.

Another encounter, in a different part of the ghetto, Zamenhof Street, took place between a Jewish group of fighters led by Yitzhak Zuckerman (figure 2.5) and the Germans. In this second encounter the Jewish fighters opened fire only when the German attackers had entered the building, offering a strategic advantage. One of the Jewish fighters was killed. The rest collected the arms abandoned by the retreating enemy and disappeared.

These two major encounters, by the Anielewicz group and the Zuckerman group, were part of the January 18, 1943, Warsaw ghetto uprisings, initiated by Heinrich Himmler's new commands, which were to destroy the ghetto. "As long as the ghetto exists, it

FIGURE 2.5 Yitzhak Zuckerman was the deputy commander of the Jewish Fighting Organization (ŻOB) and a leader of the Warsaw ghetto uprisings in January and April 1943. (Courtesy Yad Vashem)

constitutes a nest of revolt and anarchy...so the ghetto has to be finished off." Apparently he was right.[76]

The January 18 attacks upon the ghetto were turning points in the existence of the Jewish Fighting Organization. The Germans had anticipated only smooth and easy operations. Now, to their surprise, the Nazis were confronted with an unexpected loss of German lives. The ensuing losses made the Nazis realize that the battlefield was not confined to the front; it existed inside the ghetto. Zuckerman was convinced that this made possible the next ghetto uprising, which took place in April 1943.[77] The AK was willing to assist the ghetto fighters by moving them to the forest. The Jews insisted on staying in the ghetto and continuing to fight.[78] The AK's offer was, in part, prompted by the fear that Jewish ghetto fighting could spread to the Polish population in general. The AK had correctly assumed that a premature uprising was dangerous and doomed to failure.

In addition to a few successful skirmishes with the enemy within the ghetto, the Jews sent a message to the general population that confronting the Germans was a real possibility. The crises and frustrations which the fighters had experienced during the big deportations evaporated during these confrontations. Moreover, attitudes toward the Jewish fighters had also changed, both in the ghetto and beyond. Even though these skirmishes were brief, the Germans had to invest a tremendous amount of effort trying to catch the fighters. They only succeeded in catching the sick and feeble ghetto dwellers they happened to come across.

The January Aktion lasted four days. The numbers of German police who had participated amounted to 200. With additional help, the final figure came to about 800. Precise numbers about the losses are elusive; all that was evident were the constant sirens of ambulances. Probably many more Germans and their collaborators were involved than the authorities were willing to admit. All in all, an operation which the Germans had expected to take an hour or two lasted for four days. This in itself was a huge accomplishment for the Jews.

On the outside, Poles were amazed at how effectively the Jews had resisted. Several AK publications began to refer to the Jewish fighters as brave men and women, and congratulated them on how successful their resistance was. It is unquestionable that attitudes toward Jewish fighters changed. These positive appraisals about Jewish resisters helped them significantly in future encounters.

As usual, the ghetto underground took advantage of any lull in hostilities, regrouping and replenishing their weapons and ammunitions. The Germans were also preparing for a final elimination of the Warsaw ghetto. In February 1943, Himmler began to set in motion plans for the ghetto's complete destruction. His plan was to offer the demolition of the ghetto to the Fuhrer as a present for his birthday. The date of Hitler's birthday, April 19, happened to coincide with the start of the Jewish Passover.

On April 19, when the German forces reached the Warsaw ghetto, the streets were empty. Most inhabitants were hiding in their bunkers, with entrances sealed and camouflaged.[79] Zuckerman explained that "after a few days of fighting, the enemy saw that they could not conquer us easily. With this realization, the Germans attacked by setting fires. These fires spread rapidly, burning some valuable passages between Jewish positions and their possible places of retreat."[80] For the Jews, this spelled the beginning of the end.

The term "military" hardly describes the Jewish forces that confronted the powerful German fighting machine. Almost without exception, the soldiers of the Jewish Fighting Organization and the Jewish Fighting Union were young men and women who had little military training. According to some estimates, there were 750 combatants in battle units, with some 500 in the ranks of the ŻOB and 250 in the ŻZW. ŻOB members carried revolvers of various types. The Jewish fighters had from ten to fifteen rounds of ammunition and four to five hand grenades, mostly homemade. Apparently, the ŻOB had 2,000 homemade Molotov cocktails, ten rifles, and one or two submachine guns, confiscated from the Germans, along with an indeterminate supply of ammunition. ŻOB had also mined the entrances to some key positions in the ghetto area.[81]

Despite continuous appeals from the Jewish combat organization to the Polish government in London, the Poles had supplied only very limited quantities of arms, and what arms they did provide were in poor shape.[82] Moreover, the Polish underground urged its people to engage in an uprising only at the "right moment." But the "right moment" had to be fixed and decided upon by the moment itself. This meant that the Polish government would attack only when the Germans were vulnerable enough to be pushed back to their border and would not have the resources to retaliate against them.

The Polish authorities had expected the same kinds of reactions from the Jewish underground. But the Jews could not wait for the "right moment." For them, it was life or death. The Polish government-in-exile and the AK feared that the Jews might indirectly involve them in "a premature, open conflict" with the enemy. The Poles were therefore reluctant to provide the Jews with adequate weapons. This reluctance applied to all Jewish situations in the ghettos, forests, partisans, and concentration camps.

A range of considerations had dominated and complicated the Polish–Jewish wartime relationships. One of these was probably dictated by Polish anti-Semitism. From the Polish perspective the Jews were cowards. Supplying the Jews with proper arms was hardly an option. Attempts to establish more cooperative contacts with the Jews and the AK failed. In contrast, the leftist Gwardia Ludowa not only accepted Jews into their fighting units, but they supplied them with weapons and ammunition. Still, the AK and the Polish government in London were better equipped than their leftist Polish counterparts and were in a position to do far more than the GL.

For the duration of the war and throughout Poland, Jewish resistance movements were largely isolated from other resistance groups. In the course of their exposure to persecutions, practically every ghetto had to face their enemy alone. Jewish communities that were prepared to fight were faced with the tragic realization that no one would come to their rescue. On the other hand, in every place where there was even a smallest crack in their walls of isolation, the Jews were ready to stand up to their enemy. This was the case in Warsaw, Bialystok, Krakow, and a range of other communities.[83]

Indeed, there is evidence as to how gratified Anielewicz was by the initial developments in the Jewish resistance. A part of his letter to Zuckerman, dated April 3, 1943, reads: "I had a feeling of great fulfillment...things have surpassed our boldest dreams...the Germans ran away from the ghetto twice...the dream of my life has come true. I have lived to see a Jewish defense in the ghetto in all its greatness and glory."[84]

These successes had depended upon efforts to create new hiding places, as well as complex tunnels and invisible passages.[85] One of these sophisticated shelters was at Mila 18, which offered refuge to the ŻOB leaders and many of their fighters. Neither the Germans nor their deadly fires changed the Jewish fighters' determination to die with what they defined as an honorable death. At Mila 18, most of the fugitives kept their last bullets for themselves, to commit collective suicide when there was no other way out. This is what, indeed, happened.

Even the German general Jurgen Stroop, who was in charge of burning down the ghetto with all its inhabitants, was amazed by the Jewish fighting spirit. Stroop was especially impressed by the presence of the heroic women fighters who had participated equally with the men.[86] Despite Stroop's amazement, his total disregard of the loss of human lives is apparent in his last report, in which he notes drily: "The former ghetto has been completely destroyed; except for partially remaining portions of buildings....Only five walls are left standing where no explosives were set." Stroop concludes, "These ruins will yield enormous quantities of stone and scrap materials for further utilization."[87]

Up to January 1943, the Germans had acted as if the ghetto belonged to them. Gradually, as Jewish submissiveness evaporated, the Nazis had to readjust some of their tactics. Basically this meant that the Germans now had to enter the Jewish living quarters in search of their victims, who were no longer simply going to emerge willingly. When this happened the Jews would swiftly attack their enemies, depriving them of their guns and often their lives.

Zukerman describes what happened:

> The first gang of four or five Germans that entered the house at Zamenhof 58; our people were hidden—some behind doors and some elsewhere. I was sitting in a room with my gun cocked. We heard them, we heard the shouts: "Raus! Raus!" (Get out!). No one left. Then, we heard them climbing the stairs. The sound echoed in the empty house. It was very tense.... I'll never forget that picture: Zacharia Artenstein was sitting in the first room and, as I recall, he was holding a book by Sholem-Aleichem; he sat and read, facing the door. They came in and there he was, sitting and reading a book. It didn't even occur to them to tell us to put our hands up. After they entered our room, Zacharia shot them in the back. Then we shot more of them and the Germans began to run away. After the first shot, they didn't even have time to take out their guns. They were so sure of themselves. One of the fellows threw a grenade at the fleeing Germans. I took the gun from the German who fell in the room. He was still alive; it was a pity to waste a bullet on him. But we did take their guns and grenades. Right after that, we heard a few of them run into the street, which was full of Germans. They started shouting and whistling. Regular Prussian shouts, mixed with pain.[88]

It was a shame that Ringelblum was not there to witness this transformation. Despite German efforts, Ringelblum's work yielded three collections of historical texts. One of them is known by the Polish name "*Kronika*," a volume which was later discovered in the ruins of the Warsaw ghetto. This volume contains a wealth of information and is available in several languages. The second body of evidence covers the Warsaw ghetto deportations of 1942 plus the historical changes that occurred during that time. The third includes Ringelblum's book about central figures during the German occupation. An additional body of evidence involves the letters which Ringelblum and his wife Judyta exchanged with people who lived outside the bunker. As readers of these materials, we encounter Emanuel Ringelblum in a variety of roles: as a historian, as a participant in the study of the evolving wartime history, and as an individual who spread the knowledge among Jews about their wartime past.[89]

The Germans put a stop to Ringelblum's work when, on March 7, 1944, the bunker on Grojecka Street No. 81 was discovered by the Gestapo. All those who were associated with the bunker were arrested. Among them were Ringelblum and his family, their Polish protector, Morczak, his family, and his assistant Mieczyslaw Wolski. All were transferred to the Pawiak prison. According to one report, a small group of Jewish craftsmen who had worked at the Pawiak prison offered to rescue Ringelblum by dressing him as one of them and by smuggling him out. He rejected this proposal when he realized that his wife and son would not be included in this rescue.[90] All of these prisoners were executed on the ruins of the Warsaw ghetto, on March 10, 1944.

Impeccable scholarly research, exceptional organizational skills, and an ability to coordinate and expand a range of activities: all of this was compressed into Ringelblum's short life. Towering over this was his selfless dedication to the welfare of the Jewish people and the desire to improve their economic, social, cultural, and political lives. His selfless efforts improved the quality of life. He was both strong and weak. Despite his seemingly endless resources, he could not in the end save his life, nor the lives of his wife, son, and most of his dedicated coworkers. But Ringelblum's strength reached beyond his grave and the graves of those whom he loved. His life was dedicated to paying special tribute to the Jews. In the last few months, in a race with death, he wrote historical profiles of leading activists and others who selflessly plunged into actions designed to learn as much as possible from the evolving Jewish history.

While the Nazis had succeeded in murdering millions of Jews and non-Jews, they failed to destroy the fruits of their victims' compassionate labors. Just as Ringelblum and his archivists had hoped, the Jewish people became the inheritors and guardians of their well-documented history.[91]

CHAPTER THREE

The Forests

Some German attacks upon the USSR came in the form of massive onslaughts, and initially the entire Soviet Army seemed to be in complete disarray. Thousands of Russian soldiers fled into the surrounding forests, while many others surrendered to the enemy.[1] As mentioned, the Soviet Army was made up of a variety of ethnic groups—in addition to the Russians, it included Jews, Slovakians, Belorussians, and a range of others. The victorious German Army was especially eager to identify the Jews among these newly captured Soviet soldiers. Large numbers—the exact figure is unknown—of POWs, both Jewish and non-Jewish, were victims of German mass executions. Others were simply allowed to starve to death. Estimates of these Jewish and Soviet victims run into millions.[2]

For those who did not surrender, flight into the forests was common. With time, some of these Belorussian forests became a refuge to a number of military and civilian fugitives. As most of them divided into splinter groups, they referred to themselves as "partisans." Scattered throughout these forests, these anti-German groups lacked weapons, leaders, and discipline. Often, instead of fighting their German enemy, they would rob each other. Rivalry and greed would sometimes lead to murder. When confronted by easy targets they would fight the Germans, mainly in order to take arms and foods. Such early forest dwellers, though diverse in terms of background, nationality, and demographics, had much in common. None of them were driven by ideology. All were preoccupied with self-preservation. They had come to the forest because they wanted to live, not because they wanted to fight.[3]

Still, even at these early stages, some partisans were united in their hatred toward the Germans and their collaborators. The killing of Germans was equated with patriotism and heroism. Those who did not talk about waging war were subjected to ridicule and contempt. In particular, the Soviet partisans would greet the disheveled and hungry ghetto runaways with sneering comments, such as, "Why did you work for the Germans instead of fighting?"[4]

However, there was a discrepancy between the high value placed on fighting and the actual number of attacks directed against the Germans. The strong approval of fighting was unmatched by the actual number of assaults upon the enemy. This lack of correspondence between talk and action was in part responsible for some of the exaggerated claims about the extraordinary anti-Nazi escapades. Until 1942, in Western Belorussia, attacks upon the Germans by Russian partisans were rare. The few anti-enemy moves that did take place were in the form of sabotage, involving the destructions of trains, bridges, telephone lines, and installations. Infrequent and sporadic, these early anti-German ventures became more coordinated and more common after the arrival of the specially trained military personnel from the USSR in 1943. Some of them were parachuted into the area. Others flew in planes that landed at secretly constructed airports. Still, only a handful of this new breed of partisans reached the forest.

To sixteen-year-old Zvi Shefet, the German takeover of his native town, Slonim, was "a shock." He states:

> No one thought that they would come so fast. We saw so many Soviet soldiers; we thought that they were strong. There was a river near Slonim, Szczara, with a bridge, connecting the city. We heard the movements of the Russian Army, for months. There was tension, but we thought that Russia was so strong, that they will fight. There were planes, tanks and all kinds of equipment. We thought that this kind of an army could not be easily defeated.[5] Surprisingly, on the third day of the war, the Germans took over Slonim. The occupiers began their rule by destroying Soviet equipment. They brought with them many prisoners. It was pitiful to see the chaos among the Soviets. The Poles who were there received

the Germans well. Within a week or so, the occupiers issued announcements against Jews. The Gentile inhabitants committed robberies against the Jews. They robbed mills, stores, etc.[6]

Zvi was close to his mother, whom he describes as beautiful, intelligent, and resourceful. She had, he said, a way of creating good feelings around her. She tried to be in good spirits; at least outwardly. She was lively and people loved her. She kept up the morale of those around her. A graduate of a German high school, she was fluent in the German language. Her brother had lived for a while in Germany and was convinced that the Germans would never come to Belorussia. A few days into the occupation of Slonim, Zvi's uncle was arrested. Sparing no effort, Zvi's mother obtained an official order for her brother's release. She received this order in the morning, only to learn that he had been executed the night before.

The first Aktion against the Jews in Slonim took place on July 17, 1942. A special division of SS men was assigned for this task. They came in trucks and rounded up Jewish men. They had lists and tried to collect prominent figures—lawyers, architects, doctors, and so forth, and in the end had assembled 1,500 men. The Germans had confiscated all of the prisoners' personal documents and valuables. Next, they forced some of them to write undated letters, which the Germans later mailed to their families for propaganda purposes.

In no time, the Shefets found out what had happened. A forester and his wife, friends of the Shefet family, brought the news. Two days later, this couple visited the Shefets, bringing them food. When the wife reached their friend's home, she embraced those who were there and began to cry. She could not stop crying for quite a while. Those who listened tried to fill in some of the missing parts of the story. The Germans had released 300 out of the 1,500 men. In their forest dwelling, this couple had heard continuous shootings. When the noises subsided, husband and wife ventured out of their home, moving into the direction of the, by then, sporadic shootings. When they reached what they assumed was the place of execution, they were confronted by an eerie silence. Then they saw how the freshly covered ground kept moving. It was as if those who were, as yet, not dead were restless in their graves. Later on rumors circulated on how these victims were severely beaten prior to their murder. According to some witnesses who watched from a distance, the SS men reached this place in trucks filled with Jewish men. Upon arrival they roughly forced them out of their vehicles, which immediately left to get a new load. The Germans would consult their lists. They might have been checking to see whether their lists included actual and potential leaders.

When stories about these systematic murders first emerged, most people had a hard time absorbing them. Some insisted on searching for the missing men. All they found were scattered pieces of clothing. Many refused to discuss what had happened, fearing that their curiosity could lead to their own destruction. Some kept hoping that after a while the Russians would return. The realists feared for their own future. Most of them seemed to agree that they could not spend the winter in the forest.

"I thought it strange that the grown-ups were so fearful," Zvi told me. "I was blond and I did not look Jewish. When the order came to wear a Star of David, I refused to comply." Asked how he managed to do that, he replied, "I did not go out so much. I had no problems. I managed to [avoid] those who would denounce me."

Later, Zvi became more active. He substituted for his father's compulsory work. Jewish men of specified ages had to register with the Judenrat. So, if the authorities needed people for work, they would take them. There were steady and nonsteady jobs. Zvi's father was assigned to the category of nonsteady jobs. He had to be there every day and wait for orders. Those who failed to register for jobs were denied food cards. His father would register and Zvi would go to work instead of him. On many of these jobs the Germans would abuse the Jewish laborers. By taking over his father's work Zvi shielded him from assault. The family agreed with these arrangements, without much discussion.

They tried to plan for the future. Zvi remembers a conversation his parents had with a Polish woman who seemed to be cooperating with the German authorities but who was still friendly with the Shefets. Zvi recalls that this woman, with his parents, raised the issue of what should be done with "the boy," meaning Zvi. They considered a plan in which this Polish woman would take him to Warsaw and settle him there as a Gentile. He was blond and spoke Polish fluently. But Zvi strongly opposed this idea. "I was hurt that they wanted to get rid of me. I thought that I had to protect my family. I loved my mother very much and didn't want to part from her. My sister had a typically Jewish look so she could not help them much." In the end his vehement opposition to their suggestions meant that the move to Warsaw was dropped and Zvi was allowed to stay with his family.

By this point the Germans had established a ghetto into which all Jews, including the Shefets, had to move. As a part of their living quarters, the Shefets acquired a shed in which they stored wood for heating their cramped living quarters. A part of this shed was used as a hiding place. During the second Aktion, when the SS and Wehrmacht surrounded the ghetto, Zvi, his father, and several family members who felt threatened, disappeared into this newly created hiding place. From the outside, Mrs. Shefet shut carefully their shelter.

From inside, Zvi recalled that they could hear desperate cries. These were followed by the sound of someone pounding at the door to their dwelling. His mother, using her excellent German, admitted the SS men and German soldiers, who demanded to know where the men of the house were. Zvi's mother replied that her husband was at work. They wanted to know how he got to work. After all, the streets were closed. He went very early, she explained. They wanted to know if they had a yellow permit, a "Schein." Yes, Mrs. Shefet confirmed that they did, but that her husband took it with him. To this came the response, "shut the door and don't let anybody in." The Germans rushed off without searching.

At night, under the cover of darkness, they emerged from their shelter and wanted to know what had happened. They learned that the Germans had taken the grandparents, and an uncle who was hiding. This uncle had ventured out to get his coat and the Germans arrested him. The family never heard from him again. Whoever stayed in the Shefets' hiding place was safe. Relatives who were taken away from other hideouts included a blind grandmother and an elderly grandfather. During this Aktion, the Germans had collected 10,000 Jews. They had expected to find only 7,000. The authorities insisted that this would put an end to all deportations. Some people believed these assertions. Zvi's parents rejected them. This lull in the killing would only last for a short time.

After a while, people began to suspect that something was about to happen. They were suspicious about any and all changes. At the start of the German occupation, the SS had arrested large numbers of upper-class Poles.[7] The recent arrival of SS men spelled danger. Prominent Poles who had managed to survive began to search for hideouts. Some hid in the Jewish ghetto. At this time the Polish elites and the Jewish ghetto inmates were in equal danger. Some new developments took place, developments which were intended to sabotage the Germans' efforts.

Born in 1922 in Poland, Oswald Rufeisen survived World War II by pretending to be half Polish and half German. Through an unusual set of circumstances, he accepted a position as a translator and interpreter for the German gendarmerie in the town of Mir, in Belorussia. Oswald had pledged to use this job for the protection of anyone who was oppressed by the Germans.[8] And so, wearing a black German uniform and carrying weapons, Oswald was dedicated to standing up for the oppressed. He arranged a breakout from the ghetto Mir, which saved 305 Jews. He prevented a Belorussian village from being burned by intentionally mistranslating for the authorities. Oswald also managed to protect countless numbers of Soviet POWs and offered help to a large number of Jewish, Polish, and Russian underground figures.

On a particular evening, returning home from a visit with Polish friends, Oswald noticed a large number of recently arrived SS men. Equipment used for conducting surprise arrests accompanied these new arrivals. Oswald wondered why he had not been informed about these seemingly extensive preparations connected to the police station at which he worked. He suddenly realized that those in charge of this operation had purposefully excluded him from knowing about that night's operations, because these were aimed at the destruction of the Polish intelligentsia.

Convinced he had reached the right conclusion, Oswald decided to warn as many of the Polish elites as possible. Going from one Polish household to another he urged the heads of these families to spend the night away from their living quarters. He returned to his Polish hosts for that evening. Oswald explained the situation, urging the head of this Polish family to get away from the house. But this friend dismissed the danger. Subsequently, that same night the SS men picked him up. Hardly any of those Oswald had reached took his warnings seriously. Only one of these prominent Poles listened and saved his life. All the Poles who were warned but refused to act upon Oswald's urgings were arrested. Most of them ended up in concentration camps. Many did not survive the war.[9]

During the next Slonim ghetto Aktion, many of the deportees, some of them prominent Poles, objected that they were not Jewish. Their claims fell on deaf ears. The anti-Jewish attacks became a reality only several days after the arrests of the members of the Polish intelligentsia were completed.[10]

Helping the SS men who had participated in collecting the prominent Poles and ghetto inmates were Lithuanian collaborators. The Jews suspected that these Lithuanians had come to collect them rather than the Polish elites, many of whom had already been taken away.[11] The Jews had spied on the newly arrived Lithuanians and saw that at 4:00 in the morning a large contingent of them came out of their dwellings fully armed and ready for action. The ghetto inmates knew that they should hide. The Shefets had in fact two hideouts—the one located in their yard and another under the floor of their home. Hidden in the yard was an uncle with his infant daughter and a grandmother. The presence of the baby diminished the safety of this hideout. The rest of the family disappeared into the shelter located underneath the Shefets' living quarters.

The entire family group consisted of about twenty. Before they moved into their hideouts, they left some of their clothes and eating utensils in disarray. They wanted to leave the impression that they had left in a hurry. However, it seems that the Lithuanian collaborators were well informed about the number of Jews who lived at specific places. Since they found no one they waited, watching closely each ghetto home, including the Shefets' places. Because the Lithuanian collaborators could not find those they were looking for, this Aktion lasted two weeks. In the end, when waiting failed to produce the desired effects, they announced that they were going to burn the entire ghetto. The threat of a spreading fire forced many of the hidden Jews out.

The Shefets' living quarters were at the edge of the ghetto, which afforded an advantage—it meant that the fire set to the ghetto would not reach them until the evening, when they could leave under the cover of darkness. Thus, they were able to safely escape. Hoping to connect with partisan groups, they aimed at reaching the surrounding woods. Eventually, they came to the Pruszkov forest. They had heard that this and other forests housed various partisan groups. After a good night's sleep, the Shefet group began to plan for their future. They selected two men to negotiate with Russian partisans for acceptance into their group.

They had no trouble finding such groups, who were willing to accept anyone who was armed. In addition to the possession of guns—which were rare, since only Germans and their collaborators could have them, and anyone else was shot—certain other skills also assured entrance into partisan groups. Doctors were among the most valued professionals.[12]

While the "negotiators" for the Shefet group were away, those left behind discussed their chances of finding arms. Some noted that the Red Army soldiers might have thrown away some of their weapons while fleeing their enemies. Some suggested that rather than wait passively for the return of their negotiators, they should search for some of these hidden arms. After all, there was no risk in doing that. Thus, dividing into small groups, they went to look for weapons. Zvi found a shotgun. None of the others were as lucky.

Soon their two negotiators returned, announcing that only those with arms would be accepted into partisan detachments. Since these two negotiators owned guns, they were preparing for departure. Before they left, they exchanged one of their guns for the one Zvi had found. His gun was in better shape than the one they left him. When Zvi pointed this out to the two men, they assured him that they would help him and also promised to tell the commander how resourceful Zvi was. They were convinced that their support would result in his speedy acceptance into their detachment. Zvi never heard from either one of these men again.

The group continued to roam around the area. One of the Shefets' relatives, an aunt, grew up in one of the nearby villages and was therefore able to collect food from some of the local peasants. Although helped by these offers of food, the group felt compelled constantly to change places. There were young shepherds around and they were fearful that they might denounce them to the authorities. By that time the Germans had murdered about 20,000 Slonim Jews. The Shefets heard that 800 Jews continued to live in the small ghetto. Some of their group considered returning to the ghetto, but the majority opposed taking such a drastic step, and eventually, the idea was dropped.

Gradually, cracks appeared in the cohesion of this group. Not all of them had experienced the German occupation in the same way, and the pressure of the moment had made them brittle and uncertain. Nonetheless, they were bonded by their circumstances—in particular the shortages of weaponry and ammunitions.

Forest dwellers and the German authorities knew about the potential values and dangers of unattended weaponry and ammunitions. The Germans were determined to take control of the scattered portions of armaments. In western Belorussia, the authorities had established several centers that specialized in the collection and restoration of abandoned parts of weaponry and ammunitions. The biggest and best known of these centers was called Beutelager. Located close to the Slonim ghetto, Beutelager functioned as a combination of storage center and factory. Many young and able-bodied Slonim ghetto inmates worked in the Beutelager. Their job was to collect, clean, and sort the accumulated weapons parts and ammunition, regardless of what kind of shape they were in. Jewish slave laborers were charged with the restoration of these items to their optimal conditions. All along, the presence of Beutelager led to unanticipated consequences, both for the Jews and non-Jews who were directly and indirectly involved in these undertakings.

Zvi Shefet, with the rest of his family, continued to search for more permanent solutions and felt that "something was happening within our group which was unpleasant." When I asked Zvi what he meant by "unpleasant," he replied that some "dealings" had originated in the composition of their group. Zvi's uncle, his father's brother, had joined the Shefet group with his wife and several pre-teen children. In addition, the couple had two older sons who had worked in the Beutelager establishment. Through Beutelager, these two young men had accumulated weapons and ammunitions for the emergent Slonim ghetto underground. Significantly, too, with their access to arms, ammunitions, and other goods, these cousins established close contacts with Soviet partisans, most of whom were former POWs. In fact, they had supplied Soviet partisans with arms, medications, and other valued goods. When these two young men had escaped into the surrounding forests, they were automatically accepted into a Soviet partisan detachment—effectively "repayment" for past services that these Jewish youths had rendered to these early Soviet partisans. These exchanges, however, were not openly discussed.

An alert observer, Zvi could not help but notice that each visit by his two partisan cousins came with assurances that Zvi's uncle, his wife, and their young children would have a special place in their partisan detachment. But in order for this to happen the uncle, his wife, and the children had to try hard to stay away from the rest of Zvi's group. In short, the invitation to join the particular detachment did not extend to the rest of the family, which included five individuals: Zvi, his sister, both parents, and a twenty-eight-year-old woman, a relative of the family. Probably in order to not hurt his parents' feelings, Zvi had not revealed to them this uncle's and his family's plans.

Zvi had hoped that their group of five would come upon Soviet partisans who would accept them. He also thought, correctly, that his father's familiarity with this part of Belorussia was an asset for the Soviet partisans, most of whom were strangers to the region. He had hoped that their encounters with Soviet partisans would yield mutually desirable benefits. Prompted in part by these expectations, this group of five detached itself from Zvi's uncle and his family.

With this split behind them, Zvi's group moved in the direction of Kosovo, a town where supposedly the Jews were treated well. Jews continued to cling to any and all positive rumors, even when they had no connection to reality. Nevertheless, as Zvi's group continued to explore their surroundings, they made some promising encounters. At one point, Zvi recalled, "We came to a house of a forester who insisted: 'as Jews you have only one possibility for saving yourself, only by joining forest partisans. Away from the forest no Jew will stay alive.'" This decent man offered them good advice and clear directions to the partisans. Zvi remembered that when they stopped in one of the designated villages, they came across two men, "more or less in Soviet uniforms." He continued:

We were glad to meet them and asked them if we could join their partisan unit. They told us that they could not take us without the permission of their commander, suggesting that we should meet at a specified place in the forest. One of them said that we should meet at this place by noon and they would give us an answer. My father took out his watch [and] looking at it he said that in two hours we will be back. One of the partisans replied: "Give me the watch, I don't have one. This way I will know when to come to you."

This was the last time anyone in their group saw either these partisans or the watch. Having lost several hours in waiting and searching, the group of five moved in the direction of the village Okinowo, a village they heard was close to the forest and to various Soviet partisan groups. On the way, they met a Jewish man from Slonim who mentioned that Zvi's uncle and his family were already a part of a Soviet partisan unit.

Soon this group of five had reached one of the forest partisan centers, a place from which former POWs coordinated the activities of various partisan groups. Here, after several days, Zvi was accepted into a fighting unit. His parents and the rest of their group were assigned to a family detachment. Membership in such a detachment was often contingent on having a relative who belonged to a fighting unit. Sixteen-year-old Zvi was that relative.

It took Zvi no time to recognize how pervasive anti-Semitism was among the Soviet partisans. The detachment he joined, in fact, was undergoing a transformation. Referred to as Detachment 51, this unit previously refused to admit Jews, regardless of their qualifications. When the policy to reject Jews had come up for discussion, several of the commanders pointed out that Detachment 51 had benefited from supplies of indispensable goods, which they received because of Jewish efforts. Such arguments, however, made no impression upon the other members of this group. As more voices were added in support of including Jews, the anti-Semitic members of Detachment 51 stood up in protest and resigned.

A so-called "compromise" was reached. A new partisan group was formed, consisting exclusively of Jewish partisans. This unit kept the name Detachment 51. Zvi readily accepted a position in this newly created group. Zvi noticed some other changes that followed, particularly the arrival of an officer from the Soviet Union. "He was Jewish, his name was Yefim Fiodorowicz. As a newly appointed commander of Detachment 51, he made out of his partisans excellent fighters. *The best!* We also had a few women who were armed and who, with men, had participated in food expeditions. When the Germans continued to persecute the Gentile populations, more women reached our forests." [13]

Although widely publicized and backed politically by the Soviets, in reality women's participation in the Russian partisan movements was limited. The estimated proportion of women in the Soviet partisan movement ranges from 2 to 5 percent. In contrast to the pro-female governmental propaganda, the Soviet commanders argued that this small proportion of women was all the forest partisans could absorb. For women who were members of partisan groups, proper treatment was hardly a norm. [14] If women could not or would not satisfy the sexual demands of Soviet commanders, they had a hard time. These women were assigned to humiliating jobs and were discriminated against in a variety of ways. One of them, Judith Graf, a native of Slonim, struggled to stay in some of the Soviet partisan groups. It seems that the relationships that

Judith probably had with one or more of the high-ranking partisans deteriorated and she was dismissed and persecuted by a particularly vindictive commander. Most of her forest existence was characterized by continuous exposures to abusive and painful rejections. Judith was fortunate that the war came to an end at an "appropriate" time. In her case, timing might have saved her life.[15]

Women's escapes into the Belorussian forest were motivated by a mixture of fear about impending death by the Germans, death by starvation, and by varied humiliating pressures on women's daily existence. More so than their Gentile counterparts, Jewish women lived with these realities. Yet most forest women shared the desire to join the partisans, to avenge the cruelties and humiliations that were an integral part of the German occupation.

In most wartime forests, anti-Semitism and opposition to Jewish women's involvement went hand in hand. Some partisans saw all women as "service givers," there to attach herself to a partisan and to sexually satisfy him. A woman who had no male protector faced grave problems.[16] There were differences and similarities in the fate of Gentile and Jewish women who had reached the Belorussian forests. Gentile women were more likely to come to the forests because they wanted to fight the Germans. That is, they were there by choice. Jewish women, on the other hand, escaped into these forests to avoid being murdered. For many of these Jewish women, acceptance into a partisan unit was contingent upon their willingness to become mistresses of partisan commanders. These partisans' ability to accept women into their unit depended on the amount of power they had. In the forests only the powerful partisans could acquire mistresses. Most women did not qualify as mistresses. Some were accepted into a partisan detachment because they were good cooks, nurses, physicians, or simply morale-boosters.[17] Nonetheless, male partisans had little respect for women, and Jewish women were less respected than Gentile women. Since Jewish women were often the cooks, men who wanted to be fed well had to treat them kindly; but all women had less power than men and were treated with less consideration.

In part, a woman's status depended on the position of the man to whom she was attached. For example, a woman married to a doctor had a higher status. This was apparent in Mina Volkowisky's case, whose husband was a physician. The Volkowiskys came to Belorussia because of their families. As a recent graduate of the French medical school in Paris, Dr. Volkowisky found work in a hospital close to the Żyrowice estate. Several villages and patches of forests surrounded their temporary dwelling.

For Mina and her husband, the 1939 Soviet acquisition of half of Poland came as a surprise. Even more unexpected to them was the German attack upon the Soviet Union. Confronted by a rapid German expansion, the Volkowiskys relocated to Slonim, to be closer to their families. Shortages of physicians facilitated the doctor's employment in a local clinic. Mina and her husband moved to her parents' home, only to be relocated again to the newly established ghetto. This in turn was followed by an Aktion. Among the victims was Dr. Volkowisky's brother, who left behind a young wife known for her intellect and communist leanings. She, too, moved into the modest home shared by Mina's family.

Dr. Volkowisky worked in the ghetto clinic, as did Mina's mother, a dentist. For a while her father continued to run the family's tannery. Except for Mina, all the adults were employed. Mina wondered why the Slonim Jews refused to accept the obvious—that the Germans were determined to destroy them. As the only one in her family who was not working, Mina closely observed her surroundings and was surprised how detached the Slonim Jews were from the circumstances around them. For example, Mina's mother met a Jewish woman who had survived a recent German execution by managing to crawl out of the collective grave. She reached the hospital, begging for help and telling whoever would listen about what had happened. Her freedom did not last. Denounced, the woman was arrested and never heard from again. Despite the rising tide of human sufferings, the ghetto inmates continued to dismiss what they were facing.

Mina noticed that some of the people who left the ghetto for outside work failed to return. When Mina shared her observations with her husband, he tried to reassure her. As a doctor he was extremely busy and overwhelmed by the suffering he saw around him and by his inability to improve the situation. Still, with time, he was comforted by the limited help he offered. Mina learned that her beautiful sister-in-law had worked at the Beutelager and suspected that she had supplied newly emergent partisan groups with things she stole from there. One day this sister-in-law left the ghetto, only to resurface after the war.

Mina was good friends with a communist sympathizer named Dr. Slonimski. From Slonimski Mina heard that her sister-in-law had joined a group of Soviet partisans who she had over time supplied with valuable goods she stole from Beutelager. Mina confided in Slonimski that she was also eager to join a Soviet partisan detachment. The doctor discouraged her, arguing that she and her husband would not fit into a partisan unit because they were too bourgeois. He advised her, instead, to find a safe place with a peasant who would hide her and her husband for the duration of the war. But Mina was not interested in hiding. "I had too much life in me." She goes on:

> Another friend told me about a relative of ours in the woods who, if we would reach the Andrejewskie forests, would help us join his group.... This appealed to me.... Later on a policeman I knew suggested that we should leave the ghetto and join partisans who would protect us. He was willing to help. When I shared this information with my family they were angry with me. They were convinced that in the end this policeman would denounce us. Slowly, in contrast to these reactions, my husband went along with my ideas. What helped us also was the news that a group of partisans attacked a small town, Kosovo, released some Jews, and brought them to the forest. This was a known and positive incident.

The loss of her father during an Aktion convinced Mina and her friends—a group of seven, two women and five men, most of them young people who worked at the hospital—to leave the ghetto. They planned to come back later for her mother. They had been told that a Russian doctor made arrangements with a farmer to pick them up and waited for him at the designated place. It became dark and no one came. None of them wanted to return to the ghetto. "We walked towards the Andrejewskie forests and met two men on bicycles. These were Belorussian partisans who were a part of the Chapajev brigade. They wanted to take my husband and me to the brigade, but they had to get permission first. They arranged for us sleeping quarters. The rest of this group, they advised to go for help to the local partisan center."

In the morning, these men came back to the Volkowiskys with an invitation from Chapajev, the commander of the brigade, to join their unit. They accepted this offer and almost immediately the Chapajev brigade was attacked by the Germans. Soon the injured partisans had to relocate to safer places. Dr. Volkowisky had to accompany those who depended on his aid. This meant that Mina was separated from her husband. When the situation appeared more dangerous, Chapajev gave the order to split his brigade into smaller parts. Mina ended up in a group that included Krysia, who was Chapajev's mistress, and a number of his best fighters.

Krysia and Mina woke up one morning and discovered that Chapajev had disappeared. Absent also were his fighters. Left behind, in addition to Mina and Krysia, was a woman who was a cook, her teenage son, and two more partisans who were not seasoned fighters. Krysia and Mina were showered with complaints and a range of anti-Semitic accusations by the remaining Chapajev partisans. In response Krysia and Mina detached themselves from this group.

Krysia and Mina could easily pass for Gentile. Mina suggested that they approach some peasants who could help them. They seemed to be moving in circles. But Krysia was mistrustful of the local population and refused to seek their help. Next the two women met several partisans who seemed suspicious of them. When one of these men inquired what their nationality was, Mina automatically identified herself as a Pole. One of the men then recognized Krysia as Chapajev's mistress. Of the two, only Krysia owned a small gun. These partisans had promised to return promptly with an answer from their commander on what to do with them.

Left alone, the two women soon heard people approaching. Mina had guessed that these were the Soviet partisans. Krysia disagreed, suspecting they were Germans. Krysia grabbed her gun and disappeared into the woods. Mina was right; the partisans who asked them to wait had returned. Although surprised by Krysia's absence, they asked Mina to join them. As they moved around in a group, Mina was impressed with these men's sense of direction. They also knew how and whom to approach for food. Before long, news reached them that Krysia had been shot by Russian partisans.

The partisans who took in Mina treated her well. Together they would visit all kinds of different Soviet groups and their headquarters. During some of these stops, Mina heard horrible stories about the mistreatments of Jews in these forests. Russian partisans liked to repeat their accusations that if caught, Jews would divulge all and any military secrets. Many partisans blamed the Jews for all and any misfortune.

One of these newly encountered partisan groups included a Polish woman who knew that Mina was Jewish. This woman partisan shared this information with others, which radically changed their attitude toward Mina. In fact, some of Mina's so-called friends would openly refer to her as "the dirty Jew." Eventually, their anti-Semitic attitude dominated Mina's entire existence. With the winter rapidly approaching, Mina's partisans were ordered to divide up into smaller groups. None of the groups were willing to share their place with Mina. The woman who had identified Mina as Jewish felt sorry for her. She advised Mina to go to the head-quarters and to report that she was looking for her husband and that she needed help to find him.

"Nikolai Bobkov, the commander of the Sovieckaja Belorus detachment, agreed to meet me," recalled Mina. "After he confis-cated my watch, he began to ask questions. In the end, he told me that he did not know what to do with me." Another Russian, a man named Kasian, who knew of her difficulties, was willing to stand up for her. He had known Mina and her husband. "Kasian guar-anteed for me," recalls Mina. "He assured the commander that he knew me and my husband and that eventually we would be an asset to his group. This helped a lot."

For the time being, Bobkov was willing to keep Mina at the head-quarters with him. Still, things were in flux. Next morning the par-tisans were getting ready for departure. No one said anything about what to do with Mina. "I was standing there and I was too shy to say anything. The Polish woman who told them that I was Jewish urged me to follow them. She must have felt guilty. Fortunately, Bobkov turned around and called me to join them. I did."

With time, a kind of friendship developed between Mina and Bobkov. The two could even overtly discuss anti-Semitism and the mistreatment of Jews by the Soviet partisans. Sensitive to anti-Jewish prejudice, Mina was surrounded by it. The Soviets took from the Jews whatever they could, including their precious arms. The commissar in Bobkov's detachment, Yasha Gusev, who was in charge of the political policies of this unit, was an avid anti-Semite and a brutal man. Mina saw how Gusev would strip Jewish arriv-als of all their possessions and how he assigned them to the most humiliating jobs.

Often the prejudices of the Soviet partisans went beyond humili-ation. "In this area the Germans would give arms to villages sup-posedly so that they could defend themselves against the partisans. The Germans called it self-defense. One day Bobkov ordered his partisans to burn such a village. Among these partisans was a Jewish boy from Byten. He went with them on this mission. In the morning when the partisans returned they reported that they did burn the entire village but one of the partisans, the Jew, did not want to do it so they shot him. Bobkov explained to me that he could do nothing against this anti-Semitism, which expressed the anger of the people, because Jews were denouncing the partisans and the people took revenge."

Eventually, Mina was able to reunite with her husband. "When I stayed at the headquarters without my husband, it was unpleasant. Most of the partisans would have liked to sleep with me. They were watching each other. I was relieved when someone brought the news that Dr. Volkowisky was not far from us. Kasian, the man who initially stood up for me, volunteered to bring my husband to the Bobkov detachment."

After Kasian helped reunite the couple, he himself had to move to the Andrejewskie forests. The Volkowiskys were ordered to relocate to another area. Somehow they lost touch with the Bobkov detachment. Eventually, the Volkowiskys were directed to a central place from which they were supposed to reconnect with their former detachment. "In this place we met Bobkov. He was happy to see me. He had been searching for me...constantly asking around for Mina. They brought him several Minas, but he was disappointed that it was not me. He liked me and tried to convince me that he was not an anti-Semite. He also liked and approved of my husband. But his attitudes towards the Jews in general never improved, on the contrary, he seemed to be more anti-Semitic, a fact which he failed to recognize."

This was the end of 1942, when an order from Stalin came to reunite the different groups. This order saved them. "My husband became the chief physician of this brigade. This is where we stayed till 1944....Bobkov was glad to have us, glad to renew our friendship. He was also proud that his brigade had a well-trained physician. In fact, he never tired of reminding his partisans that a well-trained commander, like he, a pilot by profession, could be easily replaced. But a physician was a rare find, indeed!"

As the war was winding down, the Volkowiskys met twice with General Sikorski, the head of the entire region, which consisted of several partisan groups in Polesie. The first encounter took place several months before the end of the war. "I never met him before," remembers Mina.

This general came with his entire staff. Our headquarters was assembled there to greet him.... Such an ugly man, like an ape, fat, horrible looking. He sat next to me during the meal and started to talk. He assured me that he liked me and he promised to help my husband advance, even though I didn't ask for anything. He argued that soon the war will end and before this happens, he would like for us to move to his place. I told him that we are staying here with Bobkov and we intend to stay. But Sikorski insisted that with the end of the war, by giving my husband a higher position, my husband would become prominent after the war. The only thing we have to do is move to his place. I said no, that we wanted to remain where we were. But he continued saying that he will extend a formal invitation for us to change places. Of course, knowing how some partisans had a tendency to brag, I did not take it seriously and forgot about it.

One day, Bobkov called the couple to his headquarters to announce that they had been invited to General Sikorski's for dinner. This dinner was very festive and lavish. Sikorski gave special presents to the women. He sat next to Mina. He suddenly called on Dr. Blumovitch, who was the chief doctor, and announced that he was removing him from his position and appointing Dr. Volkowisky instead. "I was scared," recalls Mina.

I knew that my husband did not want this kind of a job. In general, he was a very modest man. We also knew that Blumovitch was talented and a good organizer. When we both pointed this out to General Sikorski, he became very angry. But my husband insisted that he did not fit into this position. Sikorski continued to argue: "You will have the position and Blumovitch will do everything for you." And when no one agreed with him, he called Prognagin, who was Sikorski's Chief of Staff. He wanted him to influence my husband to agree to the switch. But my husband refused. Angry, possibly drunk, the commander asked Prognagin to kneel and then he proceeded to hit him with a whip. Nothing helped, there was confusion, there was shouting and shooting. Most of them were probably drunk.

They ran back to their unit. After a while Bobkov paid a visit to Sikorski to ask him why he insisted on having Mina. He told Sikorski that he could have had more beautiful women than Mina. Why did he insist on having her? The General's answer was that Mina made eyes at him. He saw her as very beautiful. She had seduced him with her eyes. This brief exchange put a stop to all further contacts between General Sikorski and Mina.[18]

The chronic shortage of physicians in the forests meant acceptance of any qualified physicians, including Jewish. But the need for medical care did not automatically turn into full integration of Jewish physicians. Dr. Julian Alexandrowicz was a prominent professor of medicine at the University of Krakow. He was also a world-renowned hematologist, with important publications to his name. As an officer in the Polish Army, he had acquired excellent skills and valuable experience. At the end of 1939, as with most other Polish officers, he was warned by the Polish underground not to reveal his rank to the German authorities. Alexandrowicz was a Polish patriot, a highly assimilated Jew, who was surrounded by many devoted Polish friends. During the German occupation some of these friends were generous in extending help to him and to his family. Alexandrowicz was married and had a young son, born in the mid-1930s.

From the start of the occupation and beyond, his life was guided by his commitment to help those he could. He and his family had been relocated to the Krakow ghetto. In the ghetto he devoted himself to caring for the health of the inmates. He appreciated his close friendship with Tadeusz Pankiewicz, a Gentile who continued to manage his pharmacy within the compounds of the ghetto.[19] This pharmacy, named "Under the Eagle," served as a refuge for thousands of Jewish workers who each day moved in and out of the ghetto. In the end, most of them were deported.[20] Operating within the walls of the Podgorze ghetto, Pankiewicz offered to Jews and Christians both aid and information—a place from which to view events and hear about what was happening.[21]

Alexandrowicz showed his evenhandedness when he named thirteen Jews in the ghetto who were German collaborators.[22] Simultaneously, he named those Germans who risked their lives on behalf of the oppressed Jews and Poles.[23] Moreover, he revealed his extraordinary courage in the risks he took on behalf of ghetto hospital patients. He sadly noted how some of the Jewish underground leaders had innocently expected that everyone would simply cooperate with the Polish underground in resisting the Germans.[24]

During a ghetto deportation Alexandrowicz successfully hid some of the patients, risking his own life in the process. Also, just before the liquidation of the Krakow ghetto, he received information that all Jewish patients were to be murdered. To protect them from painful and humiliating deaths, he administered cyanide.[25] When the doctor had completed his hospital duties, he guided his wife and son out of the ghetto through the sewage system. Sadly his parents refused to join them. Alexandrowicz's father was apathetic and could not work up the resolve to leave the ghetto. His wife did not want to part from him.

Overcoming many hardships, Alexandrowicz and his wife and child succeeded in reaching the forbidden Christian world in Krakow. There they received help from Polish friends. A life filled with unexpected changes and dangerous twists began. Jews who reached the Christian world knew about the need to minimize the risks of discovery. Dividing into smaller groups was the most obvious way.

The Alexandrowicz family was among the fortunate few who had an apartment waiting for them. Officially, this apartment was rented by two Poles, who were already sheltering two older women, relatives of the three new arrivals. These Polish rescuers were employed, and from seven in the morning until four in the afternoon the five fugitives had to restrict their movements as much as possible. Surprisingly, the one best suited for this requirement was the seven-year-old boy, who was absorbed in reading his storybooks and in drawing pictures. The two oldest tenants, the grandmothers, had a hard time keeping still. The doctor wondered how long their safety would last.

Within a few weeks the inevitable had happened. It was early evening, barely past the police hour. Noises reached the door of their apartment. When they asked who was at the door, the answer was Criminal Police. The door opened and three men with guns burst into the room. One gun was shoved at the chest of Dr. Alexandrowicz. The gunmen wanted to know who they were. Instead of answering, the doctor reached into his pocket for the small bottle of cyanide he always carried with him and swallowed its contents. Convinced that he was dying, he was puzzled to hear all kinds of noises around him. His legs were numb. He had expected instant death. Then the doctor's son's voice reached him. "Daddy, I beg you, live, please live!" Alexandrowicz forced his eyes to open, to see and feel his son's face covered with tears. Shaken by the child's despair, he tried to move, but his body refused to obey. Then he felt a hand trying to pour liquid through his clenched teeth. He realized that his wife was negotiating with these men, who were blackmailers, about the amount of payment. She offered all they had. The blackmailers agreed, then even assisted her in placing a call to the nearby hospital.

The attending physician, a Dr. Zurowski, was a close friend of Alexandrowicz and took care of this unexpected new arrival. With the return of consciousness came feelings of shame. The Polish physicians who came to assist cooperated closely in restoring Alexandrowicz's health. They agreed that later he would have to move to a separate hiding place. Gestapo collaborators were closely watching. The Polish underground advised him to relocate to Warsaw, but he refused to leave Krakow. By then in good health, he relocated to new living quarters where he continued to work on his unfinished book on hematology. For safety, Mrs. Alexanderowicz and their son found shelter in a different place. Separated, they survived the war.

In his separate quarters Alexandrowicz became obsessed with the idea of joining the Polish underground, the AK. He wanted to help them take care of their wounded partisans. He knew about the shortage of physicians among the partisans and thought that he might be welcomed in the forest. Alexandrowicz's determination had probably stemmed from an official call from General Władysław Sikorski, the head of the Polish government-in-exile in London. Sikorski urged all Poles to help their underground fight the enemy in any way they possibly could.[26] Alexandrowicz's friends arranged a meeting between Dr. Alexandrowicz and a representative of the AK partisan organization. Their meeting failed to produce an arrangement. His friends continued to arrange similar meetings with other AK operatives, but they led nowhere. Refusals to accept him were phrased in a variety of ways.

While Alexandrowicz waited impatiently, he devoted himself to the health of Jews hidden in the Christian world. His contacts with these Jewish patients were arranged through Żegota, an underground organization in which Poles and Jews worked together. Alexandrowicz's work with Żegota was gratifying, but it in no way diminished his eagerness to join the AK ranks and to devote himself to saving the lives of Polish partisans. With each rejection, his astonishment continued to grow. He failed to comprehend how a physician who had behind him a great deal of military experience in performing all kinds of operations could be deemed unsuitable for the position he sought in the forest. Eventually Alexandrowicz had to conclude that within the high ranks of the AK hierarchy were those who were infected with the anti-Semitic virus.[27]

But Alexandrowicz refused to capitulate to it. Through his influential Polish underground friends, he continued to apply pressure. Eventually, an official announcement came stating that Alexandrowicz had been accepted into the "Jodla" detachment. This group was located close to the cities of Radom and Kielce. This letter reached its destination only in the spring of 1944. It came with instructions about which trains Alexandrowicz was to take to Radom and Kielce and with explanations that the meeting between this new AK member and his unit would take place in two stages.

His underground name was Dr. Twardy (which translates into "Dr. Tough"). Alexandrowicz was to come to the headquarters, where he was to be introduced to several forest commanders. At the headquarters, the pistols around the belts of the AK commanders greatly impressed Alexandrowicz. With the brief introduction behind him, one of his hosts asked him if he had any questions. "Yes," he replied. "I am eager to know when I will receive my gun?" He was told that everyone supplied their own gun. Annoyed, Alexandrowicz replied that it was much riskier to smuggle the surgical equipment bags than a small pistol. "I came armed with that which for a physician, is most appropriate for the services he can render here.... Besides, the AK unit in Krakow assured me that you would provide me with a gun."

This brief exchange in no way improved Alexandrowicz's chances for obtaining a weapon. Next came his transfer to the AK detachment in the forest. The Polish partisan responsible for this move warned him to be extremely cautious. A special guide took Alexandrowicz to what looked like the middle of the forest. There they came upon a horse-drawn wagon equipped with a peasant driver. This partisan asked Alexandrowicz to hop into the wagon, assuring him that he would be back in ten minutes. An hour passed. Alexandrowicz managed to take a nap. When he woke up, the driver, no doubt the owner of the horse and wagon, begged him to allow him to leave, assuring him that the others were about to come to fetch him. Feeling sorry for the peasant, the doctor consented to this man's departure with his horse and wagon while he had stayed behind.

Now, the doctor moved slowly around the area trying to make sure not to get lost. Soon, Alexandrowicz heard voices. "Where the hell is he?" someone asked. Another replied, "He probably changed his mind. What would you expect from a Jew, except cowardice?" This was interrupted by someone yelling, "Dr. Twardy, where are you!?" This, too, was followed by some cursing and a few derogatory assertions, that undoubtedly the doctor was a coward who must have changed his mind and escaped. They continued to call him names and curse. Convinced that these two tried to test his endurance, the doctor remained silent. Hiding behind a large tree, Alexandrowicz demanded loudly that the two should raise their hands or else he would shoot. They obeyed. The moon came out from behind the clouds and the guide who initially had brought the doctor into the forest and disappeared, recognized him. There was no point to continue the game. The Polish partisans decided that the doctor had passed the test very well. Alexandrowicz for his part told them that he would never forgive them for this prolonged and painful reception. After that, together, they moved in the direction of their partisan unit.

For Alexandrowicz, partisan life was a strange mixture of good, bad, and everything in between. When the Polish uprising in Warsaw was about to begin, partisans were ordered to send as much reinforcement as possible. Some of them hoped for the emergence of Soviet-Polish cooperation. But the Soviet-Polish cooperation happened only sporadically and not in ways that benefited the Poles. History shows how the Polish Warsaw uprising led to tragic losses of lives and the destruction of the city, movingly described and examined by Norman Davies.[28] Alexandrowicz noted how the occasional cooperative efforts between the Soviet soldiers and the Polish underground did happen, however. No matter how brief, this cooperation was on some level positive in its effects. Indeed, Alexandrowicz deplored the sporadic nature of these cooperations and blamed the leaders.[29] The Warsaw uprising began with a willingness to sacrifice. It ended with grave losses and bitter disappointments.

Still, the overwhelming sensation produced by Alexandrowicz's life in the forest was that of freedom. "My life was in my own hands and not any more in the hands of my enemies. I felt that if I perished I would do it only by fighting and not like a helpless creature without any resources nor as those who were forcefully deprived of all freedom."[30] For most Jews, such feelings were the exception rather than the rule. Most were deprived of the freedom to perish in meaningful ways, such as by helping others. Only occasionally were they in a position to help those in need of protection. For the overwhelming majority of the Jews, their aspirations and dreams faced insurmountable obstacles.

For example, when Zvi Shefet was accepted into the newly created Detachment 51, he was separated from his beloved family, which was placed into a special camp. Separated from them, Zvi, with a group of partisan fighters, was searching for places in the forest that would be suitable to spend the winter. While searching for such a place, Zvi and his fellow partisans were attacked by Germans. They were close to the marshes in Polesie. Soon Zvi's group ran out of food. The Germans burned large portions of the surrounding forests. During the battles that ensued, many comrades fell, including their commander, a Jew named Fiodorowicz. He had been a brave fighter. Reduced to forty-two partisans, Zvi's unit was leaderless. Fortunately, they met another Soviet partisan group, headed by Dziadzia Vassia, which welcomed them into their detachment.

Attacks by other partisan groups followed. Many concentrated on the destruction of family detachments. "Even early on, in 1942, a large Jewish family camp was destroyed. My family survived this raid. They perished in the next assault upon their family group, in 1943. My sister died with the rest of the family." It was not unusual for Russian partisans to attack family camps in the forests. Initially, when Zvi had joined his fighting unit, he had been assured that their partisans would concentrate on protecting his family's camp. These assurances were unfulfilled. It was common for anti-Semitism to trump obligations. Starting with the summer of 1943, rumors began to circulate about Jews. Some claimed that the Germans were sending Jews into the woods specifically to poison Russian partisans. Accordingly, rumors had it that the Germans were dispatching Jewish women infected with venereal diseases into the forests.[31] Behind these and similar accusations were assumptions that Jews would willingly let themselves be used as agents for the destruction of the Soviet partisan movement from within.

Such accusations met with opposition from powerful quarters. Among the staunchest supporters of the Jewish partisans was Hersh Smolar. Born in 1905 in Zambrow, a small town between Bialystok and Warsaw, Smolar was obsessed with the Soviet Union even as a young boy. He convinced himself that the USSR was free of anti-Semitism and would be an ideal place to live. I asked Smolar how he reconciled his Jewishness with his attachment to communism. He replied that at age eleven he became an organizer of a socialist youth organization—the Poale Zion. He was the youngest delegate his party ever had, and though he knew that in Poland involvement with communism was illegal he continued. His party's code name was "Henryk." And when he came to visit his "shtetl," the people would call him affectionately Henryk "Shmendryk."

Determined to make the Soviet Union home, Smolar's dream was thwarted. On the way he was arrested, then set free, only to try again. Eventually, at sixteen, he moved illegally to the Soviet Union. He was equally determined to work in a Jewish environment, so he relocated to Kiev, a place which had a well-established Jewish population. There Smolar immersed himself in journalism. He was particularly interested in writing for and about Jewish youths.

When I asked why, as a devout communist, he was so deeply immersed in Jewish life, he replied that he always had been. "I was a publisher of a Jewish youth newspaper, *Gwardia*, in Kharkov. This was a well-known publication for youths. At that point I met a substantial number of Soviet writers. It seems that many of them had also wanted to express themselves through youthful publications."

During the seven years he lived in Russia, Smolar continued to expand his journalism. After that the Communist Party sent him to Poland, where being a part of the party was an offense and could lead to imprisonment. Smolar indeed ended up in a Polish prison, which is where he was when the Germans invaded. All the prison administrators and guards simply abandoned the inmates. The prisoners broke down the doors and smashed windows, saving themselves.

On the outside these ex-prisoners faced more problems. Those who came from places other than the USSR knew that the Soviet authorities would not be welcoming foreign-born prisoners. Anyone who crossed the borders into the USSR without an official permit was unwelcome in the Soviet Union. Stalin refused to accept them. Throughout his life he remained suspicious of all foreigners, and at various stages of Stalin's rule the Russians were ready to deliver foreigners into German hands.

A day before Germany attacked the Soviet Union, Smolar and a coworker agreed to put up copies of the famous Molotov speech, which laid out the terms of agreement between the Russians and the Germans, all over Bialystok. Somehow it did not matter that at that point Bialystok was a deserted city. An order had to be obeyed.

At that stage, Smolar was the secretary of the association of writers for all of Western Belorussia that consisted of fifty writers, forty-six of whom were Jewish. These writers were provided with special trains to remove them to safer places. Smolar refused to avail himself of this opportunity. He and his coworker were left behind. Eventually they, too, decided to leave the deserted city. On the way they were joined by a few Polish friends. It was safer to walk in groups. They arrived in Minsk on August 1, 1941.

In Minsk, Smolar could not find the writers who had earlier departed from Bialystok. Instead, he was confronted by German policy toward the Jews, which forced him into the newly created Minsk ghetto. Here, he devoted himself to the establishment of an underground. A gifted organizer, he was gratified that by the end of August 1941, he had established the first Jewish underground in the Minsk ghetto. When I asked him what political parties were involved in establishing this underground, he assured me that the ghetto inmates were not interested in politics. Most were simply eager to enhance their military skills.

According to Smolar, the goals of the underground emerged only gradually. Initially it had concentrated on saving as many Jewish lives as possible, particularly the lives of children. Only secondarily were they interested in fighting the enemy. The organizations concentrated on destroying everything that was of value to the Germans, and this meant anything that might interfere with the promotion of Nazi goals, especially the annihilation of the Jews. The Minsk ghetto underground had identified itself as an urban partisan group.

In Western Belorussia, most ghettos lasted only for a short time. The Minsk ghetto was an exception. Smolar is convinced that the presence of skilled labor was responsible for the prolonged existence of the Minsk ghetto. The Germans relied on this labor and temporarily protected the inmates. Smolar lived in the ghetto until July 1942,[32] which coincided with the time of the big Aktion. There was nothing he could do to help. His enforced invisibility in the Minsk ghetto prevented him from helping Jews. As the head of the underground, he had to be careful. A transfer to the forest promised more cover and greater safety.

Toward the end of the summer of 1942, Smolar escaped from the ghetto. His departure was prompted by a Belorussian request that he help them create an underground in Minsk. Smolar knew that the invitation was due to his familiarity with the area, with the people, and with his fluency in several of the local languages. Smolar spent a year in the city of Minsk, helping the non-Jewish Belorussians to establish a functioning underground. Only when he was satisfied with the quality of this newly emergent resistance group did he depart for the surrounding forests. His presence in these forests was closely connected to his determination to help the neediest and most vulnerable forest dwellers: the Jewish fugitives and especially the children.

In the forest, Smolar urged members of his underground to help him transfer Jews from the ghetto into the forests. With their help, some Jews did manage to escape from the ghetto, though perhaps not as many as the 10,000 Smolar claimed that he was responsible for transferring from Minsk.[33] Initially, the underground members had no direct contacts with Russia, and they tried to work with both Jews and non-Jews. "We were responsible for the creation of an underground organization, for diverse Minsk populations. In the city, the Belorussian natives awaited orders from above. They were reluctant to act on their own." Smolar elaborated that the man in charge of the Minsk underground was a Jew, not a Russian, as some believed. "His name was Slavek. Early on, he was caught and killed by the Gestapo. As a group the underground followed my suggestions. They themselves took no responsibility for the decisions which were being implemented. Indeed, with time, we managed to create a substantial underground both in the city of Minsk and in the forest."

Tuvia Bielski (figure 3.1), about whom I have written before, was a central forest figure whose efforts resulted in the survival of over 1,200 Jewish fugitives. I was fortunate to interview Tuvia in 1987, at his home in Brooklyn, two weeks before he died. This meeting brought me closer to finishing my book, *Defiance: The Bielski Partisans*,[34] which focuses on the history of the Bielski detachment, and the largest armed rescue of Jews by Jews. I add him here because we can see in the context of other groups and individuals how extraordinary Bielski's achievements were.

The story began in 1943, in the Lida ghetto in Western Belorussia, which at the time was the center of Soviet partisan movements. Occasionally, it also served as a refuge for some of the Nazi victims. During the liquidation of the Lida ghetto, a woman named Hannah Rabinowicz was forcefully separated from her husband. He told her that she and the baby must survive: "Save yourself, run!"

FIGURE 3.1 Tuvia Bielski, Commander of the Bielski partisan unit. (Courtesy Yad Vashem)

Not quite sure how, with an infant daughter in her arms, Hannah soon found herself on a deserted country road heading toward a farm owned by a Belorussian friend. Avoiding people, she walked, hardly stopping for a rest. Only when the day was coming to an end did she knock at the familiar hut of a Belorussian woman. Though glad to see this mother and child, the woman was scared. Had anyone seen them enter the hut? If neighbors had caught sight of these newcomers, denouncement and death would follow. The entire host family would be executed. This was the German law.

Indeed, early next morning a sympathetic neighbor sounded the alarm. There was talk among the villagers that Jewish fugitives were hiding on this farm. Someone was likely to report this to the authorities. Hannah and the baby had to move on.

On leaving the village, Hannah stayed close to the edge of the woods. From time to time, she would enter a peasant's hut to ask for food and shelter. Some people fed her and let her rest a while. Others were afraid to let her in. Still others angrily chased her away. None wanted to let her stay. Those who had shown some compassion advised her to go deep into the forest and search for the Bielski partisans, a Jewish group, which they knew would take her in. But, no one could tell her their exact location.

Hannah continued to walk in the forest, heading toward an unknown destination. At night the branches offered only a semblance of warmth. Cold prevented sleep from coming and deprived her of the much needed rest. Soon the little food she had was gone. Unaccustomed to these woods, Hannah had a hard time finding nourishment. Neither the berries and mushrooms she had managed to collect nor the dew from the leaves could possibly satisfy her hunger and thirst. The baby was quiet. Perhaps she was too weak to cry. She continued to suck on her mother's dry breasts.

Hannah lost track of time, distinguishing only between night and day. Her early resolve to stay alive was slowly evaporating. Death, she began to think, might be the only solution. But, even to die she needed help. There was no one around and Hannah had no idea how she could get out of this place. Exhausted, dejected, she would spend more and more time leaning against a tree, listening, hoping, and dreading at the same time. During one of these rest periods, her ears registered the sound of breaking branches, then the rustling of leaves. These sounds were followed by a voice: "Who is there? Don't move. If you do I will shoot!" Spoken in Russian, the words had a familiar tone. Could the voice belong to a Jew? Without bothering to answer her own question, Hannah heard herself saying in Yiddish, "I am Hannah Rabinowicz from Lida. I escaped during an Aktion with my baby." A reassuring answer came, also in Yiddish. "I am here to help you, don't be afraid." Soon Hannah faced a man, who turned out to be an acquaintance from Lida. He was followed by another man, a stranger. Both carried rifles. They introduced themselves as Bielski partisans, scouts, on a mission to find Jews.

Hannah had a hard time grasping what it was all about. Even the bread and water they gave her she took without a show of enthusiasm. She let the men lead her to the Bielski encampment. There, following the custom of Jewish forest arrivals, this newcomer was introduced to the commander of the partisan detachment, Tuvia Bielski. To my question of how did Tuvia Bielski look to her, her answer was: "Like God!"

Many others must have had the same reaction.

By July 1944, when the Bielski detachment was liberated by the Red Army, it included about 1,200 Jews. Most of them were older people, women, and children, precisely the kind of fugitives who had the smallest chance of surviving the war. All of those who made it had a miraculous story to tell.

Hersh Smolar and Tuvia Bielski met in 1943 in the Nalibocka forest, a place filled with jungle-like enclaves that served as a refuge for partisans and ghetto runaways, all of whom were trying to elude the Nazi occupiers and their collaborators. Smolar and Bielski both were preoccupied with the protection of Jews from German threats.

Tuvia Bielski was the head of the Jewish partisan detachment, known for its open-door policy, admitting all Jews into its unit, regardless of age, sex, and state of health. Smolar heard that the Bielski detachment had difficulties with partisan groups that grew out of some internal and external quarrels.

The Soviet Major Vassily Chernishev, now known as General Platon, came to the Nalibocka forest in 1944, as the newly appointed head of the partisan movement for the entire Baranowicze region. Platon's and Smolar's friendship was sturdy. In the forest, Smolar had the opportunity to test this friendship, when he was warned by a Polish partisan that Soviet partisans were plotting against him. They wanted to kill Smolar by sending him on a dangerous expedition. In the forest this was a commonly used way of getting rid of unwanted enemies. Smolar dispatched an urgent message to Platon, informing him that he was being targeted for murder. Platon dispatched two partisans with orders to immediately deliver Smolar to the Platon's brigade, which saved Smolar's life.

Soon Platon shared with Smolar a letter of accusations against Tuvia Bielski, which demanded his death. Glancing over this document, Smolar suggested that instead of relying on paper accusations they should pay a visit to the Bielski detachment and directly assess the situation. Platon agreed and the two friends mounted their horses and rode to the Bielski detachment.

Upon reaching their destination, they were impressed by how all the Bielski partisans were engrossed in orderly and productive jobs. The entire detachment was divided into different workshops: a bakery, a sewing place where clothes were fixed and created, a sausage factory, a collective kitchen, and more. The visitors were full of admiration as they watched the organized activities.

Platon in particular was intrigued by the huge pots of boiling water in which animal skins were being transformed into leather. His enthusiastic comments evoke his surprise at the resourcefulness of the idea: "Making leather would benefit them in more ways than we could imagine; it would involve the making and fixing of shoes, creating all kinds of goods like saddles, belts, leather coats and hats! After all, a host of valuable articles can be made only out of leather!"

At the next day's meeting in the partisan headquarters, Platon noted that the Bielski detachment "had people who were equipped and qualified to offer indispensable services to our partisan fighters." Platon described how the Bielski detachment was capable of performing many valuable services for the entire Soviet partisan movement in the area. Smolar emphasized that both the Jewish and non-Jewish partisans would benefit from these new connections. Still, he was enough of a realist to recognize that these new ties would not erase the conflicts and hostilities which were directed at the Bielski detachment in general and at Tuvia Bielski specifically. Smolar approved of Tuvia's calm, but at the same time he understood why people envied him. Platon's recent support could diminish opposition to Tuvia, but might not eliminate it. Indeed, General Dubov, a longtime communist, remained a consistent opponent of Bielski and his partisans. Because of Platon's recent endorsement, however, Dubov curbed his hostility toward Bielski. Tuvia was delighted with Platon's support and correctly saw in him a powerful ally. For one thing, it gave him greater freedom to concentrate on the protection of Jewish lives.

Engaged in protracted struggles, the German Army from time to time would send one or two divisions of soldiers to encircle large portions of the Belorussian forests. By doing so, the Germans had hoped to achieve several goals. Successful encirclement had the potential of offering to the German Army direct access from Berlin to the Soviet German front. It would also provide an opportunity to destroy most of the partisan groups, which were active in this area. Creating a direct path between Berlin and the Soviet Union would increase their chance of victory. Those who were involved in these continuous conflicts knew that the different partisan groups would have to fend for themselves. They knew as well that not all partisan groups were equally able to face up to the Germans.

By the summer of 1943 special documents fell into Russian hands, documents that included plans about the German attack upon the Nalibocka forest. Other evidence mentioned August 1st as the official starting date for the next anti-partisan assault. Most partisans in these Belorussian forests knew that they could not defeat the Germans. Therefore, an early order went out to all partisan commanders in the area not to engage the enemy in open battles. However, each partisan detachment was asked to send some of its partisans to the headquarters. It was assumed that these fighters would participate in collective anti-German efforts. The Bielski Jewish partisan group contributed 100 armed men for such future confrontations.[35]

Despite these cooperative efforts each partisan group had its own agenda. The Poles were represented by Kasper Milaszewski, a Polish officer who had organized a separate fighting group known as Kosciuszko partisans. Most members of this group identified with the AK. Although an AK officer, Milaszewski had cooperated with the Soviet local headquarters. At the same time, less openly, he had coordinated his anti-German moves with a group of Polish cavalry fighters. These fighters and Milaszewski were each a politically strong group with strong nationalistic inclinations, which they tried to keep secret. Some of them were even affiliated with the Fascist part of the Polish underground, the Narodowe Sily Zbrojne (NSZ). The Poles preferred to keep such political leanings secret. Similarly, they had all shared a high level of Polish patriotism, which they were also reluctant to make public, as it would have placed them in a precarious situation. For quite some time, the Soviets were convinced that the Kosciuszko detachment was made up of local Poles who were free of political aspirations.

As a communist and a partisan leader, Smolar explained: "Only gradually did we realize that Milaszewski and his men were connected to the Polish government in London. I began to guess this from the kind of literature Milaszewski gave me to read. We were isolated for some time. We did not know who these Poles were and what they were after."[36]

When the encirclement of this area threatened to become a reality, leaders of the Bielski detachment, which at that point included over 700 individuals, recognized the difficulties in transferring so many people to this hard-to-reach area. Many of the Bielski members were children, older people, and people who had health problems. Nor could the Bielski detachment remain in their regular camp, which was open and accessible to the enemy. The Bielski group came up with an alternative solution, which originated with one of their partisans, Michal Mechlis.

As a professional surveyor before the war, Mechlis was familiar with most of these out-of-the-way surroundings. He suggested that the entire Bielski detachment should move to a remote place known as Krasnaja Gorka, the "red hill." This hill was located inside a large swamp, surrounded by huge and partly inaccessible forests. Mechlis argued that in addition to safety this place would offer water, a variety of mushrooms, berries, and a range of other edible growths. Secluded, out of the way, people on the run were unlikely to venture here. Few were even aware that it existed.

Preparations for a move into this remote refuge were set in motion under Tuvia Bielski's watchful eyes. His orders were simple. His people had to fill their pockets with nonperishable foods, which were usually stored in their camp. They also had to bring with them their weapons and ammunitions. In addition, they had to tie themselves to each other, with belts, thick ropes, and strings, thereby creating a moving, long, "life" chain. Young children were placed on the shoulders of adults. Directed by Tuvia, these preparations proceeded in an orderly fashion. As usual, during evacuations, he was the last to leave a place.

Here and there, as they progressed, they came upon unusual growths of weeds and strange-looking bushes and trees. Occasionally they halted. This continuously moving chain of human beings was disciplined and silent. Most seemed to concentrate on whoever was in front and behind them. Their movements were cautious, slow, and deliberate. The children, without extensive explanations, adjusted naturally. Here and there some of them rested by leaning upon each other, or on the thick growth. Some even managed to doze off. All along, Tuvia's measured voice urged them to keep moving. The same voice advised them to eat sparingly, to save their food for later. They lost track of time. Mechlis managed to mingle among them, encouraging some, promising to the rest that they will make it.

Days and nights seemed to blend into each other. The trek took more than a week. Finally Mechlis announced the end to their journey. The wild grass seemed to welcome them, as did the partially filled springs.

The new arrivals were relieved and curious about their surroundings. Some began to divide into groups, each eager to learn what this isolated place had to offer. Mechlis instructed them on how to benefit from the nourishments offered by these unfamiliar growths. There were mushrooms and a range of fruits. Their cooperative spirits were mixed with an eagerness to share. All this led to cooking and to preparation of a variety of dishes.

While it seemed to be isolated, a Belorussian woman appeared, carrying a basket. She was brought to Tuvia for interrogation. She insisted that all she wanted was to collect some mushrooms. With further questioning, she became confused. Tuvia and the others concluded that she was a spy and had to be shot. One of the partisans agreed to transport her body to a more remote place. Those who were directly involved in this incident refrained from discussing it further.

The incident was unique. Still, gradually, slowly, the food supplies began to dwindle. As a precautionary measure, the partisans dispatched a few volunteers who knew the area well to explore the situation. These investigators returned safely, but without additional food provisions. They succeeded in bringing information about the political situation, however. The news was that the Germans were preparing for departure.

In western Belorussia, as elsewhere, the Poles and the Russians were competing for the control of the region. For a while, perhaps to neutralize the situation, the local Polish underground and the Soviets maintained official contacts. During the encirclement, some Polish detachments had even coordinated their moves with the Russians. The Poles fought valiantly and lost many men as they broke the German enclosure. By September, with the end of the encirclement, considerably reduced in size, the partisans returned to the Nalibocka forest.

At that stage the Soviet-Polish cooperation became less stable, yet each side was still not prepared to challenge the other openly. As Smolar remembered, when the Poles caught a Russian partisan they would beat him up, take his weapon, and let him go.[37]

Jews who were caught by Poles were not as fortunate. Particularly the unprotected small groups of Jewish civilians, in bunkers, or Jews who were roaming the countryside, were often attacked and killed by other partisans who, more often than not, were following orders issued by the head of the Polish Home Army.[38]

Indeed the assaults of the Home Army had official sanctions in General Tadeusz Bor-Komorowski's Order No. 116, dated September 15, 1943. The newly appointed Chief Commander of the Home Army wrote: "Heavily armed gangs are continuously prowling the towns and villages, assaulting the manors, banks and commercial and industrial enterprises, houses, apartments, and larger farms. Robbery, assaults often accompanied by murders, are being perpetuated either by Soviet-based partisan detachments or by ordinary gangs of robbers. Among the perpetuators there are not only men, but also women, in particular Jewish women. . . . I have instructed the regional and district commanders to resist the element responsible for pillage, banditry or subversion, by force if need be."[39]

With Platon's support, Smolar was offered a number of interesting assignments. He recalled that around that time he shared leadership of a brigade, which included a number of detachments. "I was one of the three commanders who were at the top of this brigade. But in the Russian sources which usually listed the names of the heads of the brigade, my name was not mentioned. This was probably so because the rank I had was too high for a Jew."[40]

Involved in a wide range of partisan duties and exposed to many unusual experiences, Smolar had much to share.

> I had to travel to a lot of places, which sometimes exposed me to unusual events. . . . One day I left the forest with one of my adjutants. We had to go to a nearby village. Our walk was interrupted by loud screaming: "Germans! Germans!" First I was shocked, but when I recovered I asked: "How many are there?" . . . The answer was "one." Relieved I made the boys lead us to the place, a nearby hut. Inside I saw a young man sound asleep. The rifle stood next to him. I took the gun away, woke him up and asked who he was.
>
> He must have recognized that we were partisans. I heard him say: "I need you, to you I came." He told a story, which checked to be true. He was a reluctant soldier. He belonged to an underground organization known as the White Rose. This was an anti-Nazi, idealistic group of students who were dedicated to educating the public about the dangers of the Nazi ideology and how it undermined all human values. This idealistic, small group was ruthlessly destroyed by the Nazi regime.[41] In no time, this newly arrived German soldier explained that his socialist father urged him to desert the German army and to join the fight against Nazi Germany. From his train window he noticed signs warning German troops about the impending dangers of anti-German partisans. This soldier saw in this announcement an opportunity to fulfill his father's aspirations. He jumped off the train, in search of these forest partisans.

A distrustful Smolar listened to this soldier's story. He took the young soldier to their partisan hut, where he put him in the care of a Jewish partisan woman named Niura, to whom he explained the situation. He ordered her to watch him closely and that his work was to be limited to the kitchen. He also introduced him to a young Jewish girl. "Except for me and Niura no one else knew about this girl's Jewish identity. She was concerned that her Jewish background should not be revealed to anyone." Smolar continued,

> Occasionally I would come to visit this place and heard that this German soldier was adjusting well by becoming an active partisan. I also heard that he and the young Jewish girl were in love. At one of my visits I asked to see Fritz. When they called him in, the first thing I wanted to know was how his love affair with the young girl was progressing. He reacted swiftly: "...Ach shit, she is a Jewess!" That was all he would say. With time this former German soldier gained a reputation of a good fighter, practically a war hero. After the war I shared the story, about his love affair, with a group of people. Some of them were members of the clergy. Surprisingly my listeners responded only with total silence! [42]

As mistreatments of Jews expanded, some of it affected not only the Jews but also Russian partisans who were attached to Jewish women. This happened to Jozef Marchwinski, a Polish communist who was second-in-command of a Soviet detachment. Married to a Jewish woman, Marchwinski received a letter, signed by the head of his brigade and co-signed by General Platon, stating that his wife and one other Jewish woman, married to a partisan officer, should be transferred to the Bielski detachment. When Marchwinski's strong objections failed to stop this order, all those mentioned in this letter joined the Bielski partisan detachment. [43]

More morally devastating was the case of Fiodor Markow, the head of a brigade, who sent his partisans to the Vilna ghetto, urging Jewish underground members to come to the forest with their guns to fight the enemy. Markow argued that resistance within the ghetto would lead to the destruction of the entire ghetto population. He wanted the underground youths to move to his brigade, so that they could fight the Germans together. Markow insisted that Jewish resistance in the forest would reduce German power and prevent Jewish destruction. However, the ghetto fighters needed to bring their own guns.

After considerable soul-searching and heated discussions, a substantial number of Jewish resisters decided to join the Markow brigade.[44] On the way, some of them were killed by Germans, others by partisan groups. Those who had reached the Markow brigade faced bitter disappointments. Their prospective "comrades" turned out to be ruthless manipulators who tricked the Jews into parting with their arms.[45] In addition, these so-called "friendly" partisans insisted that the Jews must give up all valuables, including money, watches, and jewelry. These they were told had to be converted into money for the purchase of arms and ammunitions. Markow threatened that whoever would not part with their possessions would be searched and severely punished. This additional move to deprive the Jewish underground of their valuables turned out to be a hoax.[46] Many of these young people paid not only with their possessions but also with their lives.

These developments led to the emergence of different forms of resistance: resistance to save the oppressed and resistance that involved avenging Jewish murders. Outstanding among these avengers was Dr. Icheskel Atlas, who, after witnessing the murder of his family—his parents and sister—by the Germans, dedicated himself to avenging them.

For a while the Lipiczanska forest became the temporary shelter for small family clusters of unattached fugitives. Disorganized and unprotected, many of these groups lived in primitive bunkers. Unaccustomed to life in the forest, they were often attacked by partisan bands who robbed them of their meager belongings. Some Jews were murdered in the process. Occasionally, Atlas tried to help these people by warning them about impending dangers and by providing them with some food supplies and with moral support. According to one report, Atlas became depressed during his visit to one of these half-starved, defenseless family camps. He told them that he could not take them with him unless they were fit for combat. Atlas explained that all his partisans were fighters who were taking revenge for the victims of German oppression. "We are lost, but we must fight."[47] He inspired his fighters by "treating them as equals, never shouting but trying to explain and to convince. He set an example for all to follow and they did."[48]

In his dedication to punish as many Germans as possible, Atlas had the support of both the Jewish and Polish local population, who sometimes told him where there were stashes of arms left by the retreating Soviet Army.[49] He devoted all his energies to devising ingenious ways for the collection and use of these weapons.

Like so many other Jewish leaders who fought the Germans, Atlas identified with the plight of his people. Yet the help he offered was sporadic, not organized, and hence ineffective. His commitment to wage war interfered with the imperative to curtail Jewish destruction. His preoccupation with fighting the enemy made no room for saving lives. The last battle he fought was in November 1942, when he was severely wounded. His last order to his fighters was, "Pay no attention to me, go on fighting to avenge our tormented people." [50] His life as a fighter had lasted less than half a year. [51]

In contrast, Tuvia Bielski embodied an ethos of resisting by saving. Although he and his detachment took part in anti-German battles and cooperated with Russian partisans, destroying bridges and military installations, for him fighting the enemy and killing was not a priority. Resistance meant survival. By the summer of 1944, when the war was coming to an end, Tuvia's detachment had grown to over 1,200 individuals. According to Smolar, "Tuvia Bielski's wartime presence was like a glow in Jewish history, a truly exceptional phenomenon." [52] Smolar told me, "I always see the two in front of me. On the one hand Atlas, on the other Bielski. Together they represent the complexities of Jewish resistance.... Both are the two most important symbols of Jewish opposition: the fight for its existence and the fight for revenge. Atlas stood for revenge and Bielski for the preservation of life." [53]

CHAPTER FOUR

The Concentration Camps

Bela Chazan Yaari was born in 1922 into a Jewish Orthodox family in the small Polish town of Rizyszczyce. Her father died when Bela was five years old, leaving her mother to take care of her eight children. An independent woman, she opened a grocery store, which gave the family an adequate income. She insisted that her children not feel sorry for themselves nor refer to themselves as orphans. Bela's mother was a broad-minded woman, encouraging her children to become familiar with a wide range of political principles. Not surprisingly, as a young teenager, Bela joined the leftist Hehalutz organization, hoping to eventually settle in Palestine. After Germany invaded Russia in 1941, Bela and a large contingent of Zionist comrades attempted to immigrate to the Soviet Union. When they were refused entry, they returned to their home in German-occupied Poland.

After the Germans formed Jewish ghettos, Bela's Hehalutz comrades reacted by creating an underground. When she lived in the ghetto, Bela was employed as an assistant nurse, but she worked as a courier in the Hehalutz underground. This meant that she moved illegally in and out of the ghetto. Bela's Aryan looks made it easy for her to pass for a Christian. However, her somewhat limited knowledge of Polish was a problem. With time, as her underground responsibilities grew, Bela learned how to better hide her Jewish identity. She traveled extensively to cities such as Vilna, Warsaw, Bialystok, as well as to many smaller communities. Her successes gave her courage, making her feel invulnerable.

At one point her underground duties took her to the city of Grodno, where she rented a room from a Polish family. Occasionally, Bela would sneak underground comrades in need of temporary shelter into her rooms. One such man was the underground leader, Mordechai Tennenbaum. When he left, she overheard the young son of her landlady say to his mother: "Mama, Jews are coming here." Such a comment spelled danger. Unobtrusively, Bela gave up her room and relocated to the Bialystok ghetto.

Soon news reached her that one of the Hehalutz underground's most courageous and daring couriers, Lonka Kozibrodzka, had failed to return from a mission. For weeks her comrades waited for her return. Eventually someone discovered that Lonka was being held in the Pawiak prison, in Warsaw. Bela set out to find out how she might help. At a train station on the outskirts of Warsaw, two Gestapo men stopped her. They showed Bela a photograph of her in the company of Lonka and one other woman courier, whom the authorities could not identify. Bela admitted that she knew this photo and that it had been taken by the three friends as a souvenir. She told them that she had lost touch with Lonka and the third girlfriend. She was arrested. Over the course of the interrogation that followed, Bela slowly realized that the authorities were unaware that the women were Jews.

The Gestapo placed Bela in a cell in Pawiak prison. From time to time they would take her out for further interrogations. She soon learned that Lonka had befriended two imprisoned Polish underground figures. These prisoners thought that Lonka and Bela were members of the Polish underground. Lonka and Bela never revealed their secrets and were transferred to the Auschwitz concentration camp as Poles rather than Jews. They were transported together with two Polish physicians, Dr. Katarzyna Laniewska and Dr. Anna Czuperska, with whom they became friends. In Auschwitz, Lonka was employed as a German/Polish translator. Bela worked as a nurse.

Among her Jewish underground comrades, Lonka was admired for her courage and strength. She was willing to face up to all kinds of danger, relying on her outgoing and friendly personality. However, the move to Auschwitz had broken Lonka's spirit. Soon she contracted typhus. Too weak to fight the illness, Lonka gave up on life and died. Dr. Czuperska, a gentle and good-natured person, also succumbed to typhus and died.

Distraught, Bela tried to keep up her strength by concentrating on helping those who needed her help the most. Occasionally she was assigned to the job of serving soup to the starving Jewish prisoners. She overheard them commenting in Yiddish how surprised and grateful they were that this Christian prisoner (meaning Bela) served them the most nourishing soup from the bottom of the pot. Bela had witnessed several visits by Dr. Josef Mengele. During one of these, she heard him order Dr. Laniewska to prepare for him a list of names of the weakest women. Mengele's request was obvious. He wanted to send these women to the crematoria. Dr. Laniewska refused to prepare such a list. Furious, Mengele kicked her with such ferocity that she never recovered from the injuries she sustained and died.

Bela managed not to lose hope and overcame the horrors of Auschwitz. None of her Polish coworkers ever discovered her Jewishness. She recalls that when the other Polish prisoners learned after the war that she was Jewish, they were furious. "They resented me and left me all to myself. I had no one. Earlier, in Auschwitz before they knew that I was Jewish, when I offered to them help and attention, they had no trouble welcoming me. But clearly in their eyes my Jewishness made me completely unacceptable. How different these anti-Semitic Polish riff-raff were when I compared them with the noble and gentle physicians, Czuperska and Laniewska!" [1]

The concentration camps were an outgrowth of the German occupation of Poland. The idea to erect one in the Polish town of Oswiencin was endorsed by the SS, who argued that existing prisons could not accommodate the growing number of Poles who would intensify their opposition to the Third Reich. By June 1940 Auschwitz—the German term for Oswiencin—had become a reality. Initially, its entire prisoner population consisted of members of the Polish elite (intellectuals, literary figures, professionals, clergy, and army officers), but it expanded steadily, eventually including inmates from all of occupied Europe, including some satellite countries. The continuous flow of prisoners led to an expansion into three major parts: Auschwitz I, the main concentration camp, Birkenau, which became Auschwitz II, and Auschwitz III, also referred to as Monowitz.[2] With time, the entire Auschwitz complex included an estimated fifty subcamps.

Considering the horrors Auschwitz inmates had to endure, it is amazing that any of them had the strength even to contemplate resistance. Some have, indeed, argued that the only kind of opposition the Auschwitz/Birkenau inmates could be expected to have engaged in were efforts to save the lives, and/or improve the fate of, their fellow prisoners.[3] Specifically, too, it has been argued by some that chronic hunger, in itself, eroded most of the prisoners' ability to care for others. Others have pointed out that the ability to participate in any kind of underground activity was dependent on chance encounters with like-minded individuals. Still others have thought that by overcoming nightmarish circumstances some individuals would become more receptive to the needs and deprivations of others.[4] Anyone who became involved in concentration camp resistance would naturally be exposed to increased risk. And yet, the evidence suggests that by becoming resisters, some prisoners helped others overcome "the paralyzing feeling of being helplessly at the mercy of all-powerful abysmally evil forces."[5]

As mentioned, at the start of the Auschwitz/Birkenau history, the Polish political prisoners made up the vast majority of its population. Their large numbers and cultural familiarity with the camps' surroundings conferred special advantages. Unlike the subsequent groups of inmates, Poles could more easily establish lines of communication with the local population. Significantly, too, local Poles were willing to extend help to these Polish prisoners: food, information, and a range of other services.

From the beginning, one of the central figures among the Polish Auschwitz/Birkenau resisters was Witold Pilecki. A captain in the Polish Army, he had eluded capture and ignored the German order for Polish officers to come forward and register with the authorities. Pilecki was one of an estimated 20,000 Polish officers who successfully hid their prewar military rank from the Germans. As most former Polish military men, he automatically became a member of the AK. With the approval of the AK superiors, Pilecki attached himself to a street roundup of Polish men in Krakow. As a part of this group, he was transferred to Auschwitz and registered under the assumed name of Tomasz Serafinski.[6]

In Auschwitz, Pilecki began by organizing a resistance movement, identified as the Zwiazek Walki Zbrojnej, or "Union of Armed Struggle" (ZWZ).[7] He also set out to improve the lives of the Polish prisoners by smuggling extra food and medical supplies into the camp. Simultaneously, he succeeded in supplying information about life in Auschwitz to the underground in Poland and to the Allies abroad.

In one of the 1942 transports, two additional Polish underground figures arrived: Jozef Cyrankiewicz, a socialist, and Tadeusz Holuj, who identified himself unofficially as a communist.[8] Additional arrivals of new prisoners, some of whom had underground connections, created new opportunities for cooperation among a variety of groups, Polish and non-Polish. Nevertheless, true to their national traditions, the Polish underground members identified themselves with a variety of political parties.[9]

Whether a resistance group was eager to cooperate with others depended, in part, on the group's self-image. Those perceived as weak were naturally more dependent on help from the more powerful groups. For small groups, cooperation often translated into mutual help and an increase in power. Added to the diverse Polish underground groups in Auschwitz were two new small resistance groups: Czech and Austrian. Each of these wanted to cooperate with other resistance units. In contrast, other underground movements refused to have any contact with specific resistance groups. This was true of the German political prisoners, who refused to cooperate with any Polish and/or Jewish resisters. This was unusual because these German political prisoners identified themselves as communists or socialists and thus were naturally philosophically aligned with these other groups.[10] In their case, racial and ethnic prejudices overshadowed any shared political ideologies.

Needless to say, there were variations in how effective cooperation was for whom and under what circumstances. Poles were generally more likely to help Poles. Their shared nationality, however, did not always act as a unifier. Nationality was sometimes trumped by political ideology. Political and humane considerations could and did lead to mixed results. The political prisoner Hermann Langbein, an Austrian communist, had a mixed record. At certain moments he would devote himself to camp improvements that affected the fate of the entire prisoner population. On the other hand, he often made special efforts on behalf of his communist comrades at the expense of prisoners who belonged to other political groups.

In assessing the plight of Jewish prisoners, most Holocaust scholars agree with Langbein that "Jewish concentration camp inmates had the hardest, most murderous jobs, the worst food, and that they were confronted by the most horrendous living circumstances. Inevitably then, Jewish inmates were least equipped to stand up to their German oppressors."[11] Such conclusions further suggest that only a tiny minority of Jewish prisoners was ever in a position to attempt resistance.

Nevertheless, the history of the Auschwitz/Birkenau camps also points to the existence of several Jewish resistance groups, and their story underscores cooperative underground contacts between Jewish and non-Jewish resistance movements. Naturally, the German SS determined who was sent to what kind of camps at what time. Time of arrival, ethnic identification, and the size of the group affected the establishments of resistance groups. One 1942 transport to Auschwitz became the nucleus for the first and subsequent Jewish resistance groups. These arrivals included several Jewish young people from the Polish city Ciechanow. Most of them belonged to the leftist Zionist organization Hashomer Hatzair. Among them some of the recognizable names were Mordechai Bielanowicz (later known as Hilleli), Roza Robota (figure 4.1), Noah Zabludowicz, and Yakov Kaminski.

Around that time, too, the SS created a new and large group of Jewish laborers. Identified as Sonderkommandos, or Kommandos, they were a part of a group that had to perform the most gruesome

FIGURE 4.1 Members of the Hashomer Hatzair Zionist youth movement in Ciechanow on an outing in the woods, circa 1933. Among those pictured is Roza Robota (top row, left). (U.S. Holocaust Memorial Museum, courtesy of Eliyahu Mallenbaum)

tasks. These new duties were a byproduct of a diabolic German invention: the gassing and burning of Jewish victims. The Kommandos emerged in 1942, when gassing and disposing of bodies became systemic. It coincided with Yakov Kaminski's arrival, as a part of the Ciechanow group. It was, indeed, Yakov's misfortune to be appointed head of the Sonderkommando in crematorium IV, in Birkenau. Forced to take on this horrendous job, Yakov began to organize a Jewish resistance group, which expanded to incorporate workers from Birkenau crematoria II, III, IV, and V.

Only Jewish male prisoners were selected for the Kommando jobs. These men had to remove bodies from the gas chambers and burn them, either in fire pits or in ovens, which were a part of the crematoria complex. The SS were responsible for the selection of these Jewish men, as well as for their supervision. In time the Kommando inmates included Jews from a variety of European countries. These special squads lived in quarters close to the crematorium in which they worked. They were better fed than most other Jewish inmates, but isolated from the rest of the population. They were closely watched and severely punished for the slightest transgressions.

The SS kept them at their jobs for a limited and, purposely, unspecified period of time. The SS officers would decide when to retire a group of these laborers. Retirement in Auschwitz meant that they would be gassed. Kommandos who were still working were forced to burn the bodies of their comrades. The Kommando members knew that at any moment, unexpectedly and in the relatively near future, they too would be gassed and their bodies would be cremated.

Although the SS were obsessed with keeping these Kommando laborers separated from the rest of the prison population, they never succeeded in isolating them entirely. Under Kaminski's leadership, the Kommando underground groups managed to establish and maintain contacts not only with the rest of the crematoria but also with a variety of resistance groups.

By 1943, some underground groups became focused on the idea of a general rebellion in Auschwitz/Birkenau. The goal of this large uprising was to destroy the entire compound and at the same time save as many inmates as possible. The supporters of this revolt called themselves the Auschwitz *Kampfgruppe* (Struggle Group). In charge of this movement were communists, socialists, and groups from a range of other leftist parties. The *Kampfgruppe* aimed at including resisters with varying political ideologies. They argued that membership in this broad organization should not be based on size or strength. While these ideals were agreed upon in principle, they were not easily implemented. The actual planning for this revolt was still not complete as 1943 was coming to an end.[12]

The initiator and leader of the *Kampfgruppe* was the Polish socialist Jozef Cyrankiewicz. He argued that in principle those who were a part of this movement "were ready to fight for their freedom and that they shared a common respect for the right to life of every other nation, whether small or the smallest, whether the most defenseless—simply put, people and mankind."[13] Talks between the *Kampfgruppe* and those who represented the AK were set in motion. But the AK, as the biggest and best-run Polish underground, expected the *Kampfgruppe* to play a subordinate role in this large-scale uprising. During the ensuing discussions between the *Kampfgruppe* and the AK, as represented by Cyrankiewicz and Pilecki, the issue of power-sharing became the basic stumbling block. In the end, no agreement could be reached.[14]

In part, this deadlock probably convinced Pilecki that for the uprising in Auschwitz/Birkenau to be successful the AK would need help from the outside. To accomplish this, Pilecki arranged to escape from the camp, which he did—fleeing from an offsite camp bakery where he had received a night shift work detail. On the outside, at AK headquarters in Krakow, Pilecki reviewed the internal circumstances of the Auschwitz/Birkenau camps with his superiors. He tried to persuade them that with AK's outside support an overall camp uprising could be successful. But Pilecki's arguments fell on deaf ears. His superiors emphasized AK's lack of resources to pull off such a rebellion. They argued that according to their information there were an estimated 46,000 sick men and 10,000 sick women in Auschwitz and Birkenau. To parachute into the camp was out of the question. Involvement by the AK could succeed only within the context of a disintegrating German occupation. The unilateral conclusion of the AK Headquarters was such that at this point in the war—this was still early in 1943—such broad efforts would inevitably end in catastrophe.[15]

Disappointed, Pilecki had no recourse. He accepted the decision of his superiors, even though it had inflicted a heavy blow to his sense of altruism and to his profound sense of mission.[16] This meeting, in effect, terminated Pilecki's direct involvement with the Auschwitz concentration camp.

After steady involvement with the underground in Poland, he moved to Italy, but longed to return and in 1945, he did. This was a time when Polish patriotism was looked upon with suspicion by the USSR, which was in virtual control of the country. Upon his return to Poland, Pilecki was arrested on charges of treason and illegal transmissions of secrets to the Polish government-in-exile in London. He was executed in 1948. Neither the exact date nor the exact place of his execution were ever revealed. At that time, Jozef Cyrankiewicz, the former comrade and close associate of Pilecki in the Auschwitz underground, was the Prime Minister of Poland.[17]

As the Auschwitz/Birkenau camps continued to expand, additional transports kept arriving from other European countries. Inevitably, some of these new inmates were eager to join Jewish resistance groups. Among these youths were Moshe Kulka and Yehuda Laufer, both Slovakian Jews. The arrival of Israel Gutman, a Polish Jew from Warsaw, was a valuable addition to the prisoners. All three youths arrived in Auschwitz/Birkenau in 1943. An enlarged membership modified the activities and the organization of these Jewish resistance groups. What remained constant was the overall willingness by these Jewish youths to cooperate with both Jewish and non-Jewish resisters. Their illegal undertakings were guided by equally keen awareness that a resistance organization required a balance between secrecy and coordination.

Both the timing of these arrivals and the particular jobs which these prisoners were assigned led to some unusual alliances. Two rather unlikely Jewish comrades were Gutman from Warsaw and Laufer from Slovakia. Gutman, now a prominent Holocaust scholar, was a former underground Warsaw ghetto fighter who had lost an eye during the uprising. He was first sent to Majdanek and then to Auschwitz. He shrewdly avoided sharing the true circumstances surrounding the loss of his eye, explaining to the German authorities that it was the result of an accident on the job. The truth about Gutman's missing eye would have ended his life. Anyone known to the SS as having been in any way a leader was generally swiftly gassed. Despite his disability, this former rebel retained an eagerness to stand up to the Germans. After his arrival in Auschwitz, he searched for underground connections.[18] Gutman soon met Laufer, an Orthodox Jew and former Yeshiva student from Slovakia. In contrast, Gutman was a committed member of Hashomer Hatzair.[19]

These two individuals were very different yet they shared a determination to fight the Germans however they could. Both of them joined the Ciechanow Jewish resistance group.

In Auschwitz/Birkenau, rumors continued to circulate that the Auschwitz *Kampfgruppe* and the AK were planning a camp-wide uprising, which would include many of the existent underground groups in the camp. In part a pipedream, this broad, illegal undertaking was still at its initial stages. Under the leadership of Cyrankiewicz, this all-encompassing resistance movement set in motion a range of special preparations. Bruno Baum, a half-Jew and a communist, acted as a link between the *Kampfgruppe* and some of the Jewish resistance groups. Jewish resisters were eager to participate in a general uprising. Some of them had access to the gunpowder factory. They were ready to take on whatever risks were necessary for the revolt.

Jewish prisoners were "employed" in various parts of the Union factory. Of special interest to the underground was the part of the munitions factory that was involved in the final stages of the gunpowder manufacturing process.[20] The Jewish women who worked in this part of the factory were closely monitored and forbidden to have any contact with their coworkers, especially with men.[21] These restrictions did not prevent such employees from agreeing to supply their underground with gunpowder, however. Two Jewish female prisoners, Hadassah Tolman-Zlotnicki and Lusia Ferstenberg, arranged the transfers.[22] Several Jewish women laborers would steal small quantities of gunpowder by putting some of the gunpowder into tiny bags, which they then placed into several carefully selected places. Next, working as a team, Gutman and Laufer were responsible for picking up these powder bags and for transferring them out of the factory. There was never any direct contact between the women and these two men.[23]

Periodically, SS would search the departing factory employees, which included Gutman and Laufer. To accomplish safe exits, the two used the services of an inmate who was a professional tinsmith. This man prepared a "menashke," a metal soup bowl, with a double bottom. Wrapped in paper, a tiny quantity of the powder was placed between the two bottoms of the bowl. After the powder reached the outside, a part of it went to Roza Robota, who delivered it to the Birkenau Kommando. Robota worked in the Birkenau *Bekleidungskammer*, a place in which Jewish women received their camp garments before they were officially registered as camp inmates. Robota's place of employment was located across from the Birkenau crematorium IV.

The rest of this powder went to the Auschwitz *Kampfgruppe*. Laufer describes how in 1943, he would sometimes deliver gunpowder by putting it on a bed of an inmate who was a German socialist. Laufer never met this prisoner nor did he even know his name. There was safety in not knowing the name of an underground operative. All resistance groups were subdivided into small cells of three to five individuals.[24] Often members of these cells did not identify themselves by name.

One day, as Gutman and Laufer were on their way out of the factory, they noticed an SS man approaching. Laufer quickly whispered to Gutman that he had forgotten to put his gunpowder at the bottom of his bowl. Speechless, Gutman began to shake. He was convinced that this would be the end for both of them. Gutman's uncontrollable shaking continued and attracted the attention of the SS man. Like a hunter he turned to his prey, convinced he was about to uncover a crime. He ordered the trembling Gutman to step aside. Then he began to inspect his pockets, his hat, his bowl....Stubbornly, he searched and searched. Preoccupied with this suspicious-acting youth, the SS man hardly glanced at anyone else, waving them all to pass on. Laufer, with his gunpowder in his pocket, moved along safely with the other inmates. Finally, the fuming SS man ordered Gutman to leave the factory.

Preparations for the general Auschwitz/Birkenau uprising continued. The cooperating groups in these secret undertakings were the leading Auschwitz *Kampfgruppe*, a Russian underground group, and some Jewish resistance groups. Some of the arms came from the outside. A Jewish resister named Noah Zabludowicz, when working outside the camp, would smuggle out jewelry, which he then exchanged for arms.[25]

Among the Jewish groups, the Kommando in Birkenau was particularly eager to fight. They felt that at the appropriate time, and with some of the explosives and guns they had collected, they could attack the SS, confiscate their arms, and cut the camp fence to enable a mass escape of prisoners. In consultation with the Auschwitz *Kampfgruppe* a June 1944 date was set for the start of the revolt. Then, at the last moment, this uprising had to be cancelled. Someone had informed the SS. The Germans imposed cruel punishments. They executed the leader of the Sonderkommando of crematoria IV, Yakov Kaminski. The informer must have been ignorant about the identities of the remaining resisters, however, because none of the other leaders were touched. This allowed the others to carry on. In fact, the resistance leaders of the Birkenau crematoria redoubled their efforts. Following this crackdown, it now seemed to them that waiting posed the greatest danger.[26]

The SS reacted with brutal, well-coordinated determination. The political department of Auschwitz was consumed with punishing and investigating suspects. The Austrian communist Langbein, who had cooperated with the Auschwitz *Kampfgruppe*, was arrested and moved to the political Block 11 for interrogation. Shrewd and experienced, Langbein was prepared for this eventuality. His boss, the SS Dr. Eduard Wirths, rescued him. Langbein's release was followed by the arrest of the head of the Auschwitz *Kampfgruppe*, Jozef Cyrankiewicz. Again with Langbein's help and Wirths' willingness to intervene, this prisoner was also released.[27] After a while, Langbein was transferred to another concentration camp. His arrest and transfer had saved his life—but it deprived the underground of an important leader.[28] Several Poles suspected of direct underground involvement were executed. In addition, transfers of Polish prisoners to other camps followed. Most of these changes were the result of SS suspicions that local Poles had been cooperating with Polish prisoners. An unknown number of these transfers might also have been simply a reaction to shortages of laborers in specific industries.

Confronted with increased arrests and executions, the *Kampfgruppe* was reluctant to continue preparations for another uprising. They felt at this point that such a revolt could not succeed and could only be justified if the Germans were about to destroy the entire Auschwitz/Birkenau complex along with its inmate population. But for the time being there was no indication of that.

By 1944 the victorious Red Army was moving steadily in the direction of Auschwitz. A Soviet victory promised the hope of survival for some. However, the situation for the Sonderkommandos was quite different. They had no reason to believe that they would not soon be murdered well before then. They simply knew too much. In early 1944, the SS men selected 160 Kommandos from among one thousand and put them on a train, assuring the group that they were being taken to another camp for work. Instead they gassed the entire Kommando group, whose bodies were returned to the Birkenau crematoria in the middle of the night. Hoping to keep this event secret, the SS men themselves burned the corpses.

But news of the murder of these Kommandos spread all over the Auschwitz/Birkenau complex and convinced the rest of the Kommandos that sooner or later they would all be killed. They were determined to fight as soon as possible and began preparing for a final showdown with the SS. Roza Robota continued to act as a link between the Kommando resistance leaders and other Jewish resistance groups. Additional communications between the Auschwitz *Kampfgruppe* and the Kommando leaders took place via the official Birkenau food carriers. With their daily food delivery, they brought messages and prohibited goods.

FIGURE 4.2 A group portrait of six girls in leftist Zionist youth organization Hashomer Hatzair in Ciechanow. Roza Robota can be seen standing on the far left. (U.S. Holocaust Memorial Museum, courtesy of Eliyahu Mallenbaum)

As mentioned, crematorium IV was located across from the dressing room where Roza Robota worked and was a handy depository for all kinds of illegal materials, including some of the explosives made from gunpowder smuggled out of the Union factory. A Soviet prisoner named Borodin had mixed the gunpowder with special chemicals to produce a few bombs and grenades. Eventually, crematoria IV added to its growing arsenal one machine gun.

These preparations lasted several months. When in the fall of 1944 the transports of Hungarian Jews—the last major population to be deported to the death camps—came to a halt, this signaled to the Kommando leadership that time was running out. Still the leaders waited for a sign. It soon arrived. This time the SS wanted the Kommando leaders to prepare a list of 300 of their fellow coworkers who would supposedly be sent to Silesian towns that had been severely bombed. The SS order explained that the workers on the list would be employed in clearing rubble created by the recent bombings.

The Jews had no illusions. They knew that those on the list were destined to be gassed. But they also knew that an outright refusal to comply with this order could result in the murder of all the Kommandos. Those charged with the preparation of the 300 names were predominantly Hungarian and Greek Jews. Most of them were relatively recent arrivals and had not yet formed ties with the local population.

Those whose names appeared on the list announced that they were unanimously opposed to this demand and were determined to fight the SS. The other Kommandos agreed with their decision and conveyed the message to the food carriers, who delivered it to the leaders of the Auschwitz *Kampfgruppe*, which by this point was the umbrella resistance organization for the entire concentration camp. The *Kampfgruppe* replied that while they appreciated the hardships faced by the Kommandos they themselves were in no position to revolt and strongly urged the Kommandos not to start an uprising. They warned that a revolt could easily result in the murder of all prisoners. This time the Kommandos rejected the *Kampfgruppe*'s warnings.[29]

Two days passed. In crematorium IV, those men whose names appeared on the list were nervously preparing for a rebellion. They collected rags soaked in oil and alcohol, which they placed under the crematorium roof, among the wooden bunks.[30]

According to the plan they were supposed to start the uprising on the evening of October 7, 1944. But a midday conference of the Kommando in crematorium IV was interrupted by the appearance of a known SS informer. The Kommandos promptly killed him and burned his body. They knew that in no time this collaborator would be missed. They could no longer afford to wait. At 1:25 P.M., an SS man entered the block. He was attacked with hammers, axes, and stones. Next, the Kommandos set crematorium IV on fire. When those working at crematorium II saw the fire at the roof of crematorium IV, they thought that this was a signal for the uprising of the entire camp. They overpowered the head kapo, a Reich German, and pushed him and another SS man whom they had disarmed into a crematorium oven. Then, en masse, they broke down the fence of the crematorium and escaped.[31]

The prisoners in crematoria III and V did not participate in the uprising. They simply did not know what was happening. In addition, the remaining SS men were soon able to contain the situation.[32] In fact, the SS swiftly surrounded crematorium IV. Inside, the prisoners fought fiercely. Some of them escaped and reached a barn in the nearby village of Raysko. The SS guards pursued them and attacked the barn. The Kommandos returned fire. Eventually, the attackers set fire to the wooden barn. Some prisoners tried to escape through the flames and most of them were cut down. The Germans killed every Kommando they could, but a few managed to escape. They emerged the following day, when the SS had grown weary of the hunt. To investigate this uprising, the Germans temporarily spared the lives of about a dozen Kommandos.[33]

The details of this uprising are still being debated to this day. Some questions inevitably linger and may never be answered. Crematorium IV could not be used again and was shut down for the remainder of the war. All the others were restored to their pre-revolt state. While exact figures are not available, the estimated number of Jewish prisoners who lost their lives in this attempted uprising varies between 500 to 600.[34] As for SS and guard losses, some posit that three SS officers were killed and twelve were wounded.[35] Figures fluctuate. In one isolated source, the estimated number of German losses is 70, which seems to be an error.[36] Israel Gutman concludes that the precise figures for both sides will most probably never resurface.[37] Most agree that none of the organizers of this Kommando uprising survived.[38]

To the authorities in Berlin, the uprising came as a shock. They swiftly dispatched a commission to investigate the "crime." In about two weeks, this investigative body concluded that some of the gunpowder found in crematorium IV had come from a section of the camp's munitions factory.³⁹ Specifically, it was concluded that three female laborers had been directly involved with the production of this gunpowder: Alla Gaertner, Ester Wajcblum, and Regina Szafirstein. All three had been born in Poland, though Alla had lived in Belgium and arrived at Auschwitz/Birkenau on a Belgian transport. These three women were arrested and placed in the political Block 11 in Auschwitz. In the bunker of Block 11, each of the women was subjected to harsh interrogations accompanied by severe beatings. The women revealed nothing. After several days, the three returned to their barrack and their former working place in the gunpowder room. Their bruises were an obvious reminder of what had happened to each of them. And yet, on the surface, the women's release suggested a return to the pre-uprising circumstances.

For the authorities, however, this was only the beginning of an expanding, more thorough investigation. The dozen or so Kommando prisoners who had been kept alive as a potential source of information were moved to the political Block 11 in Auschwitz, and all of them were subjected to torture and lengthy interrogations. A man named Jacob, the Jewish kapo of the political Block 11, kept the Jewish underground informed about the fate of these Kommandos. One of them, whose name was Wrubel, was the first to die during the interrogation. He had revealed nothing. The rest of the Kommandos gradually followed his fate. None survived. None gave the Germans any valuable information.⁴⁰

Although the three women had been released and returned to their pre-uprising jobs, the authorities intensified their scrutiny over the three munitions employees and others. A number of spies and informers were planted among the gunpowder workers. Both the collaborators and resisters knew how important secrecy was. When Ada Halperin had delivered powder to other prisoners, she had not even known the names of her contacts. At one point, too, she was accused of sabotaging the production of gunpowder. Fortunately for Ada, her kapo, a man named Willi, stood up for her and convinced their German boss that Ada had committed an honest mistake. This incident ended with a severe beating but no further consequences.⁴¹

Naturally, after the October 7th Kommando uprising, everyone—the rebels, the authorities, and the collaborators—were all more suspicious of each other. Everyone waited for a mistake, a slipup. It was a subtle but extremely uneven confrontation. On the one side were the all-powerful oppressors and their collaborators and on the other side were the inmates, for whom the slightest misstep could easily lead to loss of lives, not only theirs but anyone connected to them.

During the investigation, a frequent visitor to the barrack where the three gunpowder women lived was Eugen Koch. Half Jewish, Koch came to the camp from Czechoslovakia. His official position was that of an assistant kapo. He had a smile glued onto his face, and that, along with his subservient behavior toward the Germans, made some prisoners suspicious. Early on, Israel Gutman was among those who identified Koch as a double agent.[42]

Eventually, it was clear to others that this frequent visitor to this barrack had attached himself to the three recently returned prisoners, Alla Gaertner, Ester Wajcblum, and Regina Szafirstein. Of the three, Koch seemed to favor Alla. Alla's friend, Herta Fuchs (nee Ligeti), felt uncomfortable about Koch's courtship. She tried to warn her friend about her ever-smiling suitor. Herta's hints had no effect on Alla; she was already under the spell of Koch. When Herta shared her concern with an underground comrade, he warned Herta not to interfere. He insisted that Herta could be in danger. Others also expected trouble. They were suspicious of Koch's gifts—the chocolates, the cigarettes, and all the attention that came with it. But neither could they openly voice their objections.[43] In the meantime, Alla herself began to feel that she might have divulged too much to Koch. Without offering clear-cut explanations, she confided in her friend Herta that she was afraid. Herta told Alla, "Whatever is going to happen to you, it is not right if you pull others down with you."[44]

What some had predicted happened. Alla Gaertner, Ester Wajcblum, and Regina Szafirstein were rearrested. Once more they were taken to the political Block 11, in Auschwitz. There in the notorious bunker, each of them was subjected to torture. Two days after the arrest of these three women, Roza Robota was also brought to Block 11. The rumor was that Alla had mentioned Roza Robota as her contact.[45]

This time the Germans had gathered more concrete evidence. Still, they wanted more. Of the four Jewish women, Robota was most knowledgeable about the underground operations. The Germans seemed to know this. Robota admitted to smuggling the gunpowder, but mentioned only Wrubel as her contact. She knew that Wrubel was already dead. She did not apologize for her actions.[46] Similar behavior has been reported about other imprisoned and tortured Jewish resisters. The rumor was that Robota refused to divulge secrets. Frustrated, the Germans intensified their efforts to extract information from her. Concurrently, they continued to search for additional clues from a range of other suspects.

On the outside a growing number of the "free" Jewish resisters were bracing themselves for the worst. How long could Robota withstand the torture? For Israel Gutman, this was the greatest fear—not death, but his ability to withstand torture. Breaking down would lead to the murder of his comrades. He seriously considered committing suicide.

Time passed. Gutman and Laufer waited as they contemplated their next moves. Both knew that their suicide would protect the lives of others. These two young resisters were filled with anxiety and indecision.

It seems that the only one who was sure that she would not divulge any secrets was Roza Robota. Each one of her smuggled messages assured her comrades that they had nothing to fear. In fact, there were loopholes in the German thoroughness. The Germans had missed a significant connection between Robota and Helen Spitzer-Tichauer, known as Zippi (figure 4.3).

Zippi was a Slovakian prisoner who had arrived at Auschwitz in the first transport of Jewish women, in the spring of 1942. By 1943, Zippi had become the official graphic designer of the women's camp in Birkenau. As a graphic designer, Zippi had access to secret information. This in turn made her a desirable contact for all kinds of resistance groups. In addition to affording her access to secret information, Zippi's position included some privileges. She had the freedom to move around in most parts of the camp, provided that an SS guard accompanied her. She liked to emphasize that she lived and worked "in the prisoners' office (*Heftlings Schreibstube*) and was known as *Zippi Aus der Schreibstube*." In Birkenau she had a separate design office, known as *Zeichenstube*. Anna, a Polish prisoner who was in charge of the Block, knew that Zippi had contacts with individuals connected to the camp's underground movements and assumed that Zippi belonged to the underground. But these two

FIGURE 4.3 Helen Spitzer-Tichauer, known as Zippi, painting letters on the Luxor Palace in Bratislava, 1938. (Courtesy of Helen Spitzer, private collection)

women never talked about it. It was much safer not to know, and not to discuss, such topics.

Zippi sometimes worked through the night, which was when visitors often came to see her. One evening Roza Robota visited Zippi's office and introduced herself as a fellow member of the Hashomer Hatzair. Robota reminded Zippi of their having once met at a Hashomer Hatzair meeting before the war. Zippi recalled that, after this brief introduction, she and Robota spoke a little.

> Then Roza said that she would visit me again. When she left, I thought that the whole visit was a pretext for something else, but it didn't matter to me. A few days later, she brought me an apron....Our uniform dress was a blouse and a skirt...only some of us had aprons. She brought me a nice apron, made out of black cloth. It was a little thing, but I appreciated it. Two weeks later she came again, with another apron, casually telling me: "I want you to have this new apron." I told her that I didn't need it, that the one I had was enough. Disregarding my comment, she said, "Give me your old apron and I'll give you the new one."...After

that she continued to exchange my apron for a new one...she did this every two weeks. These were beautifully made aprons...also occasionally, Robota would ask me to put someone in a better job, and I did it. She would ask me for other favors, and I tried to help. In fact, I encouraged her to ask me....It was not hard for me....In retrospect, it seems that Roza Robota made contact with people by supplying them with these nice aprons. I never spoke about this to anybody before....After a while I would ask myself, "Why she was so anxious to have my old aprons?" Much later, I discovered that along the edges of the aprons were those little layers...maybe, she stored her merchandise in the aprons until she delivered them? No one would have bothered her while she carried aprons. Who knows, I might have carried the powder on me....After two weeks, she came to take my apron. It just could be that way. I was probably like a live bomb! Is it possible that when she brought the apron, she had the powder in it? Could it just have been that way? But it doesn't make sense; why would she bring it to me? Some women wrote about the aprons' pockets. I remember only the special folds at the edges of these aprons.

Were these folds unusual features of these aprons? I asked her. Zippi did not think so. "That's all I know, really....This was the genius of that woman, that I did not suspect her...There are all kinds of versions about this uprising by the Jewish Sonderkommando...we know that many facts had died with those who were involved, and who might have told but did not."[47]

After the Kommando uprising, Zippi stayed away from Roza Robota and was thankful that the Germans seemed to be ignorant about her connection to her.

To ease tensions, Jacob, the kapo of the political Block 11, was willing to arrange a meeting between Robota and one representative of the underground. To neutralize the guard, Jacob needed sausages and plenty of vodka. The group selected as their representative Noah Zabludowicz, whom Robota knew from Ciechanow. When the vodka made the guard drunk and sleepy, Noah was admitted into the prisoners' cell. He could not recognize his old comrade. Her torturers had left no part of her body unscathed. Only when Robota began to speak did she begin to resemble her old self. She told Noah that she wanted to live, but was determined not to mention any names. No one should doubt her. She would not yield to the enemy. She knew that the Germans would soon execute her. She could not protect herself. All she could do was to protect others. On leaving the bunker, Noah knew that though this woman had ceased to resemble a human being, she was the most humane and magnanimous person he had met.

The public hangings of Alla Gaerten, Roza Robota, Regina Szafirstein, and Ester Wajcblum took place on January 6, 1945. To ensure the presence of the entire Auschwitz/Birkenau slave labor force, this event was divided into two shifts. The women moved to their assigned places, silently looking straight ahead. The accused and the surrounding crowds were treated to the hysterical screaming of SS man Hofler, culminating in his warning: "All traitors will be destroyed in this manner!"[48] The executions themselves happened under a cover of sullen silence. Only once was this utter silence broken—by Roza Robota's cry of "Nekama!"—"Revenge!"[49]

The deaths of these four resisters put to rest anxieties and fears of the inmates who were involved in the Kommando revolt. Had any of their names been revealed to the German authorities, each of them would certainly have shared the fate of the four women. The silence of these four Jewish women and the silence of their comrades, who were murdered in the bunker of Block 11 in Auschwitz, saved at least the lives of eighteen known Jewish participants.

Because these four victims and those who died under brutal interrogations in the infamous bunker took many secrets with them, uncovering the details is a complex process. A look at the reactions of two Auschwitz/Birkenau prisoners to the Kommando revolt yields at least some tentative insights. Wieslaw Kielar, like so many of the Polish political prisoners, was involved in the Auschwitz/Birkenau underground. Kielar's resistance contacts reached beyond Polish groups, as did his friendships and relationships. He fell in love with a Jewish prisoner, and despite his efforts to save her, she was gassed. Kielar was shattered by this loss but managed to receive some comfort from his many underground friends. Kielar and his comrades were constantly dreaming and planning all kinds of moves, including plans for escapes. He knew that a campwide uprising at Auschwitz/Birkenau was being planned.

On October 7, 1944, Kielar was with his work group outside the camp when he heard rifle shots, followed by sounds of explosives. Soon his attention was caught by smoke over a crematorium chimney. Initially, he thought that these sounds had been caused by an air attack. Next he saw a large group of SS men rushing in the direction of the burning crematorium. Bullets were flying around. For safety Kielar hid in a nearby truck. From his place, he must have seen that the crematorium IV roof was on fire. At one point, he thought that what he heard had to do with the uprising. He wondered whether partisan groups might have come to aid the camp's uprising. Kielar was pleased with this scenario—the prisoners working in unison with outside partisans.

When the shooting subsided, Kielar thought that the partisans had left. Disappointed that this had turned out to be a short-lived disturbance, he left the truck in which he had been hiding. He and his fellow workers were ordered to arrange themselves into an orderly group. Their kapo proceeded to count them and was satisfied that their number was correct. The group was ordered to turn back. On the way Kielar and his comrades heard that the shootings and fires had been caused by the Kommando revolt. Kielar checked this information with his special contact, probably a Jewish prisoner. From him he heard that this, indeed, had been the Kommando uprising. He was also told that an informer betrayed these Jewish resisters and therefore they had started their uprising early. This confusion in timing and communications diminished the uprising's effectiveness. Only crematoria IV and II had a chance to fight. Kielar was upset by the tragic outcome of this revolt and the tremendous loss of life.

Kielar had often discussed the possibilities of escaping from Auschwitz. Now, one of his close friends approached him with an urgent request to act. Kielar refused. He had serious doubts that the partisans on the outside would offer them help. Hope had somehow abandoned him, leaving him with no strength to fight. What Kielar had feared and tried to avoid before the Kommando revolt was about to happen. The following day Kielar was put on a transfer group that left Auschwitz for Germany. He seemed not to care. Just as he had anticipated, this transfer was nightmarish—overcrowding, beatings, thirst, and hunger. On the verge of collapse, pushed by his cruel handlers, Kielar's will to live seemed to be evaporating. But, somewhere in Germany, he found it again, because of an encounter with American soldiers.[50]

Another assessment of the Kommando revolt comes from Israel Gutman. He also notes that after the outbreak of the revolt, the help that the SS men received was swift and extensive. According to Gutman's estimates, two thousand well-armed German soldiers arrived at Auschwitz/Birkenau. Nevertheless, this did not prevent

Gutman from observing that during the initial stages of the uprising he saw the Germans "run around like rats during a storm."

But no one came to help the Sonnderkommandos, whose fate was sealed in advance.[51]

> And yet, despite the terrible Jewish losses...the day of the uprising of the Sonderkommando became a symbol of revenge and was an inspiration to the prisoners. In the place that had served for years as a field of slaughter for millions of victims, there fell the first Nazis in Auschwitz. And it was Jews who had done the fighting. In this gigantic camp where tens of thousands of prisoners were confined, a handful of Jews broke free of the pervasive spirit of submission and passive resignation to their cruel fate. The uprising of the Sonderkommando proved to the prisoners of diverse European nationalities that Jews knew how to fight for their lives.[52]

Inevitably, Jewish and non-Jewish undergrounds had different motivations and operated under vastly diverse circumstances. But despite these differences, they engaged in a number of similar resistance activities: the collection and dissemination of information; the forgery of a variety of documents; and the collection of arms. Up to a point they also cooperated in various planning stages of armed revolts. Auschwitz/Birkenau offers a setting in which their shared efforts were demonstrated. This is a particularly instructive case because it allows for a "controlled" comparison, one in which the setting is constant and specifically defined while a range of other variables can apply.

Within the universe of the Nazi occupation, the death camp was the ultimate means of human degradation and subjugation. In Poland, the Treblinka death camp was completed by July 1942. Early in 1943 a core of Jewish prisoners began to organize a rebellion that aimed at the destruction of the camp and at giving prisoners a chance to escape. Although precise figures elude us, of the estimated 600 to 700 Jewish inmates who took part, between 100 and 150 are known to have escaped. About seventy of them survived the war.[53]

In the summer of 1995, in Basel, my Swiss friends Martina and Vincent Frank introduced me to a number of Holocaust survivors. I was particularly eager to meet Richard Glazar, a Jewish Czech economist who lived in Switzerland. I wanted to meet him because he had participated in the uprising in Treblinka and was one of the handful who had managed to save themselves. The Franks invited the Glazars with the understanding that before dinner, in a separate part of their house, I would interview him. When we met, Richard impressed me as thoughtful and distant. He hastened to tell me that he had been interviewed by a writer for a book about Franz Stangl, the German commandant of Treblinka, and that for him this had been a thoroughly disappointing experience. Glazar felt that Gitta Sereny, the author, had distorted his account. In fact, he was still angry as he talked to me about it. He made it clear that he had not been looking forward to our interview. I listened silently as Glazar went on, suggesting that my questioning him was superfluous because his memoir, *The Trap with a Green Fence*, was about to be published in the United States. However, he continued, since he had already agreed to meet me, he would grant me a brief interview. He hoped that I would not distort his story. This was not a very promising start. But experience had taught me not to predict the outcome of such meetings.

The interview was conducted in German. I began by asking about the start of the war. He outlined his past and then quickly turned to his experiences in Treblinka, experiences which had the greatest impact upon his life. This is when I began to probe. But each time I asked a question, he countered by telling me that I would find the answer in his book. I repeated the questions by rephrasing each time. For his part, Glazar again reiterated that the book said everything I needed to know. After about three or four similar exchanges, I began prefacing my questions by saying that even though he might have dealt with the issue in his book, I would still appreciate hearing answers to what I was about to ask him. I assured him that I found it useful to listen to the same events several times. He did not argue and tried, reluctantly, to accommodate me. His answers were curt.

Gradually, however, his comments that the answers could be found in his book began to wane. Somewhere in the middle, Glazar volunteered that he regretted that before delivering the book to his American publisher he had not thought about some of the issues we were tackling. In the end, the interview was filled with thoughtful comments.

At the time unfamiliar with his book, I felt uneasy that I might have made him repeat things that he was reluctant to say. However, as he relaxed and even complimented me on some specific questions, I became conscious about the value of this interview. His comments contained important historical information, and reflections on the need for cooperation in extremis, and especially in situations that at best promise only very temporary survival. He emphasized again and again that one could not exist in Treblinka without bonding in some way. Woven into his remarks were observations about slavery, autonomy, and opposition to conditions of ruthless domination.

My subsequent reading of Glazar's memoir, valuable though it is, only reconfirmed to me how right I was to probe patiently, yet stubbornly. The interview had lasted for about two hours, but it gave me much more than I had expected. Glazer's memoir is a historically valuable and important document. Still, it does not offer some of the broader insights and implications that emerged during our conversation. He told me:

> My friend Karl Unger and I were always together. We were like twins. In this camp you could not survive an hour without someone supporting you and vice versa. We knew that we were destined to die....No individual could make it alone. Treblinka was a death camp, where people were brought to die. Here, one had to be very cautious, very alert. One had to be always sensitive to signs of danger. We tried to know which direction death might come from. We had to have a sense of how to use someone's weaknesses and how to manipulate. My friend Karl and I survived because we supported each other constantly. We divided absolutely everything, even a small piece of bread.[54]

I asked Glazar why this mutual help was so basic.

> One felt it. One knew it. This is how it was. It gave us a certain feeling of solidarity. I think this was particularly important because it was a death camp. Selfishness had no place in this camp, perhaps in different kinds of camps, but not here. Mostly, these little groups [bonding groups] were based on the country of origin. Most of us came from the same country, but not always. Because we were so close to death, we felt very down, we felt very humiliated. We knew we were in a death factory. We were so degraded because we were participating in the creation of death. We were used by the Germans as a part of their death machine....Given these horrible, degrading conditions, we had to get together with somebody else. What kept us going was the idea that we could do something. We always tried to do something to counteract this tremendous

helplessness and dependence as well as our participation in this terrible crime. While I was there, we tried to smuggle out two people, to tell the world what was happening. We wanted them to get in touch with the Polish underground.[55]

When talking about the Treblinka uprising, Glazar repeatedly emphasized the prisoners' ties and their solidarity.

There was a group of rebels, resisters, about ten people, which in time became organized. These were the ten most important people; all of them had some kind of military skills. My friend Karl and I did not have any military training at all. Because my friend and I were not military men, we were not real members of the resistance group.

However, two other Czech men, Zelo Bloch and Rudi Masarek, were an integral part of this resistance. They would inform us about a lot of things. They would also use us to do all kinds of jobs for the underground. Not as a members of the group, but as marginal members.

Many people knew something, but we were very careful not to have much contact with the Germans. It was difficult not to accidentally give something away. The plan was to start the uprising in August, 1943. All the horrors that happened, that we felt were somehow a part of each of us, somehow were cancelled out by our uprising. This is a very interesting thing. Through this desperate rebellion, we regained our pride. We regained some autonomy, some independence....And even though there were very few people who participated in planning this revolt, those who knew about it gained relief from it. It had a wonderful impact upon the rest of us just knowing about it. All of us knew something about it, and all of us somehow felt a part of it, even though many of us were not specifically involved with it....It gave us the illusion of having some control over our destiny.

There were many helpers associated with this opposition. They were not told precisely what was happening, because it would have been dangerous for them. But they had a feeling that they were a part of something. Of course, everybody, in a sense, in some way, contributed to this uprising. You cannot do this without having full cooperation.[56]

I asked Glazar if he ever worried that an inmate might denounce him. "I told you before," he replied, "that there were about three of those whom we did not really trust. Actually, even about these three, it wasn't that we thought that they would denounce us, but we thought that they might not be strong enough if they were caught not to talk. There were no explicit denouncers of whom we might have been afraid."

"Are you telling me that there was an overall solidarity among you all?" I asked.

"In a sense, yes. I am telling you that among those living there, among those slaves, yes. There was such solidarity. I think that solidarity was much stronger than in other camps because this was a death camp. But I only became aware of this distinction when I read about other camps."

"I want to see if I understand what you are telling me. Are you saying that the solidarity which existed among the prisoners made you feel or gave you the possibility of feeling like a human being?"

"Definitely. Definitely. This was a way of telling them [the Germans] that they could not fully dehumanize us, that we shared this solidarity. This realization only occurred to me later on, as I looked back and discussed and read and thought about it."[57]

I understood that Treblinka made bonding indispensable. In effect, on his own, Glazar emphasized that the more degraded life became in a camp, the greater became the need for mutual cooperation. In my research I have been finding the same thing again and again: the more dire the conditions under which one was forced to live, the greater the need for solidarity and compassion among those sharing them.

Although in some ways life-promoting, such supportive groups in and of themselves could not help people entirely to avert death. Most leaders of the Treblinka uprising did perish. Many others who died belonged to a variety of groups. Moreover, organized and armed Jewish resistance happened in at least five major concentration camps and in eighteen work camps.[58] However, most were not as dramatic as the armed resistance that occurred in Treblinka. And yet, they all had shared some similar characteristics.

With the German occupation, Glazar's parents had been convinced that their son's transfer to a remote farm where he was engaged in heavy work would protect him from scrutiny. Contrary to this expectation, by 1942 the Germans traced Glazar to the farm on which he worked.

The Nazis sent him to Teresianstadt, where he stayed one month. "After the one month, I was notified that I was being moved to another ghetto. After a few days, about a thousand people were sent to Treblinka." I asked him what he thought may have been responsible for his survival. He replied:

This question bothers me still. There are certain factors that are inherent, basic. Some are internal, some are external. Some of the external factors you have no influence over. The internal thing required us never to give up. At one point in Treblinka I had typhoid fever, and I was ready to give up. But in the end my friend and I, we ran away together, we never gave up the idea that somehow we would make it....in Treblinka a person could not make it unless he or she belonged to a group—at least a group of two.

There was an underground, but it was not easy to understand it. Sereny wrote a book about it, but I doubt she understood it at all.

Glazar wanted me to understand the culture that emerged in Treblinka.

You must understand, those who came to the camp had probably brought some valuables with them...which the Germans were aware of, and they were determined to get to these valuables. Around [these circumstances] sprang up Mafia organizations. There was a possibility of terrific profiteering from these things. This created some special situations...the poor Jews who arrived; they would have some jewelry into which they had converted all of their savings. They always had with them some kind of valuables. They had sewn into the clothes dollars, and so on, perhaps for a passage to America or Palestine, which they had saved for all their lives.

What Glazar refers to as "Mafia organizations," and the profiteering that grew out of this reality, were linked to the underground. For example, when Dr. Julian Chorazycki reached Treblinka in a transport of Polish Jews, he was assigned for work in the German dental office. Unlike some of the rest of the new arrivals, he was spared from being gassed upon arrival. The Treblinka Jewish underground was on the lookout for all such new arrivals. They could always use intelligent and energetic newcomers. In no time, the underground leaders pegged Dr. Chorazycki as an asset. The underground was busy with preparations for the August revolt. Dr. Chorazycki was suspected of being particularly gifted in the financial aspects of the resistance undertaking.

A coordinated anti-German attack called for a variety of gifts. The financial arrangements, in particular, demanded from the resistance leader very special skills. Chorazycki seemed to be a good choice; unobtrusively he collected funds for the forthcoming attack. All went well until an unexpected incident happened. One day, the SS officer and commander of Treblinka, Kurt Franz, stopped by Dr. Chorazycki's office to pick up some medication. On impulse, Franz decided to find out what this Jewish prisoner might have in his bulging bag.

He had never expected to find 150,000 zlotys, wrapped up with dollars, and a wide range of valuable jewelry. When Chorazycki realized that the SS man had discovered the money and jewelry, he ran out of the room. According to one account, during his short escape, the doctor swallowed poison, something he always had handy for just such an eventuality. The German, who was stronger and younger, caught up with him and easily overpowered and beat up the now dying doctor.

Subsequently, Franz called for a special meeting that same afternoon. The audience consisted of prisoners who were forced to witness this event. In front of the crowd stood Franz, and next to him was a bloody bundle, which had once been Dr. Chorazycki. At that point, it looked like a massive package, here and there showing red blotches of blood. Franz proceeded to hit the shapeless bundle. Fuming, he continued to hit the package next to him, counting the lashes that he administered to the lifeless body. Only when the Nazi came to fifty did he stop counting. He finished his performance with an order, "Now to the infirmary to be shot!" [59]

Despite this horrifying experience, the prisoners were determined to continue with their plans. They knew that their uprising called for additional preparations, and proceeded to carry on with the next steps. Soon, however, Glazar and Karl Unger were both incapacitated by typhoid fever. Their comrades took care of them, while keeping them informed about the progress of the preparations. The leaders of the anti-German uprising were fully absorbed in their underground operations, and all agreed that access to adequate guns and ammunition was of outmost importance. The SS men were similarly aware of the importance of arms. Indeed, the ammunition depot was located in the sturdily built SS barracks, which also served as their living quarters and included the dining room, kitchen, and sleeping accommodations, along with the special areas for storing guns and ammunition. Unlike the SS, the underground leaders spread out their resources, thereby limiting the risks.

Although the underground leaders knew the location of the ammunition depot and the guns, this did not guarantee access. The first problem they had to solve was how to gain entry to the locked depot, the keys to which were in the hands of SS officers. The underground's goal was to obtain a copy of these keys. And so, on a particular morning, one underground member slipped inconspicuously past the ammunition depot, sticking a small metal object into the lock and thereby jamming it. The SS men called on a locksmith, a Jewish inmate, to help them solve the problem. After an extensive examination, the locksmith informed them that he had to transfer the entire door to his workshop in order to fix the problem. The SS agreed, and while it was in his workshop the Jews made copies of the key.

It seems that at that time there were roughly 1,000 inmates in Treblinka. The aim of the uprising was to destroy the camp by setting it on fire, allowing prisoners to escape into the neighboring forests. To keep the preparations secret, the organizers did not involve Ukrainian guards or any potential helpers from the nearby town of Wlodawa. The leaders of the underground also felt that the uprising should take place when Kurt Franz and Kütner Miete, another experienced SS officer, were absent. Their expected leaves were to start on August 2, 1943.

At four in the afternoon on August 2, the Treblinka uprising began. A shot rang out, signaling that it had started. Most of the inmates were equipped with rakes, pitchforks, spades, and shovels. More effective weapons had to be obtained from the ammunition depot. Some prisoners were instructed to set fire to the entire building after they had removed the necessary weapons and ammunitions from the surrounding buildings. Another group was charged with the elimination of the Ukrainian guards.

Glazar and Unger managed to stay close to each other. They heard explosions coming from the Ukrainian barracks, followed by the sight of huge tongues of flames. They were herded through the fence by a prisoner whom Glazar later identified as "Lublink," and ran to the nearby river, staying underwater as long as they could to escape the flames. Gradually they saw that the flames were becoming smaller and smaller.[60] By this point the sun was beginning to set, and dusk allowed the two swimmers to venture out of the water. The bucolic surroundings and growing darkness gave them a feeling of calm, which they had not felt in a long time.

With the revolt behind them, these two young men reflected on the situation. Glazer wrote in his memoir that "the brave older fighters wanted us young prisoners to get out of Treblinka...they wanted us to live." There was, for him, no other way to explain why this "Lublink" had herded them out through the fence. "And how strange that I never saw him after that ...."[61]

Indeed, the head of this revolt, the engineer Bernard Galewski, and all the others who assisted him—Zvi Kurland, Israel Sudouwicz, Simcha, the carpenter—did not survive. Galewski made it out of the camp but after a few kilometers decided he could go no further, took poison, and died. Why? Trying to understand, Glazar and Unger reached the conclusion that the organizers of the Treblinka revolt wanted to avenge the murders of their family members. They were united in their determination to destroy Treblinka. Some valued the destruction of the camp above all else, even their own lives. Perhaps the leaders of the revolt never intended to escape.

Soon, surrounded by darkness, Glazar and Unger came upon a hut and introduced themselves to its inhabitants as Czech prisoners of war who had escaped from a camp. Over the next few days, as they roamed the countryside, they dared to enter an empty barn. Rest calmed them. Occasionally, they found scraps of food. Sometimes the scraps left them feeling ill. They tried to move in the direction of their former homes in Czechoslovakia. Later they ran into American soldiers. Somehow it did not occur to them to admit that they were Jewish. Strangely enough, after a while they felt almost relaxed with the Americans, who nudged them toward life.

When the war ended, Glazar felt an obligation to testify at some of the Holocaust trials. Specifically, he wanted to join the fifty-four Treblinka survivors who periodically came to testify at a variety of trials. As one of the fifty-four witnesses, he waited for a German witness to appear, one who would have the courage to declare that he or she participated in the murder of Jews. He longed to encounter such a German witness, but one never materialized at any of the Treblinka trials. Glazar waited in vain.[62]

Treblinka was not widely known until years after the war was over. Another little-known death camp, Sobibor, was located in the eastern part of Poland, between the cities of Chelmno and Wlodawa. Over the course of the war, Sobibor claimed the lives of a quarter million Jews. A brief look at Sobibor offers insights into the life and death of its wartime inmates.

In 1983, Karl August Frenzel, an SS officer who had been a high-ranking commander at Sobibor, asked for a meeting with Thomas "Toivi" Blatt, one of the few survivors of the camp. Frenzel had encountered Blatt at several of his postwar trials. Intrigued, Blatt agreed to meet Frenzel. As the two men faced each other after nearly forty years, Blatt asked, "Why do you want to speak with me?"[63]

"I would like to apologize to you," was the reply.[64]

When in the course of their conversation Blatt had the opportunity to repeat his question, Frenzel replied, "I can only say it again, with tears. Not only am I beside myself now, but back then too, I was greatly bothered by it all."[65] Blatt tried to engage this German in a broader conversation about guilt, but Frenzel denied any responsibility, saying: "We had to do our duty....I condemn that time."[66]

Sobibor operated from May 1941 until November 1943. Its prisoners came from Poland, Holland, Czechoslovakia, Germany, France, Austria, and the USSR. Most were gassed on arrival. The basic core of prisoners amounted to 600. They were assigned to a variety of duties.

There was a great deal of solidarity among these Sobibor inmates, despite their differences. The more established inmates were known to share food with the new arrivals, particularly the starving Dutch prisoners. Similarly, some of the old-timers were known for their efforts to keep up the spirits of the newcomers, offering not just food but survival tips, including the benefits of singing. Most of this was for naught, since the vast majority of these prisoners were almost immediately gassed.

As in most death camps, Sobibor newcomers gravitated toward and were kept in special groups, and their behavior was governed by the principle of collective responsibility. A wrong move by one inevitably led to the punishment of the entire group. All resistance was quickly and severely squelched. Despite the oppressive measures, most Sobibor prisoners were nonetheless committed to an underground. Standing out among them were such figures as Leon Feldhendler, a shoemaker; Boris Cylenski; and Shlomo Lejtman. They called their organization the Secret Arms Organization, or for short, TOB.

Together, the underground came up with a plan to destroy the camp. It also aimed at saving prisoners and eliminating collaborators. As in other camps, underground meetings in Sobibor were conducted at night. As a rule its participants were those who were most respected for their integrity and dedication.

Over time the prisoners pursued a range of plans. Early on they thought about collectively poisoning all the Germans, but this plan was soon dismissed as too difficult. Another idea was to burn the entire camp down. This, too, was abandoned as impractical. Another plan aimed at building a tunnel that would lead them to forests and partisans. This proposal was also set aside.

At first those involved in resistance worked to establish contacts with partisans. Caught with some plans outlining cooperative efforts, several prisoners were promptly tortured. Before their public executions—in front of the entire prison population—the accused called on all prisoners to avenge their deaths. They had refused to name any of their co-conspirators.

The prisoners searched for new means of resistance. Those who sorted through Jewish belongings concentrated on destroying items, such as jewelry, which were of greatest value. Some of the inmates expressed their opposition by praying nonstop, which gave some comfort to them and to other inmates.

With time, transports to Sobibor became less frequent. The prisoners had no illusions about what this meant. No transports translated into no work. No work meant hunger and death. Toward the end of September 1942, the basic core of the 600 prisoners was still intact. The majority were Polish Jews. These inmates were supervised by twenty-five SS men and 160 guards. From June 1943 on, substantial parts of Sobibor camp were mined. The authorities must have sensed that some prisoners were eager and ready to revolt.

In the summer of 1943, a large group of prisoners, somewhere around 2,000, arrived from Minsk. Of these new arrivals, eighty were retained and added to the core group of 600 prisoners. The rest was gassed. Among these new arrivals there were some former members of the Soviet military, including a high proportion of Jewish Soviet POWs, who were well-disciplined and eager to fight. Their presence improved the morale of the rest of prisoners. In this new group the Sobibor resistance saw an opportunity to restructure and improve the effectiveness of the underground.

Alexander Pieczorski, a Jewish Soviet officer, was welcomed by the underground leader, Leon Feldhendler, who as a simple shoemaker felt insecure about his ability to be the commander of the underground. Feldhendler was realistic, modest, and determined. For some time he had kept an eye out for someone more qualified than he. In Pieczorski, Feldhendler felt he had found him. At Feldhendler's insistence Pieczorski was appointed head of the underground. Feldhendler demoted himself to second in command.

As the preparations for the revolt progressed, the organizers realized that their ideal goal to save all prisoners could not be fulfilled. Instead, they moved to an examination of more realistic options. Among other things this raised the basic question of whether or not to rely on the Ukrainian guards' cooperation. In the end the leaders agreed not to trust these guards. They also had to decide how many inmates should be made privy to the preparations. To communicate the resistance plans broadly had its advantages but was dangerous. It was generally assumed that at most forty individuals knew about the underground's plans.

The prisoners were immersed in the preparations of the revolt from September to November 14, 1943. Some issues were resolved by themselves. For example, prisoners had to give up building a tunnel because the ventilation was poor and they did not know how to fix the problem. Also the date for the start of the revolt had to be adjusted because the organizers wanted to make sure that two SS men in particular—Gustav Wagner and Hubert Gomerski—were absent. Both were known to be ruthless murderers. The plan to eliminate as many of the camp's SS as possible was plausible because of the fact that some Jews had close contacts with these men.

Amid the difficulties and obstacles were also some successes. Some of these prisoners were accomplished at tailoring, shoemaking, and the manufacture of leather goods, and prisoners managed to prepare extra clothes, medication, and a supply of poison for all sorts of eventualities. They learned how to cut the electricity to cover their escapes. Some Jewish women succeeded in stealing arms from the SS men for whom they worked. Some were assigned to cover the departures of prisoners who were scheduled to escape to the forest. Arrangements were sometimes made for them to later join special partisan groups.

At one point, Pieczorski and one of his assistants were supposed to collect ammunition from a so-called safe source. Upon arrival, they discovered that the ammunition was not there and had to change plans. They ended up buying ammunition from Ukrainian guards. Such changes prolonged the preparations. On the other hand, the underground managed to find a collection of unconventional "arms" such as knives, hammers, axes, shovels, and a range of primitive objects, which could serve as weapons. The resisters finished their preparations by swearing to fight and to defend each other.

November 14th turned out to be a sunny day. The precise plans were not known even to some of those who were directly involved. The plan was that the SS men would be invited to come to various workshops, to try on clothes, shoes, and the various items, which Jewish laborers were preparing for them. And so, as an SS man was trying on a coat, the tailor cut off his head with an ax. This tailor took the man's gun and whatever things would be useful. Then, all traces of the dead man had to disappear with him.

Soon some unanticipated developments occurred. Most dangerous was the sudden reappearance of the two SS officers, Wagner and Gomerski. Gunshots were heard, signaling danger. At the main entrance to the camp the guards refused to admit a group of inmates returning from work outside the camp and had fired at them instead.

The underground responded with sporadic shootings. The inmates succeeded in killing the head of the Ukrainian guards, which intensified the fight on all sides. A small group of inmates detached themselves from the rest and entered the blacksmith's shop, where they found special scissors with which to cut the wires that blocked the inmates' escape from the camp.

At five in the afternoon, as scheduled, Pieczorski[67] arrived. He was confronted by a tense situation: the main gate was locked. Without hesitation, Pieczorski screamed, "Comrades, move forward and attack! Exit the gate!" Automatically the prisoners threw themselves at the gate. Screams and orders to hurry continued.

Confusion reigned. As noted earlier, only a minority of inmates knew about the resistance plans. Pieczorski's order to run to safety was the first they learned of it, though it was never part of the original plan. But the inmates took advantage of the opportunity and it was effective; as the inmates reached the gate they threw stones at the guards, and sand into their eyes. In another place, another group led by Pieczorski was busy cutting wires that were adjacent to the SS quarters. Eight of them were killed by gunfire and mine explosions.

It is estimated that 150 prisoners were killed in the course of this uprising and that 300 escaped. Leon Feldhendler reached the forest, and in the years that followed fought as a partisan along with other escapees. In April 1945, he was murdered in Lublin by members of the NSZ (the Polish fascist organization).[68] Pieczorski, the man who made this uprising happen, had concentrated on reaching the Soviet Union with his group of Soviet prisoners. He did, and later fought first with partisans and then as part of a penal battalion. He died in 1990. Another 150 prisoners have not been accounted for. We are uncertain as to the number of the inmates who lost their lives who had actively participated in this revolt.[69]

No one can say whether greater awareness about the forthcoming revolt would have saved—or cost—more lives. What we do know is that extreme situations preclude predictability and judgment. All we can do is celebrate resistance in the form that it took.

CHAPTER FIVE

The Couriers

Emanuel Ringelblum described Jews who served as couriers as "heroic young women who deserve the pen of a great writer....Day in and day out they face grave dangers. For protection they rely totally on their Aryan features and the kerchiefs that cover their heads, they undertake the most threatening missions without any objections, without a moment's hesitation....They recognize no obstacles." Ringelblum praised the conduct of all Jewish women, but he felt that the couriers stood out for their selfless dedication to the Jewish people.[1]

As discussed, the enforced isolation of the Jews had automatically made women more strategic to Jewish underground movements. Jewish males, because of circumcision, were in much greater danger on the Aryan side. Women's readiness to take on a variety of resistance jobs stemmed from their awareness that these risks were even greater for Jewish men. This in part accounts for the higher proportion of Jewish female couriers in both the East and the West. In general, women were less likely to be suspected of political transgressions than men. When asked to compare the threats faced by women and men, Thea Epstein, a Jewish courier in southern France, replied, "It was harder for men. A man had no right to be in the city, to move around; he was supposed to be employed in work that exempted him from military service. Or he had to study or to be in the army."[2] Another young woman, a Jewish courier who had been in a communist resistance group in France, admitted that being a girl helped her. "I took advantage of this fact."

"What were these advantages?" I asked.

"Well, for instance, when there was a control of the baggage in a bus the Germans had a tendency to pass a smiling young girl; perhaps a pretty girl could use her seductiveness....It was simply difficult to imagine that I was doing what I was doing with the way I looked. I didn't look like a scout. It's a good question, but I never before thought about it."[3]

Jewish female couriers functioned as the glue that held an underground together. Born in Poland, Leah Silverstein's life experiences illustrate these functions (figure 5.1). When Leah was five, her mother died in 1928 in Praga, a suburb of Warsaw. She had two older brothers, her father, and two sets of grandparents. Four years after Leah's mother died, her father remarried, which led to a string of painful experiences. As the youngest member of her family, Leah was particularly vulnerable. She recalls that, as in the fairy tales, her stepmother was wicked. "She was truly wicked. At one point she tore up all my schoolbooks, which I treasured. I liked to study. I loved school. We ended up fighting each other physically."

Her father's passivity and her stepmother's behavior threatened Leah's safety. Help came from her maternal grandmother, an intelligent and deeply religious woman. She invited Leah to share her modest apartment. Despite their poverty, the old woman and the young girl felt comfortable with the life they shared. Leah continued to study diligently. She completed elementary school and dreamt about attending high school, though in Poland at the time enrollment into high school cost money and no one in the family had the necessary resources. Leah heard about a contest in which young girls could compete for two free places in one of the local high schools. She entered this contest and won one of the prizes. For the next two years, she attended, free of charge, the Zydowskie Gymnasium. For Leah, this was a dream come true.

She continued to live happily with her grandmother. Most of their neighbors and friends were poor, yet poverty in no way interfered with their extensive participation in a wide range of political and cultural pastimes. A large proportion of these local youths belonged to the Jewish Scout association, and a variety of Zionist organizations, especially Hashomer Hatzair. Many of these local groups had close ties to the liberal Polish Christian Scouts Association. Leah's Orthodox grandmother encouraged her granddaughter's participation in all these diverse activities. Leah would often express her gratitude for the many things she had learned from her membership in these groups. She was convinced that these contacts had given her something to believe in. She also felt that through these organizations she became more intellectually active, able to form new and vibrant friendships. As a member of the Jewish Scout organization, Leah appreciated the ties she had made with some Polish Scouts and continued to cherish her memories of these friends. Before and during World War II, some Polish Scouts were supportive of their Jewish counterparts, often under most trying circumstances.

Among those who returned to their homes after the German invasion in 1939, which, as we have seen, created a mass exodus, many were Jewish youths, members of various Zionist organizations. Leah's grandmother, remembering World War I, comforted whoever would listen that they had nothing to fear from the German occupation. Reality, of course, proved otherwise.

Singled out for early and vigorous assaults were members of the Polish elites, which was part of Hitler's plan, as Ian Kershaw has put it, to deprive the Polish intelligentsia of any chance "to develop into a ruling class."[4] For example, in Krakow, the entire faculty of Jagiellonian University was invited to come to a large assembly hall. All faculty members were asked to appear on November 6, 1939, to discuss issues related to the start of the new academic year. After the distinguished faculty reached the designated place of assembly, the German police invaded the hall. Without any explanations, the police pushed the waiting faculty, 106 in all, out of the hall and into vehicles and disappeared with them. When information reached students and family—the rumor was that they had been taken to Sachsenhausen and Dachau—seventeen were already dead.[5]

The Central Welfare Council (Rada Główna Opiekuńcza, or RGO) headed by Jerzy Roniker, worked incessantly to help. Roniker knew that the Germans defined Polish officers, some of whom were returning home, as elites and ordered them to register with the authorities. As mentioned earlier, the newly created Polish underground warned these officers what this meant and told them to conceal their identities. By not revealing their military past, many Polish officers survived; these underground warnings saved lives.[6]

The focus of oppression, of course, soon became the Jews, who early on were targeted for progressive degradation that led to the construction of ghettos. By October 1940, the Germans completed the construction of the Warsaw ghetto, and by November 15th, it was sealed, meaning that its Jewish inhabitants could not enter or leave the area unless they had special permits.[7] Officially, the death sentence applied to any Jew who left or entered the ghetto in an unauthorized way. The death sentence also applied to Gentiles caught helping Jews.

Like most ghetto inhabitants, Leah Silverstein's family had settled in dilapidated apartments. One was assigned for her father and his family, and the other was allotted to Leah and her grandmother. Asked to describe the Warsaw ghetto, Leah's unhesitating assessment was that it was "hell on earth." Over 300,000 Jews were crowded into a small neighborhood: "Eventually, these rundown spaces had to accommodate about half a million Jews. Similarly, the amount of food allotted to the ghetto inmates was way below the subsistence level. All ghetto inmates were exposed to dirt, hunger and a range of debilitating conditions, including the spread

FIGURE 5.1 Leah Silverstein poses holding a bicycle at the Hashomer Hatzair Zionist collective in Zarki. (U.S. Holocaust Memorial Museum, courtesy of Leah Hammerstein Silverstein)

of deadly diseases....Occasionally, Jewish inmates were driven from their dwellings to the public baths, for the so-called de-lousing."[8]

Like others, Leah tried to renew her past associations. She elaborates: "In the ghetto, former members of the Hashomer Hatzair tried to contact each other. Earlier these organizations had been divided by age groups. So I tried to find friends who were my age. We started meeting in groups. When some of our former leaders returned from their failed attempts to escape to the East, they began to reorganize our youth groups. Each time, we would meet in some other home."

Leah joined a group of Hashomer Hatzair members who referred to themselves as a kibbutz. Compared to ghetto life in general, she saw her situation in this group in a positive light. "Life in our kibbutz was good, compared to what was going on in other family groups. We kept ourselves clean, even though the premises were overcrowded. We also engaged in extra work." In the evenings and on Shabbat, Leah and the other members of the kibbutz would gather for discussions. "We benefited from all kinds of presentations by various literary figures who visited our kibbutz. And so, we were politically and intellectually active, in spite of the terrible conditions that surrounded us." She continues:

> Every Jew had a right to a certain amount of food allotments. We didn't go to the store individually. One person collected food coupons and through certain channels we were supplied with food. This person saw to it that we should be provided with the food. There was a system, according to which each youth organization was getting a certain amount of food. Some former members of our organization used to come to visit our group, although they lived with their respective families. Many of them were already starving. With some of them we tried to share our food.

> Officially, our members would get in the morning two slices of bread, with some substitute marmalade and a bowl of soup. In the middle of the day there was another bowl of soup, usually the same kind of soup, and in the evening again, a piece of bread and soup. The soup was usually made out of grouts, Kasha. Occasionally it came with potatoes, very seldom with a piece of fat. Very rarely was there butter or some other kind of fat...I remember that the grouts were of a special kind. They were coarsely ground so that

the husks were swimming in the soup, to eat the soup you had to separate the husks from the grains so you had a wreath around the plate of the husks. Our group had no place to grow vegetables. Only occasionally were we allotted a few vegetables.

Leah's kibbutz had up to twenty members. They all worked hard; the young men were authorized to engage in heavy work on the roads, in factories, and in airports. For some of these jobs, the Judenrat paid them limited amounts of money.

The young women in our kibbutz took on domestic jobs inside the ghetto. In the ghetto, a small minority could still afford maids. There were differences among people. Some would buy food, which was smuggled into the ghetto. People who in the ghetto became immediately pauperized were usually cut off from their professions. Many of them were forced into the ghetto from the surrounding, smaller communities. They were definite candidates for death by starvation. In Poland, even before the war, a large proportion of Jews had been poor. Many of them lived in poor communities. To be sure, the Judenrat and various ghetto organizations tried to help the poor and the starving. However their needs were much greater than the resources necessary for the elimination of death by starvation.

Leah saw her life in the ghetto kibbutz as "an oasis in that horrible...cesspool of humanity." She felt fortunate because she was a part of a fine group of people, whom she valued and looked up to. Her kibbutz comrades gave her a sense of family. Among the leaders of the ghetto underground—the ŻOB—were Mordechai Anielewicz, Joseph Kaplan, and Shmuel Breslaw. Among the women leaders in the ghetto, she most vividly remembers Tosia Altman, Miriam Heinsolor, and Civia Lubetkim. Most of these women worked as underground couriers.

Although most couriers were women, one exception was Jan Karski, a Polish courier and an international emissary. He was aware of the precariousness of the women. "The average life of a woman courier did not exceed a few months....It can be assumed that their lot was the most severe, their sacrifices the greatest, and their contributions the least recognized. They were overlooked and doomed. They neither held high ranks nor received any great honors for their heroism."[9] And yet, it was the contributions of couriers, both Jewish and non-Jewish, that enabled the underground movements to coordinate and integrate their efforts. Their efforts contributed greatly to keeping various underground movements alive.

Kibbutz members made concerted efforts to keep order by adhering to a consistent division of labor. In line with established traditions, the young women were assigned to the kitchen. In addition to their internal work, these women had domestic jobs outside their kibbutz. Members of the kibbutz cooperated fully, making their lack of food less demoralizing. They listened to music, sang, and discussed the issues that were of special interest to them.

Comparing the life Leah had in the ghetto kibbutz to that of her family provides a startling contrast. Her father came to the ghetto in October 1940; by the following March he had died from starvation. Leah notes that once he was forced into the ghetto he had no possibility of earning a living. "Terrible hunger settled in my father's house. Sometimes I would run from the kibbutz to see how he was. And it was a sight which I will never forget. I would also run to see my grandmother, whom I loved, because she was my mother substitute."

Occasionally Leah would save a slice of bread or a boiled potato and bring it to her father. She knew that this would not change much, but it was all she could do. She herself was hungry.

> It's not a big deal to share food with others when you have plenty, but it's very difficult to share with others when you are yourself hungry. Very hungry! Gradually my health deteriorated to a point where I fainted and I was taken to a clinic. And, of course, the doctor said that I needed better nutrition, that I should not work so hard. But I could not follow any of these recommendations.

> The sight of my father and of my grandmother dying from starvation and the deplorable hygienic conditions are pictures which haunt me till this day. These things happened over half a century ago but they torment me through terrible nightmares to this very day....I would find my grandmother lying in a soiled bed because she had been unable to move from her bed. I remember she said to me in Yiddish, "Look what state I am in." And I stood there, a young girl, with tears running down my cheeks. I couldn't help it.

Throughout the ghetto, there was widespread starvation. But it takes months before death relieves the sufferings of the starving individuals. Leah remembers how it happened with her father: "One day a girl came to tell me that my father was dead. So, I ran over there, and there he was in that basement apartment...you can't even call it an apartment. He was on the floor in a pool of his excrement. And the stepmother stood next to him. Well, I didn't have much sympathy for her, but that's how it was."

In 1940, those in the ghetto could still have a burial if they paid the Jewish council fifteen zlotys. For this sum, they would provide a hearse and carry away the dead person. Leah had no money, however. The day after her father's death, in the hope of finding his body, she went to the cemetery. There a huge pile of dead bodies confronted her. They were in different stages of decay. She searched for her father, but did not find him. Horrified, defeated, she turned around and went back to her kibbutz. When she came close to her living quarters, she understood that she could not even share her experiences with her comrades. Many of them had lost different family members to starvation. Others expected to lose more still. She, too, was just as unfortunate with the fate of the rest of her family. They all perished without a trace.

Sometime in 1941, through the efforts of Joseph Kaplan, a member of the Hashomer Hatzair, a group of young members were sent to the Zarki farm, located close to Czestochowa. As a group, they moved to Zarki to farm the land.

Some members of the Hashomer Hatzair moved to Zarki legally, others illegally. Leah was one of those who had welcomed the opportunity to exchange her ghetto existence for farm work. To her and to some of her comrades this experience promised more and better food and possibly preparation for a future life in Palestine. The Zionists viewed farm work as a preliminary step in the preparations for future jobs on farms in Palestine. Sadly, the long-range hopes that emanated from Zarki never happened. Eventually this entire experiment was dissolved, and its Jewish participants were scattered into a variety of directions.

Before this happened, however, at Zarki Leah fell in love with Jurek (Arieh) Wilner, a bright and tragic star of the Jewish underground. Leah tried to recollect how their lives touched at Zarki:

> I don't want to claim that I was his fiancée. It was not official at all....In those days everything was temporary. We didn't know what the next day would bring. Arieh (Jurek) came to Zarki in the spring of 1942. I met him and fell in love. Maybe we were ten days or two weeks, together. I don't know. In those days two weeks

was a lifetime....Now from a distance...I ruminate...about those times....I search for images of those who were close to me, boy-friends and girlfriends...the face of Jurek Wilner stands out vividly among them. I see him as young, handsome, with light hair...when we met, Jurek was on his way to Bendzin and he stopped at Zarki for a few days. My enchantment was instantaneous. For me, he expressed all that was beautiful, energetic, and pulsating with life.

I can say this today that I still smell the grass on which we rested, close to each other, in the vegetable garden. I see how he chewed on a blade of grass, smiled, lightly absorbed in an examination of the sky, sprinkled with scattered clouds. I patted his blond hair, enraptured by the youthful magic of love. He spoke little, probably determined to unwind from the many burdens he carried. His eyes contained an overall weariness. With a full open mouth he breathed the country air. This was followed by the incredible sweetness of his kisses. How I longed to stay with him forever. His smile and caresses meant life which, for me, pressed so tightly to him, took on a happy glow, despite the raging war.[10]

At the start of 1943, the Gestapo arrested Wilner. This hap-pened on the Aryan side, where he acted as a courier and had passed for a Christian Pole. Leah received a letter from her friend Tosia Altman, also a courier, who wrote about Wilner's arrest, insisting that for safety Leah had to change her living quarters and switch jobs. One could never be sure if and when, under torture, Jurek would break down and divulge secrets, which could lead to Leah's arrest. Leah followed Tosia's suggestions.

Later on, through underground sources, they learned that Wilner, although severely tortured, had divulged no secrets. His close friend Henryk Gradowski, a member of the Polish Scouts organization, miraculously saved him. Gradowski not only risked his life to save Wilner, he insisted on bringing him to his home on the Aryan side. But Wilner refused this friend's generous offer. Instead, he was determined to join his comrades in the Warsaw ghetto. With them he wanted to fight. With them he wanted to die fighting. As we saw in chapter 2, preparations for an uprising began in earnest in Warsaw after the massive summer deportations of 1942. At that point, the Jewish resistance groups knew about the mass shootings of Jews in Ponary and the mass gassings in Treblinka, Auschwitz, and Chelmno.

Leah managed to reach the Warsaw ghetto a week before the start of the uprising. Her first stop brought her to Wilner's dwelling. Here she found a totally changed man. Wilner seemed half asleep. Worse still, he gave the impression of having neither the will nor the strength to talk or to communicate in any way. Unable to recapture even a glimmer of their past closeness, Leah left his place without uttering a word. She was, however, eager to stay and fight in the ghetto. But her underground comrades wanted her to return to the forbidden Christian world. They argued that the ghetto underground lacked arms and would not be able to supply her with a gun. Besides, as a courier who spent most of her time in the forbidden Christian world, she lacked the training of a guerrilla fighter. She could be more useful to them from the outside, by procuring guns.

Disappointed, Leah returned to the Aryan side, where she tried to reconnect with the few underground contacts she had. On April 19, 1943, a week after Leah's departure, the Warsaw ghetto uprising began. It was the first urban, armed rebellion initiated and executed by the Jews and it unexpectedly grew into a fierce struggle. For some on the outside, the fighting ghetto turned into a growing spectacle. Large crowds of onlookers surrounded the ghetto as it burned, and Leah became a part of this curious crowd. "On the outside I stood there with a smile on my face. Yet I continued to cry on the inside. I went there...every day. I was driven to this place by a force." What drove her repeatedly to the ghetto was fear for her friends and for the man she had fallen in love with, and continued to love.

Jewish underground members and specifically couriers such as Leah would slip in and out of the ghettos. As long as they could return to it, they retained a sense of belonging. But with the Warsaw ghetto transformed into a heap of ruins, all that came to an end. Leah, for whom the Warsaw ghetto was home, described how she felt when this happened and she had to live alone in the Aryan world: "With nobody to console you, with nobody to tell you it's okay, it will be better, hold on, you are in total isolation. Total loneliness. You know you are among people, and yet you are like an island. You have to make life-and-death decisions all by yourself...you never know whether your choices would be successful or not. It is like playing Russian roulette with your own life. And it is not one incident; it [was] this way from the moment I came to the Aryan side. Day after day." [11]

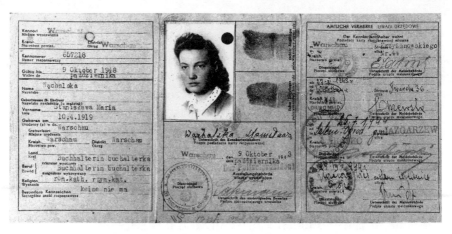

FIGURE 5.2 Many couriers carried false identification cards. This one, issued in the name of Stanislawa Wachalska, was used by Vladka Meed during her work as a courier for the underground. Her tasks included obtaining arms for the ŻOB, finding hiding places for Jewish women and children, and assisting Jews already in hiding with food, clothing, documentation, and medical care. (U.S. Holocaust Memorial Museum, courtesy of Benjamin Miedzyrzecki Meed)

Fortunately for Leah, her past periods of isolation were mixed with interruptions during which she was reconnected with some of her underground contacts. The fall of 1942 had been one of these lonely times on the Aryan side. She found employment as a kitchen helper in a rehabilitation hospital that specialized in tending to German soldiers wounded at the various fronts. The place was called Soldatenheimat, a home for soldiers.

Passing for a Polish Catholic, Leah's document identified her as Leokadia Bukowska.[12] She shared a modest room with a stranger, who turned out to be a professional prostitute. Leah's job was demanding and dull. All day long she had to wash and peel vegetables, clean pots, and contribute continuously to the spotless appearance of the kitchen. Leah showed an overall willingness to do favors for her Polish coworkers. She had hoped to win their support through her accommodating attitudes and extensive work.

One day on her way home, she met Tuwia Szengut, whom she remembered from their prewar participation in Hashomer Hatzair, the leftist Zionist organization. Currently he was known under the Polish name Tadek. He explained that through underground channels he had heard about her living and working in Warsaw and had decided to reconnect. He told Leah that he belonged to an underground in Tarnow, made up of young people eager to fight the Germans. They needed guns. Then, almost casually, Tadek suggested that perhaps here Leah would steal a gun for them. The German hospital in which she worked had offered her such opportunities.

Leah remembered that at this point she began to shake. Was it Tadek's request that she should steal a gun? Was it the strong wind? Or was it simply the fact that she was not wearing a coat? Tadek noticed this and decided it was because of the lack of a coat. He would find her one. Indeed, when they met several days later, a coat was hanging on his arm. Although it was too big, it was warm. Leah was grateful and touched.

At their next meeting, Tadek did not even mention the gun. But by now Leah was preoccupied with the idea of appropriating one for Tadek's group. She knew enough to understand that possession of one gun could lead to the acquisition of more. She also realized that this could end as a suicidal gesture. At the same time, she could not help but see that getting them a gun could make a huge difference in the lives of these young Jews. She continued to vacillate between her desire to steal a gun and fear for her life. Leah was well aware that with the many military men around her, there were ample opportunities, but she had no idea how to do it. "Yes gun" and "no gun" became Leah's obsessions. They inevitably translated into sleepless nights. The brief walks between Leah and Tadek continued, and though Tadek did not refer to the gun again, Leah was hardly able to think about anything else. Yet she did not dare to mention it to Tadek nor to anyone else.

Then one morning at work, as Leah was moving from the kitchen to the bathroom, she passed next to a few empty rooms. Some of these rooms were being used by recovering German soldiers, others by some German guards. The place was silent. Without thinking, Leah entered an unoccupied room and walked over to a closet. When she opened the door of the closet, she saw a pistol. It was as if it had been waiting for her. She took it and placed it under her dress, and then quickly moved into the bathroom. When she locked the door behind her, she was both happy and miserable. What should she do now? She looked around. By standing on the toilet seat, she found she could look through a small window in front of her. The window opened with a gentle push out onto a roof. She took off her underwear, wrapped the gun into it, and placed it on the roof.

Leah left the bathroom, forcing herself to act normally. She resumed her place and work in the kitchen. She was silent, but she usually was. She knew that she had to remove the pistol from the roof. When it was her turn to dispose of potato peels, she went outside. Assuring herself that no one was around, she retrieved the gun. She knew that she had to act quickly. In the back of the hospital was a door that led to the hospital grounds. The door, rarely used, was surrounded by all kinds of tall weeds and thick grass. Leah pushed it open and put the gun, still wrapped in her panties, into the thick growth, where it was lost next to the tall weeds and grass. Leah returned to the kitchen.

After half an hour she became aware of a commotion. An announcement came that there had been sabotage and that all employees would be searched. She knew that no one would suspect her; and even if they did, they would find nothing. The gun was under the grass and weeds close to the back door. Then the search began. A German who knew her and seemed to like her looked into her bag and declared that she was free to go. Slowly she moved in the direction of the unused gate. No one was around her. When she doubly reassured herself that no one was around, she reached quickly for the gun and put it into her bag, then opened the gate and left. Slowly she moved in the direction of her house. The next morning, when she came to work she heard that the German soldier to whom the gun belonged had been accused of stealing and selling it.

Tadek was delighted when Leah presented him with the gun. He promised to treat it with due respect. Soon Leah heard that they had used it in an attack on a police station that yielded more guns and ammunition. Eventually, according to rumors, this gun played important roles in several subsequent actions. When Tadek and Leah met, they would invariably touch on how helpful getting this first gun was.

I asked Leah whether she had considered keeping the gun for herself. She was taken aback by my question. No, she never once thought about keeping the gun. After all, she had no use for it. When I suggested that it might have made have her feel more secure, her "No" was very definite. Again she said that she would not have known what to do with it. Also, because Tadek initiated the stealing of the gun, it was proper that his group should benefit from it.

Between March and August 1944, the date of the Polish uprising, Leah was actively working as a courier. "I was delivering money, and documents, and I was going to Skarzysko Kamienna [an important railroad town located 90 miles south of Warsaw]. I would go to Starachowice [another town south of Warsaw], and I was helping families in Warsaw who were in hiding. My reason for going there was to deliver documents in case people had an opportunity to run away, that they should have Polish papers to do it with."[13]

Leah had limited contact with other couriers during the war because it was potentially so dangerous. "At one point I returned to the Aryan side of Warsaw and reconnected with my friend, Julcia. She was also a courier. Actually as couriers we tried to keep our contacts to a minimum because knowing other couriers had a potential of discovery. The less information we had about each other, the safer we were in case of an arrest." One of these couriers, whom she met only after the war and admired greatly, was Hela Schupper (figure 5.3).

Hela Schupper was born in Krakow and was eighteen when the Germans invaded Poland. She had finished her schooling with a business degree. She was popular and her friends valued her honesty and her independent spirit. For some time, she had been involved

FIGURE 5.3 Jewish youth on a train taking them from Germany to Belgium. In the middle is Hela Schupper, a daring female courier. (U.S. Holocaust Memorial Museum, courtesy of Dola Kogan and Josef Horowitz)

in Zionist activities and hoped eventually to settle in Palestine. Schupper's looks, manners of speech, and courage made her a perfect candidate for becoming an underground courier. Her devotion to her Jewishness, together with her membership in Akiva, a moderate Zionist organization, offered her special opportunities to cooperate with Jewish youths who were similarly inclined. On one of her visits to Warsaw, she met Lutek Rotman, a young leader of the Warsaw ghetto underground; they fell in love. Often separated by their underground duties, to those around them Hela and Lutek seemed like a perfect couple.

Hela was ready to take on any underground assignment. By August 1942, she was constantly on the move between Krakow and Warsaw. She was in effect a full-time courier. Indeed, playing the part of a Christian Pole, Hela would accompany Jews who, for a variety of reasons, had to move between Warsaw and Krakow. Hela's Aryan looks and relaxed manner offered invaluable protection to those whose underground duties required frequent relocations. In addition to transferring people, she also smuggled false documents, money, and arms.

She considered herself fortunate that she happened to be in Warsaw during the ghetto uprising. As Lutek's girlfriend, Hela stayed in the bunker, which served as the headquarters for the ŻOB underground. Lutek also brought to this bunker his mother, known to others as Mrs. Maria. Maria, a widow, was closely attached to her only son. Other underground leaders also brought those who were close to them to this bunker.

By May 1943, the Germans had intensified their search for bunkers. They were particularly eager to locate the one that served as ŻOB's headquarters. At one point, with many of its fighters engaged elsewhere, the ŻOB fighters left in the bunker sensed a nearby fire. This could spell the destruction of all those inside. After discovering a bunker, the Germans would pump gas into it, suffocating those who hid within. The Germans counted on burning the Jews out of their shelters. As those inside the ŻOB headquarters contemplated their next move, they suddenly realized that the German soldiers were getting ready to depart. The soldiers started singing, generally proof that they were done for the day. Finally, from their hiding place, the Jews could see the Germans leaving—yet they still smelled fire.

Everyone at the ŻOB headquarters had agreed that the Germans should not take any of them alive, and that the last bullets in their guns should be reserved for their own suicide. As they smelled the fire approaching, some concluded that the end was near. Lutek's mother had poison in her hand. Hela, who was with her, urged her not to swallow it, insisting that the time was not yet come. They removed themselves to a part of their cellar where there were fewer fumes. As they were thinking over what to do next, Lutek and several underground fighters entered their bunker, bringing with them news: the entire ŻOB headquarter had been invited to relocate to the bunkers at Mila 18 street.

As mentioned in chapter 2, the Mila 18 address was a network of bunkers that had once belonged to a group of Jewish thieves. In preparation for the ghetto uprising, the Polish underground had collectively acquired a spacious area underneath the ghetto, extending over a number of cellars, which had been transformed into networks, divided, and reinforced, and was now being used for a variety of functions. Mila 18 was well-equipped and supplied with food, water, electricity, and arms. At the head of this syndicate was Shmuel Iser. Aware that the ŻOB headquarters were in danger of being burned or attacked, some members of the Polish underground wanted to help the Jewish fighters. Indeed, the accommodations that they offered to the ŻOB were luxurious in comparison to the spaces they had used previously. With time the generosity of these hosts extended further, including offers of food as well. The help given to ŻOB was critically important and greatly appreciated. The bunkers at Mila 18 attracted ŻOB fighters who were forced from their own bunkers by fires; they sought shelter there usually as a last resort.

Jewish fighters and the Germans operated at different hours, as we have seen. Less familiar with the ghetto, the Germans and their collaborators limited their activities to the daytime. For the Jewish fighters most activities began in the evening. Some of the fighters went off in search of food and supplies in houses that the Germans had not yet destroyed. Others went to the Aryan side in search of help. Some groups were exploring the possibilities for moving the ghetto youths to forests, where they might join the partisans. But no positive responses had reached the ghetto from the forests—and no responses meant no options.

The burning of the ghetto continued, reducing the availability of grenades, Molotov cocktails, and other ammunitions. Small arms with limited amounts of ammunition were ineffective. However, with each group that managed to escape to the Aryan side, hope was reinspired among the rest. Jewish fighters continued to hope that their representative on the Aryan side, Antek Zuckerman, might help with some of the problems they faced. All the ghetto fighters were eager to do something useful, yet often there was little one could do. The leaders did not give up, however. They were constantly sending more underground members to the Aryan side, usually through the sewage system.

On May 7th, Mordechai Anielewicz approached Hela, asking her to leave the ghetto with a group of people for the Aryan side. Her Aryan looks would be helpful to her and to those who would come with her. Hela told him that she would prefer to remain in the ghetto. Anielewicz assured her that while he would not force her to leave, he viewed her departure as her duty. Hela said that she would like to discuss this with Lutek.

That day Lutek was acting as a watchman for the main entrance to their bunker. Hela approached him and asked if he knew what Anielewicz had told her.

"Yes, I know."

"What is your opinion?" Hela asked.

"You should follow his advice," came the answer.

Hela told him that she wanted to stay with him until the end. Mira, Mordechai's girlfriend, was refusing to leave the ghetto and staying on.

"Mira could not as easily pass for a Gentile as you," Lutek replied. "Besides, she has no experience with life on the Aryan side."

Hela asked whether Lutek wanted her with him.

"You are the most important person in my life," was his reply, "but you should leave the ghetto."

Choking on her tears, Hela said that she would go.

Having made the decision, Hela went to the room in which people were prepared for ghetto exits. It had a hairdresser chair in the middle. Next to it stood a hairdresser, helping people prepare for their departure to the Aryan side. Hela was given a bottle of hair dye to bleach her hair and was soon transformed into a blond. Around her, people were teasing her about it. No one would recognize that she was a Jew.

Earlier, someone brought a big bag of used clothes that they had collected in some of the abandoned houses. Hela settled on a blouse, a sweater, and a skirt. She reasoned that one could not run quickly while wearing a coat and did not take one. She cleaned herself up as well as she could, and then went to say goodbye to

Maria, Lutek's mother. Both wept. Hela assured Maria that she would soon come back and take her and Lutek to the forest or a village. "I do not count on this," said Maria. "You are young and you will live to see a different world. I won't leave this place anymore." They kissed goodbye and Hela left.

Most escapes from the ghetto happened via the sewage system, which had a complicated structure of special exits known only to a few people. Before the group was about to leave, each of them received a piece of sugar and a slice of stale bread. The trip through the system was an ordeal: the smell was overpowering; the ground was uneven, wet, and covered with slime; and the tunnel was too low for people to straighten up. It was dark, and there was the ever-present possibility of stepping into something horrible. The first exit the group came to was blocked, and they had to turn back and start again.[14]

For Hela's group, eleven in all, however, reaching the Aryan side offered the hope of bringing aid to the comrades who had stayed behind, and this propelled them to keep moving. For part of the way, Cywia Lubetkin and Chaim Fryman accompanied the group. Their job was to make sure that the group would receive help from a special guide on the other side. Only when they secured such a promise did Cywia and Chaim return to the Mila 18 bunker. Two other ŻOB members, Regina Feuerstein and Lutek Rosblat, stayed with the group for as long as they could. In the end, they, too, returned to Mila 18.[15]

In the middle of the night, the group reached the Aryan side, where they were immediately accosted by a group of Polish policemen who were waiting for ghetto escapees in order to press them for bribes. As Hela was climbing out of the sewer, she heard the policemen insist that the new arrivals should enter the gates of the nearby building, casually adding that this is where they would conduct their business. From experience, Hela knew that going through this gate meant danger. It might cost them their lives. She refused, arguing that she was only willing to give them money out in the open. She wanted to know how much they wanted. Hela and Pavel, an underground comrade, stood next to each other. As the Polish policemen continued to pressure the arrivals to go through the gate, they heard a German shout, "Halt!" It was followed by several shots.

For Hela, Pavel, and most of their group, the interruption offered a chance to run, which they did. Behind them they could hear footsteps heading in a variety of directions. They came upon the ruins of a house and took shelter there. Contemplating their next move, they saw a German soldier running toward them, a gun in each hand. Somehow they managed to blend into the partial ruins. The German ran past them, shooting in another direction.

They resumed running. Hela scrambled over a wall and was confronted on the other side by two Poles. Screaming, "Leave me alone!" she struck at them and they ran off. Puzzled as to how she had succeeded in getting rid of both, she entered a large yard and was immediately enveloped by silence. Hela found some water and splashed it on her face. She changed her stockings and washed her knee, which was bleeding. She wanted to look normal. Finally, slowly, casually, she moved out of this yard. She came upon a train station. A woman looked at Hela closely. She asked Hela whether she was all right. She was so pale! Hela explained that she had just seen Germans chasing after an escaping Jew whom they were about to shoot.

Later, when Hela managed to reach Antek Zuckerman's apartment, he was not there. She left a message and went off in the direction of another address she had been given. She was to meet a Jewish courier by the name of Stenia or Schifra, who also had been a member of the Hashomer Hatzair. (In fact, Stenia hoped to write a history of their movement.) She was renting a room from a Polish family. She welcomed Hela, though the two had never met. Exhausted, Hela fell asleep, waking up when Antek arrived. Antek assured her that people were being dispatched to the ghetto to organize escapes for the other underground members.[16]

Only much later could Hela piece together what had happened to her comrades at Mila 18. On either the 10th or 11th of May, the Germans discovered the entrance to the bunker of Mila 18 and pumped gas into it. A handful of people miraculously survived; all the others were killed. When those inside smelled gas, they panicked. About a hundred people pushed toward one single exit, though the bunker had five of them. The result was chaos, only interrupted by an order from Wilner to use the last bullet: "The Germans will not take any of us alive!" This started a process of mutual killing.

One of the stories Hela heard was that Lutek had offered his mother a chair, kissed her, gave her poison, and then shot her. Next he shot himself.

Some of those who knew Mordechai Anielewicz well knew that he had not been in favor of collective suicide. If there was even a slight possibility that they might survive, they should try to take advantage of it. He encouraged methods like placing a wet rag on your face, which could protect a person against the effects of gas. Soldiers at the front in World War I had used this method; wet rags might save lives. No one knew how Mordechai Anielewicz died.

Tosia Altman, Jehuda Wengrover, and a few other fighters who were close to the exit miraculously got out. When this small group later heard about the fate of most of their comrades, they wept. Those who could departed from this unmarked Jewish graveyard.

When the news about the Warsaw ghetto reached the ŻOB comrades on the Aryan side, they, too, wept bitterly. Hela was overcome by exhaustion, rage, and powerlessness. As if these tragic losses were not enough, their supposedly reliable Polish landlady suddenly asked the group of ŻOB comrades to vacate their apartment. She explained that the Germans had intensified their hunt for Jews. Whenever they came upon hidden Jews, they would destroy not only the "guilty tenants" but would also demolish the entire building as well with the rest of the tenants. There was ample evidence for these assertions. Poles who wanted to protect the Jews were pressured by Polish friends and families to stop exposing themselves to the danger.

Around that time, the Germans had made a seemingly plausible proposal—swapping Jews for Germans imprisoned in Russia and other countries. The Germans offered to issue passports for Jews with visas to a number of countries, mostly in South America. In exchange, the Jews were asked to pay large sums of money for these passports, in the form of gold, diamonds, and other articles of value. The details of this proposal were not clearly spelled out. The Jews who would participate in these exchanges could temporarily move to a Warsaw hotel, specifically the Hotel Polski. There the Jews would wait until the arrangements for these transfers were "completed."

There were ambiguities in these plans and loose ends, which were never tied up. Jews wanted to believe in the proposal, but distrust and questions lingered. The Germans managed to enlist the support of certain prominent and respected members of the Jewish community. Among them was the director of the Jewish Joint, David Guzik. He lived at the Hotel Polski and worked hard at helping people acquire foreign passports. He even gave money to those who were in need. Deeply involved in the entire process, he was eager to send his wife and children on one of these exchange transports.[17] Abraham Gancwajch, a known collaborator, sent his wife on one of these transports.[18] The involvement of these two men, Guzik and Gancwajch, seemed to lend legitimacy to the process. In the end, however, the overwhelming majority of those who were a part of the exchange processes ended up in concentration camps. Many were sent directly to the gas chambers in Auschwitz.[19]

After the uprising, Hela and several of her ŻOB comrades had difficulty finding even temporary living quarters. These money-for-passports exchanges seemed to offer the opportunity for a permanent existence. But they had no money to buy documents that would entitle them to South American passports. Some friends who were involved in these schemes urged them to wait, because Jews who paid for these documents sometimes failed to pick them up. Some of them might have been arrested. Others might have found a permanent and safe hiding place and given up the idea of traveling to another country.

In the end Hela and her Hashomer Hatzair comrades, despite serious reservations, moved to the Hotel Polski. They had no other options. All of them ended up in the concentration camp Bergen-Belsen, an experience Hela and some of her comrades survived, in part because they had each other to depend upon.[20] They also survived because the war came to an end.

Most Jewish couriers did not survive the war. Among the best-known and most courageous was Sonia Madejsker, who was actively engaged as a courier in Vilna and the surrounding forests. Shortly before the Nazi retreat, Sonia was arrested. She attempted suicide and was transferred to a hospital, where she died without revealing any names of her underground comrades.[21]

The history of the period is filled with descriptions of couriers whose lives were cut short. Their names and deeds are scattered throughout the Holocaust literature.

One of the most prominent names is the previously mentioned Tosia Altman. Born in 1918, she was involved in Hashomer Hatzair activities. Together with Lea Kozibrodzka, she organized resistance groups in the Vilna ghetto and contributed to activities in various parts of occupied Poland. She fought bravely in the Warsaw

FIGURE 5.4 Tosia Altman, a leader of the Jewish underground in the Warsaw ghetto. With few exceptions, all of the couriers were women. (Courtesy Yad Vashem)

ghetto's uprising and succeeded in escaping from a bunker to a more secure location near Mila 18. When the Germans attacked with gas, Tosia saved herself by escaping through the sewers with a group of ŻOB fighters. In a weakened condition, Tosia hid for several days in a Warsaw factory, which contained highly flammable photographic materials. When a fire broke out in this factory, Tosia was badly burned, which prevented her from escaping with her comrades. Transferred to a nearby hospital, she was interrogated but refused to supply the German authorities with any damaging information. She died during these interrogations.

Frania Beatus, born in 1926, was transferred by the Germans to several ghettos around the town of Ostrowiec and eventually joined the Jewish underground ŻOB as a courier. In the Warsaw ghetto, Frania took on the dual roles of fighter and courier.

Moving among her ŻOB comrades, she spent time in the Warsaw ghetto and on the Aryan side, and would help transfer Jews from one place to another. For a while she worked closely with Yitzhak Zuckerman. During one of her missions, she heard that the Warsaw ghetto underground ceased to exist and she committed suicide. The specific timing and circumstances of her death are unknown.

Another courier, Marylka Rozycka from Lodz, was a member of the Communist Party and a wartime legend. In Bialystok, Marylka, whose looks and manner were typical of those of a Polish peasant, established contacts between the Party and the Bialystok ghetto underground. After the liquidation of the ghetto, Marylka maintained close ties with both the underground on the Aryan side and the forest partisans, some of whom had been ghetto resisters. Compassionate and fearless, she insisted that all jobs were important and none were too dangerous. Marylka survived the war and settled in Bialystok. She died in a car accident in 1992.[22]

The Holocaust literature is filled with many couriers who still await source recognition.

CHAPTER SIX

The Special Case of Jan Karski

As we have seen throughout this book, the plan to annihilate the Jews was tied up with Hitler's determination to destroy the Polish elites. Hitler was eager to "prevent Polish assimilation into any parts of the newly conquered territories," [1] as well as to prevent them from developing into a ruling class. Basically, the brutality which the Nazis had brought to occupied Poland was aimed at the liquidation of anyone with leadership capacity, whether the nobility, the clergy, or the intelligentsia. [2] Moreover, convinced that the Wehrmacht had treated the Poles too gently, Hitler replaced them with the ruthless SS. [3]

However, the Germans were by no means the only enemies facing the Poles. Stalin saw the German invasion as an opportunity to acquire Polish territories, while tightening controls over Poland in general. America's entry into the war on the Allies' side after the German invasion of Russia strengthened his hand, shifting the balance of power. In addition, the 1941 widely publicized German discovery of mass graves in the Katyn Forest helped to deepen the long-standing divide between the Poles and the Russians. These graves contained the bodies of 4,321 Polish officers murdered by the USSR. [4] The Soviet Union vehemently denied any involvement in these killings. Indeed, Stalin accused the Germans of having committed these crimes to frame Russia. In protest, Stalin summarily cut off all communications with the Polish government-in-exile in London.

These developments only confirmed Polish suspicions of Soviet power and the implications that this could potentially have upon

FIGURE 6.1 Jan Karski in 1943, taken during his mission to the United States to inform government leaders about Nazi policy in Poland. (U.S. Holocaust Memorial Museum, courtesy of Jan Karski)

the Allies. The Allies in turn had assured the Poles that they would prevent the USSR from taking control of Poland. Again and again they assured Poland that it had nothing to worry about, and that Polish lands would be fully protected. Due to the ever-changing military realities, these assurances turned out to be hollow. In the end, Stalin shrewdly manipulated circumstances to his advantage. History shows how, incrementally and systematically, the Soviets gained political control over Poland. Despite the Poles' determination to resist the Nazis, the result of which was a strong and effective underground movement, they were losing ground.

Among the most heroic Polish underground figures was Jan Kerski, born in Lodz in 1914. He was a courier and deeply involved with the Polish underground. Known as Jan Karski, he was a devout Catholic who served as an emissary, a link between the underground and the Polish government-in-exile in London. Among the numerous honors bestowed upon him after the war was Poland's highest military decoration, the order of Virtuti Militaris.

In Jerusalem, Yad Vashem paid tribute to Karski by distinguishing him with the title of the Righteous among the Nations (in Hebrew: Hasidei Umot Haolam). Karski's story offers significant insights into wartime developments in Poland.

While still a young boy, Karski lost his father. His brother, Marian, eighteen years his senior, became a surrogate father and encouraged Jan's educational and professional ambitions. His mother instilled in her younger son a tolerance for outsiders, including Jews. With this tolerance came an equally strong concern for social justice. And while Catholicism played an important role in Karski's life, he placed an even higher value on the human spirit.

With his university degree, the aspiring young diplomat entered the Polish Foreign Service. In 1939 Karski enlisted in the Polish army with a rank of second lieutenant. Taken prisoner by the Soviets, he escaped to Warsaw, where he joined the newly established AK.

Karski was selected to be an international emissary. He may have been chosen for this kind of work because of his diplomatic background, impressive physical stamina, and photographic memory. Karski modestly described his role as follows: "I was only a courier. My duty was to transport information. In a sense I acted as a mailbox or a gramophone record. I hurried from one side of the front to the other. Everybody had me swear that I would tell what I heard to authorized people only."[5]

As discussed, the Polish government-in-exile was primarily made up of four prewar parties—the Peasant Party, the Christian Labor Party, the National Party, and the Socialist Party.[6] Of these, the socialists had the richest, most continuous tradition of fighting for independence.[7] Karski notes that during the war, the Poles, unlike the French, for example, refused to become a part of the Nazi General Government, a separate administration region of occupied Poland.[8]

Karski outlined the basic principles guiding them all:

1. No collaboration with the enemy, under any circumstances.
2. The military army of the Polish underground was to coordinate its activities with the Polish government-in-exile.[9]

As a supporter of parliamentary democracy, Karski saw in this newly created wartime government in London an improvement over the earlier Polish governments. It had returned to the older tradition of parliamentary democracy, and in the end it offered more freedom than the prewar so-called democracy.[10] Still, these changes did not mean that this newly created government was free of prejudices and abuses. The powerful Nationalist Party was characterized by anti-Semitism, and in general the government-in-exile was guided by self-interest rather than concern for any of its minority constituents, least of all the Jews.[11]

Additionally, official positions do not necessarily reflect reality in its entirety. For example, a statement made in 1942 by Tadeusz Bor-Komorowski, deputy commander and then commander of the AK, claimed that the AK had offered assistance to the Warsaw ghetto underground with supplies of ammunition and arms, and Jewish underground leaders had rejected the offer. Israel Gutman and Shmuel Krakowski reject the veracity of this claim entirely, calling it a "fiction from beginning to the end." "It is difficult," they add, "to understand the motives in fabricating such a tale." [12] In 1943, the Jewish underground in the Warsaw ghetto did receive some guns and other aid from the AK. However, this help came only after Jewish resisters had successfully fought off the German attack on January 18, 1943.[13]

Turning to the earlier stages of the war and the initial German attacks upon Poland, it is usually accepted that a substantial number of Polish Jews joined the escaping crowds. No exact figures are available. According to some estimates, about 200,000 Jewish refugees reached Soviet-occupied Poland.[14] Poles who lived in the eastern part of Poland suspected the Jewish newcomers of being communist sympathizers or, worse, Russian spies, however much they protested that they were propelled by fear of the Germans. Ironically, many of these Jewish refugees were sent by the Russians to Siberia. With the subsequent German occupation of this area, the remaining Jews were caught in the net of annihilation.

In 1940, at the age of twenty-five, Karski left for his first mission in France. There, in addition to the information he submitted to the government-in-exile, at the request of his superiors, he wrote a report about life in Poland under the German and Soviet occupations. A portion of this report dealt with the Jewish plight and the German occupation's effect on the Jewish-Polish relations. In this document Karski called for the creation of a common front, an alliance through which the weaker partners—the Jews and the Poles—might work together against their deadly enemy, the German occupational forces. He argued that such an alliance would be morally advantageous to all Poles. At the same time, he deplored the fact that the Polish masses did not seem to sympathize with the Jews. Already insightful and concise, he surmised long before most that the Germans had targeted the Jews for total destruction.[15]

Karski returned to Poland via Hungary and Czechoslovakia. Within a few weeks, he was sent to France again. This time, however, the Gestapo arrested him in Slovakia. Although tortured, Karski revealed no secrets. Still, he feared that eventually he might succumb. At the first opportunity he had, he retrieved some razor blades he had hidden in his shoes and cut his wrists—only to be revived by the Germans. The brutal Nazi interrogation resumed. Shortly thereafter, however, it was interrupted by a daring and successful rescue operation executed by a Polish commando group. After he recovered, Karski continued to serve the AK.[16]

Karski was preoccupied by the Nazi annihilation of the Jews and was ready to do what he could to alleviate Jewish suffering. He took advantage of an opportunity to alert the leaders of the free world to the systematic murder of the Jews. In the latter part of 1942, in preparation for a transatlantic journey, Karski met with Jewish leaders in Poland and agreed to deliver their messages to Allies and others whom they deemed influential.

To add credence to this part of his mission, with the help of these Jewish underground leaders, Karski was first smuggled into the Warsaw ghetto, in order to gain first-hand knowledge of the Jewish plight. To report on another phase of Jewish destruction, Karski, dressed as a guard, was smuggled into the transit camp Izbica Lubelska. Jews from all over Europe were brought to this camp, which served as a traffic regulator for Jews destined for the death camp Belzec. In Izbica Lubelska, the Jewish prisoners were robbed of their possessions, humiliated, brutalized, and often simply murdered. Some of the Jewish survivors were transferred to Belzec and gassed upon arrival.[17]

Not only was Karski risking his life through these visits, he also endangered his psychological health. His biographers, E. Thomas Wood and Stanislaw Jankowski, describe how while in Izbica Karski suffered a kind of breakdown, weeping and gesticulating, essentially losing self-control. Only his escort's angry shouts of "Follow me! Follow me!" roused him from his stupor. Hustling Karski from the camp, the guide vented his fury through clenched teeth: "You acted like you were crazy in there! With your crazy gestures! You endanger people! You've got no business being here! Come on!" [18]

Subsequently, in England and in the United States, Karski met with many world leaders, including President Roosevelt, Prime Minister Churchill, and the British foreign minister Anthony Eden. He also met with such dignitaries as Szmuel Zygielbojm, a Polish-Jewish leader of the socialist Bund, who had escaped from Poland and established himself in London in order to mobilize support for the Jewish people. However, Zygielbojm was never successful in obtaining any significant guarantees of aid. After many failures, disheartened by the lack of sympathy, and in protest, Zygielbojm committed suicide. In a letter, he explained himself, arguing "that the responsibility for the crime and murder of the whole Jewish nationality in Poland rests first of all on those who are carrying it out, but indirectly it falls also upon the whole of humanity, on the peoples of the Allies, on their governments, who to this day have not taken any real steps to halt this crime." [19]

Karski's reports about the plight of the Jewish people and the messages from the Jewish Polish leaders who pleaded for help also fell on deaf ears. For the Allies, as for other governments, the systematic murder of the Jews by the Germans was not a primary concern. Years later, commenting on this mission, Karski described it as "an obvious failure. Six million Jews died, and no one offered them effective help. Not any nation, not any government, not any church. The help they did receive, heroic help, was provided only by scattered individuals." [20]

The 1942 meetings with high-ranking governmental officials convinced Karski that the Jews had been abandoned by the world's governments, and he said as much on multiple occasions. However, his experiences also convinced him that while the murderers of Jews by far outnumbered those who wanted to save them, the Jews were not entirely alone. "We hear it said that the Jews were abandoned by governments, social structures, church hierarchies, but not by ordinary men and women." [21]

Significantly, Karski was convinced that in reflecting on and studying the Holocaust, it was counterproductive to concentrate only on the murderers and ignore the minority that was determined to save Jews. He argued that we must adhere to the historical truth by showing how thousands of Christians tried to save Jews and were often prepared to die doing so. Some did. Karski was convinced that overlooking those who risked their lives to save the oppressed only perpetuated the idea that "everybody hates the Jews."[22]

Karski believed that for the Jewish people, focusing exclusively on their wartime destruction would develop into a psychic wound that would never heal. He identified with Jewish suffering and with their apprehension that with time the Holocaust would become one of those forgotten historical events, lost among so many other human tragedies. He therefore understood Jewish fears of the Holocaust becoming trivialized and the resulting single-minded focus on Jewish destruction. Nevertheless, he felt that this emphasis on Jewish annihilation, while understandable, was ultimately counterproductive. First, because historically it was untrue; many people opposed Jewish annihilation. Second, because it perpetuated the notion that anti-Semitism was universal.

Karski's humanism extended to other oppressed groups and individuals as well. His identification with the downtrodden grew out of his moral convictions and having witnessed the suffering of various groups. Still, it was the Jewish annihilation that preoccupied him. His first report for the Polish government-in-exile, then in France, written in 1940, was filled with vivid examples of helplessness and humiliation. Karski reported:

One time I was at the Gestapo to obtain a pass of some sort. A Jewish woman came in, a member of the educated class, very frightened. She was expecting a child. She was requesting a pass for herself or for her doctor to be on the street after 8:00 pm should it be necessary to begin delivery then.

The female secretary, a Volksdeutsche, responded, "You don't need a pass. We are not going to facilitate the birth of a Jew. Dogs are dying from hunger and misery, and still you want to give birth to Jews? *Heraus! Heraus!* [Get out of here!]"[23]

In another part of this same report, Karski wrote:

I was in the Kercelak (a kiosk stand in Warsaw). A frozen Jew is the proprietor. A German soldier comes by. He takes socks, combs, soap—wants to walk off without paying. The Jew demands money. The soldier pays no attention. The old man raises his voice; his frightened neighbors hold him back and calm him; they are afraid for him. The old man shouts, or rather howls: "What will he do to me? What will he do to me? He can only kill me. Let him kill me. Let him kill me. Enough of all this! I can't go on any more."

The German walked away; he didn't pay. As he was leaving, he muttered, "*Verfluchte Juden.* [Damned Jews]."[24]

Karski was also sensitive to and identified with the dangerous and life-threatening conditions of low-ranking underground workers. In his book, *Story of a Secret State*, his reports are full of compassion. "Pitiful were the young girls who distributed the underground press. It was a thankless job—this was a simple mechanical task—men did not want it; men insisted on playing more important roles. The death rate among these girls was very high."[25] Couriers had a slightly higher status than those who distributed illegal literature. As we have seen, most were women. Karski was keenly aware of the special dangers that female couriers faced. A courier's job, he noted, required that many people "knew every detail of her life—and in clandestine work that was bad.... They were overloaded with work and doomed from the start."[26]

Late in 1943, Karski's position in the Polish underground changed drastically. On the way to Poland, he stopped in London and was told that Germans were aware of his trip to the United States and were issuing broadcasts that Karski was a Bolshevik agent paid by American Jews to slander the Third Reich by spreading lies. The Polish prime minister Stanislaw Mikolajczyk determined that Karski's return to Poland would be too risky. "I was marked by the scars on my wrists. Actually, the Polish government did not know what to do with me. I knew too many secrets."[27]

Karski wound up working in Washington on the Polish Embassy staff. He remembered those years as the busiest of his life. He delivered some two hundred lectures, and in 1944 wrote *Story of a Secret State*. "In most of the lectures, interviews, articles, and in my book, I informed the public about what was happening to the Jews in Poland."[28] Karski was continuously frustrated by the Allies' refusal to do anything about the systematic annihilation of the Jewish people. The end of the war proved how right he had been, and, perhaps in a gesture of defiance and rage, Karski stopped talking about the Holocaust altogether.

The United States became Karski's permanent home. By 1952 he had earned a Ph.D. at Georgetown University, where he stayed on as a professor, teaching courses on Eastern Europe, government, and international affairs. Soon surrounded by a circle of devoted

FIGURE 6.2 Jan Karski at Georgetown University in 1982. The same year, Karski was honored by Yad Vashem and designated as one of the Righteous among the Nations for his work as a resistance fighter. (U.S. Holocaust Memorial Museum, courtesy of Carol Harrison)

students, Karski became an admired figure on the Georgetown Campus. In 1962, he married Pola Nirenska, a distinguished dancer and choreographer, and a Polish Jew.

He revisited his past only at the insistent urgings of Claude Lanzmann, the director of the film *Shoah*. An admirer of Lanzmann's talents, Karski regretted that the film did not include the story of Christians who had risked their lives to save Jews. He thought there should be a special film focusing exclusively on the rescue of Jews by Christians, which he believed was necessary for those generations that had not witnessed the Holocaust, Jew and Gentile alike, "in order not to lose their faith in mankind."[29]

Karski speculated that of the Jews who survived the Holocaust in Europe, an estimated half a million had received some help from non-Jews. The rescuers came from every quarter—nuns, peasants, workers, and so on. "The organized structures fell short of expectations, but not the ordinary people. And there were perhaps millions of such individuals. In this lies a hidden source of optimism, and this optimism should be passed on to those generations for whom the Holocaust is not more than a page from a history textbook."[30]

When asked to comment about the postwar reaction to the Holocaust, Karski's consistent answer was that while he read about how Western leaders—"statesmen and generals, church hierarchies, civic leaders" –claimed that they had no knowledge about the Nazi genocide, they knew. "According to them, the murder of six million Jews was a well-guarded secret. This version of wartime events persists in many quarters even today. This version is no more than a myth. They knew."[31] In Karski's estimation,

> Anybody who wanted to know about German crimes against the Jews could have known, and not only through me. There were many other sources. But this truth could not get through. This was not only due to ill will. The Holocaust, this systematic extermination of an entire nation, happened for the first time in the history of mankind. People were not prepared for such a truth. And that is why these truths were rejected, even subconsciously. The most trustworthy witnesses were rejected. There are things which minds and hearts refuse to accept.[32]

Jan Karski's death in 2000 deprived the world of a humanitarian whose courage and selfless dedication gave hope to many.[33] He proved that Christian and Jewish passivity during the Holocaust was a myth. In most wartime settings—ghettos, forests, concentration camps—conditions were not conducive to resistance, and yet, in myriad shapes and guises, both Jews and Christians found the strength to stand up to German oppression. They found a way to cooperate, and to oppose the enemy.

Conclusion

"Not Alone"

Wartime cooperation against the Germans was expressed in a wide range of efforts that frequently moved beyond the expected and often took the form of acts of kindness. The Holocaust offers many examples of such acts.

Self-preservation, autonomy, and actual survival are intricately connected in ways that are often unclear. I have asked many survivors what *they* thought was responsible for their survival. Almost without exception their initial answers were luck, chance, and fate. They wished to convey the idea that their survival was not contingent on their talent or intelligence.

When I continued to probe, however, they offered additional reasons. Most agreed that central among these secondary reasons was cooperation with others. Most of these prisoners were at one time or other part of a group—whether formal or informal—that involved mutual support. For most of them, being a part of these groups translated into being alive.[1]

The final liquidation of the Vilna ghetto began on September 23, 1943. What happened on that day followed an established pattern. First, the population was divided by age and sex. Older men were thrown into a group with older women and women with children. Dina Abramovicz, a teenager at the time, watched from afar as her elderly mother struggled with her oversized bundles. Then Dina spotted a teacher whom she and her mother knew. He was crippled from the waist down and walking on crutches. Because he was an invalid, the Nazis pushed him into the group of older women and children. Dina realized that he would be expected to climb a hill along with the crowd. He looked around imploringly, as if asking for help. Dina tells what happened next:

> Someone responded to his pleading and it was my mother. She put down all her bundles and took the arm of the crippled man, who leaned heavily on her. As they moved toward the steep hill together, the tall, crippled man, and the elderly, frail woman, their faces glowed with a sublime light—the light of compassion and humanity that overcame the horror of their destiny. This is the light in which I remember my mother and which will not disappear from my memory as long as I live.

On the way to the concentration camp, Dina and a group of young people jumped off the moving freight train that was transporting them. Miraculously, they landed near a forest and survived the war as partisans.[2] After the war Dina became a respected librarian at YIVO, now the Institute for Jewish Research in New York. She helped me and many others with finding materials for research.

Arieh Eitani was a teenager in wartime Poland brought to the Kaufering work camp. Like most other victims, he was preoccupied with finding food. Here and there he came upon some additional food, which he occasionally shared with others. Although resourceful and self-reliant, one day he was overcome by circumstances that were stronger than his ability to deal with them. He recalls:

> I had diarrhea and couldn't stop running to the bathroom. My clothes would not dry from the previous night. I had no shoes....I knew of a shoemaker in the camp that had extra shoes, but he would not give me any....It was raining, it was cold. I had enough. I thought that I was finished. I wanted to die and stopped working...just stood there. A kapo saw this and started beating me. Blood was streaming down my head.
>
> A German guard, a soldier, came over, and asked the kapo, "Why are you hitting him? What's going on?"
>
> The kapo said, "He doesn't want to live; he wants to give up. He doesn't want to work or do anything. He wants to die."

The German ordered, "Release him to me."

I thought to myself, "Well, at least the end will come soon."

The soldier took me to his place. He put me next to the stove so my clothes would dry. He gave me his sandwich and he asked, "Tell me, what is the problem?" I told him. I told him everything, everything, explaining that I just didn't want to live any more. He said, "All this will be over soon." [This was the winter of 1944.] Then he talked about himself. "Look, when I was in Russia at the Front, it was also very difficult. I also had diarrhea, and we as soldiers would cut our pants in the back and wore them like this." I can't remember all he said...he talked about himself a lot...what was important to me was the heat, the sandwich, the fact that I wasn't working...Who knows?...all this did something to me. Next day, after work, this German came over, took me to his barrack. He gave me food and let me sit near the stove. But then, after the second day, I never saw him again. I don't know what happened. I looked for him, hoping for a sandwich and some warmth but never saw him.

This German offered help and a glimmer of compassion in a chain of humiliations and depravations that had pushed Arieh to the brink of suicide.[3] Perhaps the rarity of these incidents increased their effectiveness.

Tonia Rotkopf tells about a similar experience. After the 1944 liquidation of the Lodz ghetto, she was first transferred to Auschwitz and from there with a group of Jewish women to a work camp in Freiburg. In this place food was distributed once a day; bread and soup. The portions of the bread kept shrinking.

Tonia worked in a plane factory. She thought of her job as "horrible." She remembers:

We had to cut aluminum and I didn't know how. They laughed at me....All the supervisors were German men or German women. We were not allowed to go to the toilet alone; we always had to go in a group of fives. The main supervisor, a Nazi, was a terror. A typical brute....Then, from cutting aluminum they assigned me to work with a German, not a Nazi; this German was some kind of a prisoner and was not allowed to talk to me. I would bring the nails and hold them out. He used my hands for the job. I worked with the end part of the airplane. He and I were a team; we had to work together. I had to complete the job because my hands were small. Whenever he wanted to say something to me, he would look in a different direction and mumble under his breath.

Once Tonia went for a drink of water without asking permission. Her absence was noticed. "When I came back, the Nazi supervisor was there, and he screamed at me: 'How the hell can you drink water? You will get sick from it!' then he slapped me across my face four times. I could see his ring with the Nazi emblem on it. The German prisoner with whom I worked and other co-workers were there. I was ashamed to be hit in the face, in front of everybody... but then hoped that possibly no one had noticed... with the noise and all."

Tonia was convinced that such a public humiliation would push her toward suicide. She just looked at those present. "When the German master turned around, I saw one tear drop flow from his eye. One tear, from one eye. This is how I realized that only one of his eyes was real. I also realized that he was my friend.... Later on he asked me, 'Why didn't you tell me that you wanted water?'" From then on, Tonia's friendship with this German made hunger, hard work, and humiliations more bearable.

For both Arieh and Tonia, a crisis was followed by compassion, which reestablished a balance and gave each of them some strength to continue. It gave them a sense of community and the realization that they were not alone.[4]

The fate of the children in the Bernson and Bauman Hospital in the Warsaw ghetto was different. I recount this story in my book *Resilience and Courage*, but it bears repeating here. Dr. Anna Brande-Heller was the hospital chief. Among the women physicians who played a special role during the deportations was Dr. Anna Margolis, a pediatrician in charge of the children's TB ward, and her young assistant—she was barely out of medical school—Dr. Adina Szwajger.

At the height of the deportations each head doctor received a ticket that entitled him or her to an exemption. Supposedly holders of these tickets were shielded from deportation. Each head of a hospital received a few additional tickets with an order to distribute them among members of their staff. Such tickets were scarce, covering only a small portion of hospital employees. This in turn meant that a head doctor was burdened with the decision of whom to select for an exemption from deportation, which everyone knew meant death.

At first, Dr. Heller refused to take on this responsibility. But her staff urged her to distribute the tickets, for if she didn't, the tickets would go to other heads of hospitals. In the end, Dr. Heller distributed the tickets to her people.

When Dr. Szwajger reached the building on that fateful September day, deportations were in full swing. Except for the very young children and patients who could not walk, everyone seemed to have disappeared. Soon, however, from different directions, from nooks and corners, older children patients reemerged. They surrounded Dr. Szwajger. One of these youngsters stepped out. "Doctor, we all know that we have no mamas and no papas anymore. And that we are not going to live through it either. But will you stay with us to the end?" Szwajger assured them that she would.

That morning Dr. Heller decided to give the five tickets to the younger people on the staff. Among them was Dr. Margolis and her daughter Ala, who worked as a nurse; Marek Edelman, a hospital employee and an underground leader; and Dr. Szwajger. After Szwajger received the news, she sat on the ward and watched a young nurse trying and failing to administer an injection. This nurse turned to Szwajger and begged the doctor to do it. The patient was the nurse's mother. "I beg you, please. I don't want them to shoot her in the bed and she can't walk." Szwajger agreed. The old woman smiled and offered her arm.

Once this was done, Szwajger asked the nurse whether they had a big supply of morphine. They had enough, the nurse replied. There was no need to say more. They understood. Szwajger told Dr. Margolis of her plan to give morphine to the children. Margolis agreed. Working together, the two doctors moved among the youngest children and babies, injecting them with the morphine solution. Next, they turned to the older children and told them that the medicine they had for them would make all the pain disappear. The children drank from the glasses. When they were told to undress and go to bed, they did so quietly.

Outside the door came a commotion. People were shoving and pushing. The noise was coming closer. In a daze, with the ticket pinned to her white coat, Szwajger left. She does not know if she had glanced at the children or not. From total silence she moved into a nervous chaos. There Szwajger bumped into a teacher she knew. The older woman asked in a hard voice if Szwajger had a ticket. The doctor kept silent and moved on. Later, those who were spared tried to send their tickets back to the hospital for others.

Szwajger was active in the ghetto resistance and subsequently, on the Aryan side, she worked as a courier. After the war she stayed in Warsaw and became a pediatrician. For decades she never told anyone the story of the children whom she had helped to die. What was critical in her memory was the way in which they had worked together—she, the nurse, Dr. Margolis, and her daughter, Ala Margolis. Their complicity was a compassionate response. They had been pushed to making life-or-death decisions, and their resistance was to choose the most humane path they could.[5]

In the end, there was no more extreme place than the concentration camps, where life hung by a thread. There, friendships were particularly valuable, and indeed invaluable. For many they were family. It was common for young Jewish women in the concentration camps to form powerful attachments. Two such young girls in Auschwitz became closely attached to each other. One of them developed a violent cough, which was observed by a kapo. He insisted that the sick girl be moved to the Auschwitz medical ward. The healthy friend would come to visit her every day after work, risking being herself interned in the medical ward. Occasionally she would bring her water or a little slice of bread.

One day as the girl was returning from work she noticed a raspberry bush next to the road. She approached the bush to confirm that it was real. Verifying this fact, she was filled with a desire to bring the fruit to her sick friend, but knew that if the Germans found out it would be confiscated and she would be punished. So she gently placed the fruit into her closed palm in a leaf. As soon as she arrived at the camp, she rushed to her friend with the news that she had a surprise. The raspberries, however, clutched tightly in her hand, had become a paste. Nevertheless, when the sick young girl saw what was in her friend's open palm, her face lit up with happiness. Such an individual gesture of kindness, an act of resistance in its own way, proved to each girl that she was not alone and rekindled hope for life.

Acknowledgments

My involvement with resistance grew out of my personal interest in questions touching on wartime resistance. In a sense, this book developed from a prolonged journey marked by a range of expected and unexpected detours and revelations. Some of the obstacles and road bumps I encountered during this process were smoothed by a range of generous aid from a variety of sources. Inevitably, I welcome this opportunity to thank the multitude of individuals whose care and involvement improved the quality of this book.

A special and important role in my endeavor to complete this book was played by Timothy Bent, my editor at Oxford University Press, who so generously supported the production of this book with the help of his assistant Keely Latcham. Moreover, the publication of this book has greatly benefited from the continual support of Niko Pfund, president of Oxford University Press (USA).

My research efforts in this project relied on the help of a number of research institutions that invited me to participate in their various projects, broadening and facilitating my involvement in Holocaust research. Initially, both my position as a Fellow at the International Institute for Holocaust Research at Yad Vashem in Jerusalem and my research positions held at the Holocaust Museum in Washington, D.C., paved the way for my exploration of Jewish and non-Jewish resistance during the Holocaust.

I am fortunate to have had my family's unwavering support. Indeed, I am indebted to my family, my husband Leon Tec and my children Leora and Roland Tec, for their support of my research. I have particularly benefited from my son's eager contributions to my Holocaust research and have often relied on his insightful and creative comments.

I deeply admire those individuals who, during different stages of my research, so generously shared with me the stories of their painful pasts. Many of these stories became integral parts of my different publications. Others still await personal recognition.

N.T.

Notes

Introduction

1. For some discussion of collaboration, see Yehuda Bauer, *Rethinking the Holocaust* (New Haven: Yale University Press, 2001), 144–149. Alice Kaplan, *The Collaborator* (Chicago: University of Chicago Press, 2000).
2. Dina Porat, "The Vilna Proclamation of January 1, 1942 in Historical Perspective," *Yad Vashem Studies* 25 (1996): 99–136.
3. Ibid., 116.
4. Ibid., 113.
5. Bruno Bettelheim, "Individual and Mass Behaviors in Extreme Situations," *Abnormal and Social Psychology* 38 (1943): 417–452.
6. Bruno Bettelheim, *The Informal Heart* (New York: Avon, 1960), 248–249.
7. Ibid., 251.
8. For a discussion of life in the forbidden Christian world, see Nechama Tec, *When Light Pierced the Darkness* (New York: Oxford University Press, 1986), 25–69.
9. Hannah Arendt, *Eichmann in Jerusalem* (New York: Viking, 1963), 125.
10. Ibid., 118. John Lukacs, in his book *The Hitler of History* (New York: Random House, 1997), refers to H. Arendt's, *The Origin of Totalitarianism*—as a flawed and dishonest book (113).
11. Raoul Hilberg, *The Destruction of the European Jews* (New York: New Viewpoints, 1973), 168–174.
12. Arendt, *Eichmann in Jerusalem*, 125.
13. Raul Hilberg, *The Destruction of the European Jews* (New York: New Viewpoints, 1973), 1:20–21.
14. Ibid., 3:1005.

15. Yitzhak Zuckerman, *A Surplus of Memory* (Los Angeles: University of California Press, 1993), 79.

16. For a different and interesting comment about Arendt's participation in the Eichmann trial in Jerusalem, see Deborah E. Lipstadt, *The Eichmann Trial* (New York: Schocken, 2011), 148–187.

17. For an additional perspective, see Lipstadt, *The Eichmann Trial*, 169. She discusses Hannah Arendt's concept of the banality of evil and notes that in the Eichmann case, Arendt's analysis is strangely out of touch with the reality of his historical record.

18. Primo Levi, *The Drowned and The Saved* (New York: Summit Books, 1986), 48–49.

19. Nathan Eck sees Hilberg's assessment of Jewish passivity as an insult to the dead and as an act of "Jewish self-hatred" ("Historical Research or Slander," *Yad Vashem Studies* 6 [1967]: 385–430).

20. For a slightly different perspective, see David Engel's review of a book related by Steven E. Aschheim, ed., *Hannah Arendt in Jerusalem*. Engel's review appeared in *Jewish Quarterly Review* 95.4 (2005): 685–693.

21. See a most recent publication by Norman Davies, *Rising '44* (New York: Viking, 2004).

22. Philip Friedman, *Roads to Extinction: Essays on the Holocaust*, ed. Ada J. Freidman (Philadelphia: Jewish Publication Society of America, 1980).

23. Isaiah Trunk, *Judenrat: The Jewish Councils in Eastern Europe under Nazi Occupation* (New York: Stein and Day, 1977).

24. Reuben Ainsztein, *Jewish Resistance in Nazi-Occupied Eastern Europe* (New York: Barnes & Noble, 1974).

25. Yuri Suhl, ed., *They Fought Back: The Story of the Jewish Resistance in Nazi Europe* (New York: Schocken Books, 1975). A very recent addition of this kind of an approach is Adam Rayski, *The Choice of the Jews under Vichy* (Notre Dame, Ind.: University of Notre Dame Press, 2005).

26. What follows is just a brief illustration of their work: Yizhak Arad, *Ghetto in Flames: The Struggle and Destruction of the Jews in Vilna in the Holocaust* (New York: Holocaust Library, 1982); Bauer, *Rethinking the Holocaust*; Shmuel Krakowski, *The War of the Doomed: Jewish Resistance in Poland, 1942-1944* (New York: Holmes and Meier, 1985); Dov Levin, *Fighting Back: Lithuanian Jewry's Armed Resistance to the Nazis, 1941-1945* (New York: Holmes and Meier, 1985).

27. Israel Gutman, *Resistance: The Warsaw Ghetto Uprising* (New York: Houghton Mifflin Company, 1994).

28. Lucjan Dobroszycki, "Polish Historiography on the Annihilation of the Jews of Poland in WW II: A Critical Evaluation," *East European Jewish Affairs* 23.2 (1993): 47.

Chapter One

1. Rytel's wartime experiences are described on pp. 267–271 in *This One Is from My Country*, in Wladyslaw Bartoszewski and Zofia Lewinowna, *Ten Jest Z*

Ojczyzny Moje (Krakow: Wydawnictwo Znak, 1969). I interviewed Zygmunt Rytel in the Jewish Historical Institute in Warsaw in 1978.

2. Rytel's rescue of Jews for which he was recognized by Yad Vashem as a Righteous among the Nations, on January 24, 1967 (*Encyclopedia of the Righteous among the Nations* [Jerusalem: Yad Vashem, 2004], 689).

3. From now on whenever I quote Z. Rytel, what he says is based on the interview I conducted with him in 1978; for a description of Yad Vashem and the distinctions it offers, see Tec, *When Light Pierced the Darkness*, 3–4.

4. When pursuing his resistance activities, Rytel relied on the Polish Socialist Party (PPS).

5. For the Third Reich, the decimation of the Polish elites was a top priority. Hence, the murder of the Polish elites was systematic. See Ian Kershaw, *Hitler: 1936-1946 Nemesis* (New York: Norton & Co., 2000), 2:241, 245. See also Saul Friedlander, *The Years of Extermination* (New York: HarperCollins, 2007), 12–13.

6. This Law was introduced in German-occupied Poland on October 15, 1941. See Tec, *When Light Pierced the Darkness*, 22–24. See also Lucy S. Dawidowicz, ed., *A Holocaust Reader* (West Orange, N.J.: Behrman House, Inc., 1976), 67.

7. For an illustration of what life was like for the Jews in the forbidden Christian world, see Nechama Tec, *Dry Tears: The Story of a Lost Childhood* (New York: Oxford University Press, 1982).

8. Symon Rudnicki, *Ruwni ale nie zupelnie* (Equal but not quite) (Warsaw: Biblioteka Midrasha, 2008), see specifically 153–156.

9. Ibid., 124.

10. Nechama Tec, *Resilience and Courage* (New Haven: Yale University Press, 2003), 206–207.

11. Israel Gutman and Shmuel Krakowski, *Unequal Victims: Poles and Jews during World War II* (New York: Holocaust Library, 1986), 29.

12. Ian Kershaw, *Hitler: 1936-1946 Nemesis* (New York: Norton & Co., 2000), 245.

13. Tec, *Resilience and Courage*, 21.

14. For a historical overview of initial Jewish destruction in the freshly conquered Eastern territories, see Hilberg, *Destruction of the European Jews*, 191–219. Martin Gilbert, in *The Holocaust* (New York: Holt, Rinehart and Winston, 1985), 154–212, concentrates on Eastern Europe in 1941; he includes descriptions of Jewish reactions to these initial assaults.

15. Ibid., 244.

16. Ibid., 244, 245.

17. Tec, *Resilience and Courage*, 21.

18. Ibid., 22.

19. Ibid.

20. Tec, *Dry Tears*, 154, 155.

21. Unless otherwise specified, when I describe or quote, it is based on the personal interview I conducted with Bleichman in 1996 in New York.

22. On how the Soviet government responded to this situation, see Tec, *Resilience and Courage*, 272–273.

23. Ibid., 282–283.

24. Jan Karski, *Story of a Secret State* (Boston: Houghton Mifflin, 1944), 233–237.

Chapter Two

1. Artur Eisenbach, "Wstep," in Emanuel Ringelblum, *Kronika Getta Warszawskiego* (Chronicle of the Warsaw Ghetto) (Warsaw: Czytelnik, 1983), 5–27. Nechama Tec, "Unheralded Historian Emanuel Ringelblum," *Yalkut Moreshet* 75 (April 2003): 32–37.

2. Eisenbach was married to Ringelblum's sister.

3. This is my translation from the Polish of Artur Eisenbach's essay: "Wstep," in Ringelblum, *Kronika*.

4. Ringelblum, *Kronika*, 11–12.

5. David Engel, "Writing History as a National Mission: The Jews of Poland and Their Historiographical Traditions," in *Emanuel Ringelblum, the Man and the Historian*, ed. Israel Gutman (Jerusalem: Yad Vashem, 2010), 119–120; Barbara Engelking, "Moral Issues in Emanuel Ringelblum's Writings from World War II," in ibid., 227.

6. Recent publication deserves closer reading in Gutman, ed., *Emanuel Ringelblum, the Man and the Historian*.

7. J. Noakes and G. Pridham, eds., *Nazism, 1919-1945*, Vol . 3, *Foreign Policy, War and Racial Extermination* (Exeter, Devon: University of Exeter, 1988), 1050–1053 (quote on 1052).

8. Trunk, *Judenrat*, xxv-xxxv.

9. Ibid.

10. Ibid. Except for a few clerical positions, women are conspicuously absent from most Judenrat positions.

11. Ibid. 20–21.

12. Jean Amery, *At the Mind's Limits: Contemplations by a Survivor on Auschwitz and its Realities* (Bloomington: Indiana University Press, 1980), 21–40; Terrence Des Pres, *The Survivor* (New York: Oxford University Press, 1976), 53–71.

13. Personal communication, Israel Gutman.

14. This is my free translation of Ringelblum, *Kronika*, 67.

15. Ringelblum, *Polish-Jewish Relations*, 42.

16. Jacques Adler, *The Jews of Paris and the Final Solution* (New York: Oxford University Press, 1987), 5–9; Calel Perechodnik, *Am I a Murderer* (Boulder, Colo.: Westview, 1996), 8.

17. Raul Hilberg, Stanisław Staron, and Josef Kermisz, eds., *The Warsaw Diary of Adam Czerniakow* (New York: Stein and Day, 1982), 200–220.

18. See Hilberg, *Destruction of European Jews*, 166–168, 174.

19. Chaim Kaplan was particularly critical of the Judenrat, see *Scroll of Agony*, trans. and ed. Abraham I. Katsh (New York: Collier, 1973), 337–339. See also Philip Friedman, "Social Conflicts in the Ghettos," in *Roads to Extinction*, 145–150; Israel Gutman, *Jews of Warsaw* (Bloomington: Indiana University Press,

1982), 78; Hersh Smolar, *The Minsk Ghetto* (New York: Holocaust Library, 1989), 53.

20. Friedman, "Social Conflicts in the Ghettos," 150.

21. Ibid. 144–145. See also Alan Adelson and Robert Lapides, eds., *Łódź Ghetto: Inside a Community under Siege* (New York: Viking, 1989), 175; Lucjan Dobroszycki, ed., The Chronicle of the *Łódź* Ghetto: 1941–1944 (New Haven: Yale University Press, 1984), 93.

22. Yitskhok Rudashevski, *The Diary of the Vilna Ghetto* (Israel: Ghetto Fighters' House, 1973), 67, 31, 32, 33. For more information, see the more recent publication of material from Rudashevski's diary in Laurel Holliday, ed., *Children in the Holocaust and World War II* (New York: Washington Square Press, 1995), 137–183.

23. Sara Zyskind, *Stolen Years* (Minneapolis: Lerner Publications Co., 1981), 42–44.

24. Tec, *When Light Pierced the Darkness*, 52–69.

25. Marc Dworecki, "The Day to Day Stand of the Jews," in *The Catastrophe of European Jews*, ed. Yisrael Gutman and Livia Rothkirchen (Jerusalem: Yad Vashem, 1976), 367–399.

26. Charles G. Roland, *Courage under Siege* (New York: Oxford University Press, 1992); Dawid Sierakowiak, *The Day of Dawid Sierakowiak: Five Notebooks from the Lodz Ghetto* (New York: Oxford University Press, 1996). These are examples of books that discuss starvation and hunger in ghettos. They can be further multiplied.

27. Adina Blady Szwajger, *I Remember Nothing More* (New York: Simon & Schuster, 1990).

28. Rudaszevski, *Diary of the Vilna Ghetto*, 65.

29. Tec, *Resilience and Courage*, 39–40.

30. Hilberg, *Destruction of the European Jews*, 174.

31. Lucy Dawidowicz coined the phrase with publication of her book *The War against the Jews* (New York: Holt, Rinehart, Winston, 1975).

32. See Tec, *Resilience and Courage*, 163–166.

33. Dobka Freund-Waldhorn, personal interviews, Kvar Shmariahu, Israel, 1995, 1996.

34. Ringelblum, *Kronika*, 347.

35. Ibid.

36. See "Historical Perspective: Tracing the History of the Hidden Child Experience" in Jane Marks, *The Hidden Children* (New York: Ballantine, 1993), 273–291.

37. According to an additional source, the Germans received 2,613 calories per day, the Poles 669 calories, and the Jews 184 (Gutman, *Resistance*, 86).

38. For descriptions of welfare activities in the Warsaw ghetto, see Gutman, *Resistance*, 62–70.

39. Slapakowa had to interrupt her research because she was deported to Treblinka, where she was gassed. See Ringelblum, *Kronika*, 473–474.

40. Yad Vashem, JM/25/5. My translation from Polish.

41. Ringelblum, *Kronika*, 462–463.
42. Ibid.
43. Ibid., 393.
44. Ibid.
45. Ibid., 395.
46. Ibid., 402.
47. Ibid., 507.
48. Gutman, *Resistance*, 47.
49. Ringelblum, *Kronika*, 470.
50. Yisrael Gutman, "Adam Czerniakow—The Man & Destiny," in *The Catastrophe of European Jewry*, ed. Y. Gutman and L. Rothkirehen (Jerusalem: Yad Vashem, 1976), 451–489; Raul Hilberg, Stanislaw Stram and Josef Kermicz, *The Warsaw Diary of Adam Czerniakow* (New York: Stein & Day, 1982).
51. Ringelblum, *Kronika*, 447–448.
52. Ibid., 451.
53. Ibid., 452.
54. Ibid., 453.
55. Ibid., 431.
56. Ibid., 409. This comment seems surprisingly cold, surprisingly unfair.
57. Ibid., 409.
58. Ibid., 23.
59. Ibid. Contrary to the previously established pattern, during the big deportations all documents showing working affiliation with shops failed to protect the Jews who had them.
60. Ibid. Remba was deeply touched by the fate of Korczak and his orphanage, which he described in Ringelblum, *Kronika*, 603–607.
61. Ibid., 404.
62. Introduction to *Kronika*, by Anthony Eisenbach, 18.
63. Ringelblum, *Kronika*, 421.
64. Gutman, ed., *Emanuel Ringelblum, the Man and the Historian*, 34. Ringelblum is emphasizing in his comment that the Jewish underground, the Jewish Military Union (ZZW), was a group which politically was more to the right than Ringelblum's group (ZOB).
65. Zuckerman, *Surplus of Memory*, 273–274.
66. Ibid., 202–203.
67. Ibid. Most references to Lejkin's assassination assume that his killer was not identified. I. Gutman suggests that the Jewish underground, ZOB, ordered Lejkin's killing. See Gutman, *Resistance*, 169.
68. Youths cooperated greatly and successfully (ibid., 126–130).
69. Tec, *When Light Pierced the Darkness*, 22. Also Nechama Tec, "Life in the Ghetto," in *Resilience and Courage*, 338–339. This is an example of how one Jewish woman was murdered because she failed to follow this law. The Holocaust literature is filled with such sad examples.
70. The Jews did not prepare for withdrawal (ibid., 199).

71. The young relied too much on the view of the older generation. For an enlightening discussion of these issues, see Ringelblum, *Kronika*, 500–503.

72. Gutman, *Resistance*, 195.

73. Ringelblum, *Kronika*, 441.

74. Gutman, *Resistance*, 152–153.

75. Ibid., 199.

76. Zuckerman, *Surplus of Memory*, 287.

77. Gutman, *Resistance*, 183. Gutman refers to "Zuckerman as saying that the revolt in January made possible the ghetto uprising in April."

78. Zuckerman, *Surplus of Memory*, 349–350.

79. Gutman, *Resistance*, 204.

80. Zuckerman, *Surplus of Memory*, 310.

81. Ibid., 204.

82. Joseph Kermish in Ringelblum, *Polish-Jewish Relations*, 302.

83. Ibid., 304–305.

84. Zuckerman, *Surplus of Memory*, 357.

85. Ibid., 196–197.

86. General Stroop was imprisoned with an AK officer Kazimierz Moczarski, who was eventually released from prison. In contrast, General Stroop was convicted and hanged on March 6, 1952, for the crimes committed against the ghetto and its inhabitants. For more information, see *The Stroop Report: The Jewish Quarter of Warsaw is no more!* (New York: Random House, 1979). See also Kazimierz Moczarski, *Rozmowy Zkatem* (Warsaw: Panstwowy Instytut Wydawniczy, 1978). Moczarski collected the material from Stroop while the two shared the prison cell in Warsaw.

87. *The Stroop Report* (New York: Pantheon Books, 1979), Warsaw, May 24, 1943, Report.

88. Zukerman, *A Surplus of Memory*, 236.

89. These distinctions were clearly presented by Barbara Engelking and I found them both useful and interesting. See Engelking, "Moral Issues in Emanuel Ringelblum's Writings from WWII," 207–227, in *Emanuel Ringelblum, the Man and the Historian*.

90. Israel Gutman, "Emanuel Ringelblum, the Chronicler of the Warsaw Ghetto," *Polin: A Journal of Polish-Jewish Studies* 3 (1988): 7.

91. Tec, "Unheralded Historian Emanuel Ringelblum," 41–42. See another article, "A Glimmer of Light—Reflections on the Past Challenges for the Future," in *The Holocaust and the Christian World: Reflections on the Past Challenges for the Future*, ed. Carol Rittner, Stephen D. Smith, and Irene Steingeldt (London: Kuperard, 2000), 151–154.

Chapter Three

1. Obedience to rules does not fit well into the lives of guerrilla fighters. In contrast to regular soldiers, partisans are freer and more independent. And since they only very reluctantly bow to authority, they are much harder to control

than regular army men. Because partisans are usually well acquainted with the surroundings, they also have much greater freedom of movement than regular soldiers. In part greater mobility and familiarity with the environment counteract the disadvantages that stem from small size and inadequate military equipment. By definition, guerrilla fighters are not as big or as well equipped as a conventional army that they oppose. See John A. Armstrong and Kurt DeWitt, "Organization and Control of the Partisan Movement," in *Soviet Partisans in World War II*, ed. John A. Armstrong (Madison: University of Wisconsin Press, 1964), 73–139, at 73; Henri Michael, "Jewish Resistance and the European Resistance Movement," in *Jewish Resistance during the Holocaust*, Proceedings of the Conference on Manifestations of Jewish Resistance (Jerusalem: Yad Vashem, 1972), 365–375.

2. Violence also becomes a part of the guerrilla fighter's life. Use of violence is often backed up by moral rationalizations. See J. K. Zawodny, "Guerrilla and Sabotage: Organization, Operations, Motivations, Escalation," *The Annals of the American Academy of Political and Social Science* 341 (May 1962): 8–18.

3. Nicholas P. Vakar, *Belorussia: The Making of a Nation* (Cambridge, Mass.: Harvard University Press, 1956), 174–175.

4. For a few examples, see Reuben Ainsztein, *Jewish Resistance in Nazi-Occupied Eastern Europe* (New York: Barnes & Noble, 1974), 307–308; Krakowski, *The War of the Doomed*, 28–58; Levin, *Fighting Back*, 206–227.

5. Zvi Shefet, personal interview, Tel Aviv, 1995.

6. Ibid. Unless otherwise specified, discussions about the fate of the Shefet family are based on this interview.

7. Hitler's attitudes toward the Poles were extremely negative. He insisted that "the Polish Intelligentsia were to be deprived of any chance to develop into a ruling class." See Kershaw, *Hitler, 1936-1945: Nemesis*, 245. Saul Friedlander emphasizes how orderly and determined Hitler was in promoting the murder of the Polish intelligentsia. See Friedlander, *Years of Extermination*, 13–14.

8. Nechama Tec, *In the Lion's Den: The Life of Oswald Rufeisen* (New York: Oxford University Press, 1990).

9. "Working for the Authorities," ibid., 92–105.

10. Zvi Shefet interview.

11. The first anti-Jewish Aktion took place on July 17th. It was known as "Bloody Thursday." For a description, see Alpert Nachman, *The Destruction of the Slonim Jewry* (New York: Holocaust Library, 1989), 45–49.

12. Michael Temchin, M.D., *Memoirs of a Partisan* (New York: Holocaust Library, 1983) emphasizes how this shortage of physicians gave him certain advantages. Leon Berk, *Destined to Live: Memoirs of a Doctor with the Russian Partisans* (Melbourne: Paragon, 1992) shows that his medical degree did not necessarily result in an acceptance into a partisan unit (97). This issue will come up again.

13. For a discussion of issues related to the fate of Jewish women in the forest, see Nechama Tec, *Defiance: The Bielski Partisans* (New York: Oxford University Press, 1993), 154–169.

14. For a broader discussion of Jewish women and resistance, see Tec, *Resilience and Courage*, 256–339.

15. I would like to thank Zvi Shefet for sending me a tape in Hebrew of Judith Graf's testimony, Yad Vashem No. 2978, group 220.

16. These ideas were emphasized by Zvi Shefet during my interview with him in Tel Aviv in 1995.

17. Becoming a mistress of a commander has not necessarily protected women from suffering. In Soviet partisan units, the birth of newborn babies led to their "mysterious" disappearances. One such case is touchingly described by Berk, *Destined to Live* 163–164; another case was a baby girl born to the Chief of Staff Prognagin and his mistress Irka. They took away the child from her and she was never able to find it. This mother is currently a professor in the United States. I heard about this case from Mina Volkowisky, who met her with the newborn baby in her arms in the forest when she was visiting Sikorski's Brigade.

18. General Sikorski employed Michael Pertzof as his translator and interpreter. I interviewed Michael Pertzof in Israel in 1995. Pertzof concurs that Sikorski was always drunk. Once he was called by this general in the middle of the night. As usual the general was drunk. The German soldier who was there was on the verge of death. He uttered no words. Michael explained: "The General demanded that I should first talk to the German and then shoot him. It was terrible. He was dead.... yet I had to shoot him ... but after that I could not eat, I could not sleep so, if I were to write about something like this? Would anybody believe me?"

19. Tadeusz Pankiewicz wrote a memoir, *The Pharmacy in the Cracow Ghetto* (New York: Holocaust Library, 1987).

20. On February 10, 1983, Yad Vashem had recognized Tadeusz Pankiewicz as the Righteous among the Nations. See Tadeusz Pankiewicz, *The Encyclopedia of the Righteous among the Nations: Rescuers of Jews during the Holocaust, Poland* (Jerusalem: Yad Vashem, 2004), 2:579.

21. About expressions of hopes, struggles, and cooperative efforts in the Krakow ghetto and beyond, see *Every Day Lasts a Year*, ed. Christopher R. Browning, Richard S. Hollander, and Nechama Tec (Cambridge: Cambridge University Press, 2007).

22. Julian Alexandrowicz, *Kartki z Dziennika doktora Twardego* (pages from Dr. Hard) (Krakow: Wydawnictwo Literackie, 2001), 29.

23. Ibid., 29–30.

24. Ibid., 40.

25. Ibid., 47.

26. Ibid., 61.

27. Ibid., 62.

28. Davies, *Rising '44*.

29. Alexandrowicz, *Kartki z Dziennika doktora Twardego*, 78.

30. Ibid., 74.

31. Hersh Smolar, personal interview, Tel Aviv, 1989. Both these allegations are discussed in Tec, *Defiance*, 155.

32. Smolar, *Minsk Ghetto*. This book indeed proved very valuable.

33. Nechama Tec, Hersh Smolar, personal interview, Tel Aviv, 1989.

34. Nechama Tec, *Defiance: The Bielski Partisans*, Oxford University Press, 1993.

35. Tec, *Defiance*, 115.

36. Personal interview, 1990.

37. Nechama Tec, Hersh Smolar, personal interview, Tel Aviv, 1990.

38. Ibid.

39. Yisrael Gutman and Shmuel Krakowski, *Unequal Victims* (New York: Holocaust Library, 1986), 123–124. For further evidence of these issues, see Tadeusz Bor-Komorowski, *The Secret Army* (London: Victor Gollacz, 1951).

40. Personal interview, Smolar, 1990.

41. Ingel Scholl, *The White Rose: Munich 1942-1943* (Middletown, Conn.: Wesleyan University Press, 1970), 4.

42. Personal interview, Smolar, 1990.

43. Tec, *Defiance*, 111.

44. Rachel Margolis, *Wspomnienia Wilenskie* (Memories of Vilna) (Warsaw: Zydowski Instytut Historyczny (Jewish Historical Institute), 2005).

45. Ibid., 138–139.

46. Ibid., 140–143.

47. *Sefer Hapartisanim Hajehudim* (*The Jewish Partisan Book*) (Merchavia: Sifriath Poalim, Hashomer Hatzair, 1958), 1:337, 346.

48. Leonard Tushuet, "The Little Doctor, A Resistance Hero," in *They Fought Back*, ed. Suhl, 257.

49. Samuel Bornstein, "Dr. Yehezkel Atlas, Partisan Commander," in *Anthology of Holocaust Literature*, ed. Jacob Glatstein et al. (New York: Atheneum, 1982), 300.

50. Gilbert, *The Holocaust*, 385.

51. Ibid., 259.

52. Personal interview, Smolar, Tel Aviv, Israel, 1989.

53. Ibid.

Chapter Four

1. Personal interview, Bela Chazan Yaari, 1995.

2. Israel Gutman, "Auschwitz: an Overview," in *Anatomy of the Auschwitz Death Camp*, ed. I. Gutman and M. Berenbaum (Bloomington: Indiana University Press, 1994), 16–19.

3. Hermann Langbein, "The Auschwitz Underground," in *Anatomy of the Auschwitz Death Camp*, ed. Gutman and Berenbaum, 485.

4. Hermann Langbein, *Against All Hope* (New York: Paragon House, 1994), 392. For a theoretical discussion of these issues, see Tec, *Defiance*, 204–209.

5. Ibid., 392.

6. Danuta Czech, *Auschwitz Chronicle 1939-1945* (New York: Henry Holt & Company, 1989), 29.

7. Pilecki felt that the very existence of ZWZ and AK (Home Army) would lift the spirits of the Polish prisoners; Jozef Garlinski, *Fighting Auschwitz* (New York: W. W. Norton, 1975), 54 and 60.

8. Henryk Swiebocki, *The Resistance Movement*, Vol. 2, *Auschwitz, 1940-1945*, ed. Waclaw Dlugoborski and Franciszek Piper (Oswiecim: Auschwitz-Birkenau State Museum, 2000), 104.

9. For descriptions of the varied Polish underground groups, see Garlinski, *Fighting Auschwitz*, 60–105 and Swiebocki, *The Resistance Movement*, 65–106.

10. Hermann Langbein, *Die Starkeren* (The strong ones) (Frankfurt: Bund Verlag, 1982), 214–215.

11. Ibid., 122. Tec, *Resilience and Courage*, 174–175.

12. Swiebocki, *The Resistance Movement*, 129–133.

13. Ibid., 130–131.

14. Ibid., 133–134.

15. Garlinski, *Fighting Auschwitz*, 223–230.

16. Ibid., 231.

17. Ibid., 348–349.

18. Yehuda Laufer, "A Yeshiva Bocher Turned Resistance Fighter," in *The Union Kommando in Auschwitz*, trans. and ed. Lore Shelley (Lanham, Md.: University Press of America, Inc., 1996), 177–183.

19. Israel Gutman, "A Warschauer of the Ciechanow Group," in ibid., 144–160.

20. "Preface," in ibid., p. xiv.

21. Gutman, "A Warschauer of the Ciechanow Group," 153–154.

22. Laufer, "A Yeshiva Bocher Turned Resistance Fighter," 182.

23. Ibid.

24. Ibid., 181.

25. Noah Zabludowicz, "A Comrade of the Hashomer Hatzair Talks about Roza Robota," in *The Union Kommando in Auschwitz*, trans. and ed. Shelley, 293–294.

26. Filip Müller, *Eyewitness Auschwitz* (Chicago: Ivan R. Dee, 1979), 152–153.

27. Garlinski, *Fighting Auschwitz*, 288–290.

28. Ibid., 311, 337.

29. Zabludowicz, "A Comrade of the Hashomer Hatzair," 295.

30. Müller, *Eyewitness Auschwitz*, 153–155.

31. Czech, *Auschwitz Chronicle 1939-1945*, 725.

32. Ibid., 726.

33. Raya Kagan, "The Investigation as Seen by an Inmate of the Political Section," in *The Union Kommando in Auschwitz*, trans. and ed. Shelley, 286–290; Swiebocki, *The Resistance Movement*, 120–121 and 249.

34. Zabludowicz, "A Comrade of the Hashomer Hatzair," 294–295.

35. Langbein, "The Auschwitz Underground," 500–501.

36. Krzysztof Dunin-Wasowicz, *Resistance in the Nazi Concentration Camps 1933 1945* (Warsaw: Polish Scientific Publishers, 1982), 236.

37. Gutman, "A Warschauer of the Ciechanow Group," 156.

38. Langbein, "The Auschwitz Underground," 500–501.

39. Raya Kagan as an employee of the political section had access to the reaction of the Berlin authorities ("The Investigation as Seen by an Inmate of the Political Section," 286–290).

40. Ibid., 288.

41. Ada Halperin, nee Neufeld, "I was Hoarse the Day I Auditioned to Sing for the Birkenau Orchestra," in *The Union Kommando in Auschwitz*, trans. and ed. Shelley, 77–80.

42. Gutman, "A Warschauer of the Ciechanow Group," 157–158.

43. Zabludowicz, "A Comrade of the Hashomer Hatzair," 295.

44. Herta Fuchs, nee Ligeti, "Camp Love with a Capital L," in *The Union Kommando in Auschwitz*, trans. and ed. Shelley, 71–76.

45. Kagan, "The Investigation as Seen by an Inmate of the Political Section," 288–289.

46. Gutman, "A Warschauer of the Ciechanow Group," 158.

47. Personal interview with Helen Spitzer-Tichauer, known as Zippi, 1994.

48. Czech, *Auschwitz Chronicle 1939-1945*, 775.

49. The literature includes a great variety of these executions. I tried to include the least obtrusive one.

50. Summaries of Kielar's last stages of his slave-like existence under the German occupation are described in the last forty pages of his memoirs; Wieslaw Kielar, *Anus Mundi* (New York: New York Times Book Co., Inc.,1972), 260–300.

51. Gutman, "A Warschauer of the Ciechanow Group," 156.

52. Ibid., 156–157. Right after the end of the war, a moving testimony was offered by the woman, Birkenau prisoner Mania Kampel, about the uprising in the Sonderkommando in Betti Ajzensztajn, *Ruch Podziemny W Ghettach I Obozach* (Underground movements in ghettos and camps) (Warszawa: Centralna Żydowska Komisja Historyczna w Polsce, 1946), 197–200.

53. See Alexander Donat, ed., *The Death Camp Treblinka: A Documentary* (New York: Holocaust Library, 1979) and Zabecki Franciszek, *Wspomnienia Dawne I Nowe* (Warsaw: Instytut Wydawniczy Pax, 1977).

54. Richard Glazar, personal interview, Switzerland, Basel, 1995. See also Glazar's *A Trap with a Green Fence* (Evanston, Ill.: Northwestern University Press, 1995), 36. The quotes in the text come from this interview and Gitta Sereny, *Into the Darkness from Mercy Killing to Mass Murder* (New York: McGraw Hill Co., 1974).

55. Tec, *Resilience and Courage*, 189.

56. Ibid., 190.

57. Ibid., 191.

58. See Gutman and Krakowski, *Unequal Victims*, 106. These authors mention that "serious armed resistance organizations were set up in the five major ghettos: in Warsaw, Wilno, Bialystok, Cracow and Czestochowa; as well as in forty five other ghettos." While this book mentions many ghettos in which resistance took place, other sources increase the number of ghettos and concentration camps in which organized Jewish resistance happened.

59. Glazar, *Trap with a Green Fence*, 100–101.
60. Ibid., 147.
61. Ibid., 148.
62. Richard Glazar, personal interview, and Glazar, *Trap with a Green Fence*.
63. Thomas Toivi Blatt, *Ashes of Sobibor: A Story of Survival* (Evanston, Ill.: Northwestern University Press, 1999). See also Thomas Toivi Blatt, *Sobibor, the Forgotten Revolt* (Bern: H.E.P. Verlag, 1998); Jules Schelvis, *Sobibor: A History of a Nazi Death Camp* (London: Berg Publishers, 2007); and Richard Rashke, *Escape from Sobibor* (Boston: Houghton Mifflin Company, 1982).
64. Ibid., 235.
65. Ibid., 236.
66. Ibid., 235–242. Frenzel failed to throw any additional light on this initial statement, claiming to be fair in the performance of his concentration camp duties.
67. The name Pieczorski appears with different spelling in various sources.
68. Ajzensztajn, *Ruch Podziemny W Ghettach I Obozach* (Meterialy I Dokumenty), 187.
69. Adam Rutkowski, "Resistance at the Death Camp of Sobibor," *Bulletin of the Jewish Historical Commission* 65-66 (1968): 42.

Chapter Five

1. Ringelblum, *Kronika*, 337–378.
2. Thea Epstein, personal interview, Tel Aviv, 1995.
3. Claire Sokolowski, personal interview, Paris, 1995.
4. Ian Kershaw, *Hitler: A Biography* (New York: W. W. Norton, 2010).
5. Adam Ronikier, *Pamietnik, 1939-1945, Memoirs* (Krakow: Wydawnictwo Literackie, 2001), 40.
6. Among those who talked to me about exposure to these warnings was Jan Karski, *Story of a Secret State*; Albin Kazimierz, *Warrant of Arrest* (Oswiecim: Auschwitz-Birkenau State Museum, 2003), who had the same experience as practically all the other Polish officers who spoke to me about their homecomings.
7. Dawidowicz, *A Holocaust Reader*, 67; Tec, *When Light Pierced the Darkness*, 52–69.
8. For illustration of these circumstances, see the following few examples: Gutman, *The Jews of Warsaw*; Roland, *Courage under Siege*; Sierakowiak, *The Diary of Dawid Sierakowiak*.
9. Karski, *Story of a Secret State*, 281.
10. Leah Silverstein gave me a Polish copy of this essay; it was also translated into Hebrew in its entirety, published in *Yalkut Moreshet* 50 (1991). This is my free translation from the Polish.
11. Leah Silverstein, U.S. Holocaust Memorial Museum Archive or Leah Silverstein, personal interview, see previous note.
12. The story about obtaining a gun is based on the book by Leah Silverstein, written in Polish under her name, Leokadia Silverstein, *Tak Wlasnie Bylo* (This is how it was) (Warsaw: Jewish Historical Institute, 2002). Based on the chapter by the title of "Parabellum," 83–104.

13. Personal interview, Washington, D.C., 1996.
14. Hela Schupper-Rufeisen, *Pozegnanie Milej 18* (Goodbye to Mila 18) (Krakow, 1996), 109–113.
15. Ibid., 113.
16. Kazik (Simha Rotem) describes and attempts with some successes and some failures to bring out members of ZOB through the sewers. See Appendix: Kazik, *Memoirs of a Warsaw Ghetto Fighter* (New Haven: Yale University Press, 1994), 155–169.
17. Abraham Shulman, *The Case of Hotel Polski* (New York: Holocaust Library, 1982), 42.
18. Ibid., 43.
19. Ibid., 158.
20. I interviewed Hela Schupper-Refeisen in Israel 1989.
21. Yizhak Arad, *Ghetto in Flames: The Struggle and Destruction of the Jews in Vilna in the Holocaust* (New York: Holocaust Library, 1982), 456.
22. Chaika Grossman, *The Underground Army: Fighters of the Bialystok Ghetto* (New York: Holocaust Library, 1987).

Chapter Six

1. Kershaw, *Hitler:1936 1946 Nemesis*, 245.
2. Ibid., 241.
3. Ibid., 247.
4. Norman Davies, *God's Playground: A History of Poland*, Vol. 2, *1795 to the Present* (New York: Columbia University Press, 1984), 452. For a more detailed description of the Katyn massacre, see J. K. Zawodny, *Death in the Forest: The Story of the Katyn Massacre* (New York: Hippocrene Books, 1962), 235.
5. Karski, *Story of a Secret State*, 329.
6. E. Thomas Wood and Stanislaw M. Jankowski, *Karski: How One Man Tried to Stop the Holocaust* (New York: John Wiley & Sons, Inc., 1994), 64.
7. Ibid., 129.
8. Ibid., 234.
9. Ibid., 134.
10. Ibid., 131.
11. David Engel, *In the Shadow of Auschwitz: The Polish Government in Exile and The Jews, 1939 1942* (Chapel Hill: University of North Carolina Press, 1987), 203.
12. Gutman and Krakowski, *Unequal Victims*, 154–155.
13. Ibid., 160.
14. Nechama Tec, personal communication, Israel Gutman, 2009.
15. Ibid., 9–10.
16. Ibid., 326.
17. Ibid., 128–130.
18. Ibid., 127.
19. Ibid., 333.
20. Ibid., 333.

21. Ibid., 334.
22. Jan Karski, personal communication, 1999.
23. Ibid., 7–8.
24. Ibid., 8.
25. Ibid., 283.
26. Ibid., 266.
27. Ibid., 334.
28. Ibid., 9.
29. Jan Karski, personal communication, 1999.
30. Jan Karski, personal communication, 1999.
31. Ibid., 9.
32. Ibid., 334.
33. Tec, *A Glimmer of Light*.

Conclusion

1. Tec, *Resilience and Courage*, 203–204.
2. Ibid., 79–80.
3. Ibid., 151–152.
4. Ibid., 152–153.
5. Szwajger, *I Remember Nothing More*.

Works Cited

Abramsky, Chimen, Maciej Jachimczyk, and Antony Polonsky, eds. *The Jews in Poland*. New York: Blackwell, 1986.

Adelson, Alan, and Robert Lapides, eds. *Łódź Ghetto: Inside a Community under Siege*. New York: Viking, 1989.

Adler, H. G. *Theresienstadt, 1941–1945*. Tübingen: Mohr, 1960.

Adler, Jacques. *The Jews of Paris and the Final Solution: Communal Response and Internal Conflicts, 1940–1944*. New York: Oxford University Press, 1987.

Adler, Stanisław. *In the Warsaw Ghetto, 1940–1943: An Account of a Witness*. Jerusalem: Yad Vashem, 1982.

Ainsztein, Reuben. "The Bandera-Oberlander Case." *Midstream* 6, no. 2 (Spring 1960): 17–25.

———. *Jewish Resistance in Nazi-Occupied Eastern Europe*. New York: Barnes and Noble, 1974.

———. "The Jews of Poland Need Not Have Died." *Midstream* 4, no. 4 (Autumn 1958): 2–4, 101–103.

———. *The Warsaw Ghetto Revolt*. New York: Holocaust Library, 1979.

Ajzensztajn, Betti, ed. *RUCH PODZIEMNY W GETTACH I W OBOZACH* [The underground in ghettos and camps]. Warszawa: Centralna Żydowska Komisja Historyczna w Polsce, 1946.

Akavia, Miriam. *An End to Childhood*. Ilford, Essex: Vallentine Mitchell, 1995.

Alpert, Nachum. *The Destruction of Słonim Jewry: The Story of the Jews of Słonim during the Holocaust*. New York: Holocaust Library, 1989.

Amarant, Shmuel. *Nevo Shel Adam* [The oasis of man]. Tel Aviv: Published privately with the help of Misrad Hahinuch V Tarbut, 1973.

Améry, Jean. *At the Mind's Limits: Contemplations by a Survivor on Auschwitz and Its Realities.* Trans. Sidney Rosenfeld and Stella P. Rosenfeld. Bloomington: Indiana University Press, 1980.

Anderson, M. L., and P. H. Collins, eds. *Race, Class and Gender: An Anthology.* Belmont, Calif.: Wadsworth, 1992.

Anderson, Susan Leigh. *On Mill.* Belmont, Calif.: Wadsworth, 2000.

Anissimov, Myriam. *Primo Levi.* Woodstock, N.Y.: Overlook, 1999.

Apenszlak, Jacob. *The Black Book of Polish Jewry.* New York: American Federation of Polish Jews, 1943.

Arad, Yizhak. *Bełżec, Sobibór, Treblinka: The Operation Reinhard Camps.* Bloomington: Indiana University Press, 1987.

———. *Ghetto in Flames: The Struggle and Destruction of the Jews in Vilna in the Holocaust.* New York: Holocaust Library, 1982.

———. *The Partisan: From the Valley of Death to Mount Zion.* New York: Holocaust Library, 1979.

Arad, Yitzhak, Israel Gutman, and Abraham Margalit, eds. *Documents on the Holocaust: Selected Sources on the Destruction of the Jewry of Germany and Austria, Poland and the Soviet Union.* Jerusalem: Yad Vashem, 1981.

Arad, Yitzhak, Shmuel Krakowski, and Shmuel Spector, eds. *"The Einsatzgruppen Reports: Selections from the Dispatches of the Nazi Death Squads" Campaign Against the Jews, July 1941–January 1943.* New York: Holocaust Library, 1989.

Arditti, Leon. *The Will to Live.* New York: Shengold, 1996.

Arendt, Hannah, *Eichmann in Jerusalem: Reflections on the Banality of Evil.* New York: Viking, 1963.

Arieti, Silvano. *The Parnas.* New York: Basic Books, 1979.

Armstrong, John A., ed. *Soviet Partisans in World War II.* Madison: University of Wisconsin Press, 1964.

Aschkenasy, Nehama. *Eve's Journey.* Philadelphia: University of Pennsylvania Press, 1986.

Ash, Timothy Garton. *The Uses of Adversity.* New York: Random House, 1989.

Aubrac, Lucie. *Outwitting the Gestapo.* Lincoln: University of Nebraska Press, 1993.

Barkai, Meyer, ed. *The Fighting Ghettos.* New York: Lippincott, 1962.

Bar-Oni, Bryna. *The Vapor.* Chicago: Visual Impact, 1976.

Bartoszewski, Władysław. "EGZEKUCJE PUBLICZNE W WARSZAWIE W LATACH, 1943–1945" [Public executions in Warsaw, 1943–1945]. *BIULETYN GŁÓWNEJ KOMISJI BADANIA ZBRODNI NIEMIECKICH W POLSCE 6* (1946): 211–224.

———. *1859 DNI WARSZAWY* [Warsaw's 1859 days]. Kraków: Wydawnictwo Znak, 1974.

———. *STRACENI NA ULICACH MIASTA* [Lost on the streets of the city]. Warszawa: Książka I Wiedza, 1970.

Bartov, Omer. *Hitler's Army: Soldiers, Nazis, and War in the Third Reich.* New York: Oxford University Press, 1991.

Bauer, Yehuda. *A History of the Holocaust.* New York: Franklin Watts, 1982.

———. *The Holocaust in Historical Perspective*. Seattle: University of Washington Press, 1978.

———. *The Jewish Emergence from Powerlessness*. Toronto: University of Toronto Press, 1979.

———. *Jews for Sale?* New Haven: Yale University Press, 1994.

———. *Rethinking the Holocaust*. New Haven: Yale University Press, 2001.

Bauman, Janina. *Winter in the Morning: A Young Girl's Life in the Warsaw Ghetto and Beyond, 1939–1945*. New York: Free Press, 1986.

Bauman, Zygmunt. *Modernity and the Holocaust*. Ithaca, N.Y.: Cornell University Press, 1989.

Baumel, Judith Tydor. *Double Jeopardy: Gender and the Holocaust*. London: Vallentine Mitchell, 1998.

———. "Social Interaction among Jewish Women in Crisis during the Holocaust: A Case Study." *Gender and History* 17, no. 1 (April 1995): 64–84.

Bauminger, Arieh L. *The Fighters of the Cracow Ghetto*. Jerusalem: Keter, 1986.

Bauminger, Roża. *PRZY PIKRYNIE I TROTYLU: OBÓZ PRACY PRZYMUSOWEJ W SKARŻYSKU KAMIENNEJ* [The forced-labor camp Skarżysko-Kamienna]. Kraków: Centralny Komitet Żydow Polskich, 1946.

Beckwith, Francis, ed. *Do the Right Thing: A Philosophical Dialogue on the Moral Issues of Our Time*. Boston: Jones and Bartlett, 1996.

Benisch, Pearl. *To Vanquish the Dragon*. Jerusalem: Feldheim, 1991.

Berenstein, Tatiana, et al., eds. *EXTERMINACJA ŻYDÓW NA ZIEMIACH POLSKICH W OKRESIE OKUPACJI HITLEROWSKIEJ* [Jewish extermination on Polish soil during the Hitlerite occupation]. Warszawa: Żydowski Instytut Historyczny, 1957.

Berg, Mary. *Warsaw Ghetto*. New York: Fischer, 1945.

Berger, Zdena. *Tell Me Another Morning: A Novel*. New York: Harper, 1961.

Berk, Leon. *Destined to Live*. Melbourne: Paragon, 1992.

Berkowitz, Sarah Bick. *Where Are My Brothers? From the Ghetto to the Gas Chamber*. New York: Helios, 1965.

Bierman, John. *Righteous Gentile: The Story of Raoul Wallenberg, Missing Hero of the Holocaust*. New York: Viking, 1981.

Birenbaum, Halina. *Hope Is the Last to Die*. Armonk, N.Y.: Sharpe, 1996.

Bluel, Hans Peter. *Sex and Society in Nazi Germany*. New York: Lippincott, 1973.

Bor-Komorowski, Tadeusz. *The Secret Army*. London: Gollancz, 1951.

Borowski, Tadeusz. *This Way for the Gas, Ladies and Gentlemen*. New York: Penguin, 1976.

Bożykowski, Tuvia. *Between Falling Walls*. Ghetto Fighters' House, Israel: Ghetto Fighters' House, 1972.

Brand, Sandra. *Between Two Worlds*. New York: Shengold, 1982.

———. *I Dared to Live*. New York: Shengold, 1978.

———. *Roma*. New York: Shengold, 1992.

Brenner, Rachel Feldhay. *Four Women Confronting the Holocaust*. University Park: Pennsylvania State University Press, 1997.

Bridenthal, Renate, Anita Grossman, and Marion Kaplan, eds. *When Biology Became Destiny*. New York: Monthly Review Press. 1984.

Browning, Christopher R. *Nazi Policy, Jewish Workers, German Killers*. New York: Cambridge University Press, 2000.

———. *Ordinary Men*. New York: Harper, 1992.

———. *The Path to Genocide*. New York: Cambridge University Press, 1995.

Buber-Neuman, Margarete. *Milena*. New York: Schocken, 1989.

Buchler, Yehoshua. "First in the Vale of Afflictions: Slovakian Jewish Women in Auschwitz, 1942." *Holocaust and Genocide Studies* 10, no. 3 (Winter 1996): 299–325.

Cantor, Aviva. *Jewish Women, Jewish Men: The Legacy of Patriarchy in Jewish Life*. San Francisco: HarperSanFrancisco, 1995.

Cargas, Harry James, ed. *When God and Man Failed: Non-Jewish Views of the Holocaust*. New York: Macmillan, 1981.

Chevrillon, Claire. *Code Name Christiane Clouet*. College Station: Texas A&M University Press, 1995.

Cholawski, Shalom. *Soldiers from the Ghetto*. New York: Herzl, 1980.

CHOROBA GŁODOWA [Starvation illness]. Warsaw: American Joint Distribution Committee, 1946.

Cohen, Elie A. *Human Behavior in the Concentration Camp*. London: Jonathan Cape, 1954.

Czech, Danuta. *Auschwitz Chronicle, 1939–1945*. New York: Henry Holt, 1989.

Dallin, Anthony. *German Rule in Russia, 1941–1945: A Study of Occupation Policies*. New York: Octagon, 1980.

Datner, Szymon. *LAS SPRAWIEDLIWYCH* [The forest of the righteous]. Warszawa: Książka I Wiedza, 1968.

———. *WALKA I ZAGŁADA BIAŁOSTOCKIEGO GETTA* [The struggle and destruction of the Białystok ghetto]. Łódź: Czytelnik, 1946.

David, Janina. *A Square of Sky/A Touch of Earth: A Wartime Childhood in Poland*. New York: Penguin, 1981.

David, Kati. *A Child's War: World War II through the Eyes of Children*. New York: Four Walls, Eight Windows, 1989.

Davies, Norman. *God's Playground: A History of Poland*. 2 vols. New York: Columbia University Press, 1982.

Dawidowicz, Lucy. *The War against the Jews, 1933–1945*. New York: Holt, Rinehart and Winston, 1975.

Dawidowicz, Lucy, ed. *A Holocaust Reader*. New York: Behrman House, 1976.

De Jong, Louis. *The Netherlands and Nazi Germany*. Cambridge, Mass.: Harvard University Press, 1990.

Delbo, Charlotte. *None of Us Will Return*. New York: Grove, 1968.

Des Pres, Terrence. *The Survivor: An Anatomy of Life in the Death Camps*. New York: Oxford University Press, 1976.

Distel, Barbara, ed. *Frauen im Holocaust*. Gerlingen, Germany: Bleicher Verlag, 2001.

Dobroszycki, Lucjan, ed. *The Chronicle of the Łódź Ghetto: 1941–1944.* New Haven: Yale University Press, 1984.

Dobroszycki, Lucjan, and Jeffrey S. Gurock, eds. *The Holocaust in the Soviet Union: Studies and Sources on the Destruction of the Jews in the Nazi-Occupied Territories of the USSR, 1941–1945.* Armonk, N.Y.: Sharpe, 1993.

DOCUMENTY ZBRODNI I MęCZEŃSTWA [Documents of crimes and torture]. Kraków: Żydowska Komisja Historyczna w Krakowie, 1945.

Donat, Alexander. *The Holocaust Kingdom: A Memoir.* New York: Holt, Rinehart and Winston, 1965.

Donat, Alexander, ed. *The Death Camp Treblinka: A Documentary.* New York: Holocaust Library, 1979.

Draenger, Gusta Davidson. *Justyna's Narrative.* Ed. Eli Pfefferkorn and David H. Hirsch. Trans. Roslyn Hirsch and David H. Hirsch. Amherst: University of Massachusetts Press, 1996.

——— *PAMIETNIK JUSTYNY* [Justyna's diary]. Kraków: Wojewódzka Żydowska Komisja Historyczna, 1946.

Druks, Herbert. *The Failure to Rescue.* New York: Speller, 1977.

———. *Jewish Resistance during the Holocaust.* New York: Irvington, 1983.

Dunin-Wąsowicz, Krzysztof. *Resistance in the Nazi Concentration Camps, 1933–1945.* Warsaw: Polish Scientific Publishers, 1982.

Dwork, Debórah. *Children with a Star.* New Haven: Yale University Press, 1991.

Dwork, Debórah, and Robert Jan van Pelt. *Auschwitz: 1270 to the Present.* New York: Norton, 1996.

Eckman, Lester, and Chaim Lazar. *The Jewish Resistance: The History of the Jewish Partisans in Lithuania and White Russia during the Nazi Occupation, 1940–1945.* New York: Shengold, 1977.

Edelman, Alina Margolis. *ALA Z ELEMENTARZA* [Ala's childhood]. London: ANEKS, 1994.

Ehrenburg, Ilya, and Vasily Grossman, eds. *The Black Book: The Ruthless Murder of Jews by German-Fascist Invaders throughout the Temporarily Occupied Regions of the Soviet Union and in the Death Camps of Poland during the War of 1941–1945.* New York: Schocken, 1981.

Eibeshitz, Jehoshua, and Anna Eilenberg-Eibeshitz, eds. *Women in the Holocaust: A Collection of Testimonies.* Vol. 1. New York: Remember, 1991.

Eisenberg, Azriel, ed. *Witness to the Holocaust.* New York: Pilgrim, 1981.

Elias, Ruth. *Triumph of Hope.* New York: Wiley, 1998.

Elkins, Michael. *Forged in Fury.* New York: Ballantine, 1971.

Engel, David. *In The Shadow of Auschwitz: The Polish Government in Exile and the Jews, 1939–1942.* Chapel Hill: University of North Carolina Press, 1987.

Engelking, Barbara. *NA ŁACE POPIOŁÓW: OCALENI Z HOLOCAUSTU* [On the field of ashes: Saved from the Holocaust]. Warsaw: Wydawnictwo Cyklady, 1993.

Engelking, Barbara, and Jacek Leociak. *GETTO WARSZAWSKIE* [Warsaw ghetto]. Warsaw: Wydawnictwo, IFISPAN, 2001.

Erlichman-Bank, Sujka. *LISTY Z PIEKŁA* [Letters from Hell]. Bialystok: Krajowa Agencja Wydawnicza, 1992.

European Resistance Movements, 1939–1945. International Conference on the History of the Resistance Movements. New York: Pergamon, 1960.

Fackenheim, Emil L. *From Bergen-Belsen to Jerusalem: Contemporary Implications of the Holocaust.* Jerusalem: Hebrew University of Jerusalem, 1975.

———. "The Spectrum of Resistance during the Holocaust: An Essay in Description and Definition." *Modern Judaism* 2 (1982): 113–130.

Fein, Helen. *Accounting for Genocide: Victims—and Survivors—of the Holocaust.* New York: Free Press, 1979.

Fenelon, Fania. *Playing for Time.* New York: Berkeley, 1983.

Ferderber-Salz, Berta. *And the Sun Kept Shining.* New York: Holocaust Library, 1980.

Ferencz, Benjamin B. *Less than Slaves: Jewish Forced Labor and the Quest for Compensation.* Cambridge, Mass.: Harvard University Press, 1979.

Fink, Ida. *The Journey.* New York: Farrar, Straus and Giroux, 1992.

———. *A Scrap of Time and Other Stories.* New York: Schocken, 1987.

Flinker, Moshe. *Young Moshe's Diary: The Spiritual Torment of a Jewish Boy in Nazi Europe.* Jerusalem: Yad Vashem, 1965.

Fogelman, Eva. *Conscience and Courage.* New York: Doubleday Anchor, 1994.

Frank, Anne. *The Diary of a Young Girl: The Definitive Edition.* New York: Doubleday, 1995.

Frankl, Viktor. *Man's Search for Meaning.* New York: Simon and Schuster, 1962.

Fraser, Kennedy. *Ornament and Silence.* New York: Knopf, 1996.

French, Marilyn. *The War against Women.* New York: Ballantine, 1992.

Friedl, Ernestine. *Women and Men: An Anthropologist's View.* New York: Holt, Rinehart and Winston, 1975.

Friedländer, Saul. *When Memory Comes.* New York: Farrar, Straus and Giroux, 1979.

Friedman, Filip. "ZAGŁADA ŻYDÓW POLSKICH W LATACH 1930–1945" [Destruction of the Polish Jewry, 1930-1945]. *BIULETYN GŁÓNEJ KOMISJI BADANIA ZBRODNI NIEMIECKICH W POLSCE* 6 (1946): 165–208.

Friedman, Philip. *Roads to Extinction: Essays on the Holocaust.* Ed. Ada J. Friedman. Philadelphia: Jewish Publication Society of America, 1980.

———. *Their Brothers' Keepers.* New York: Crown, 1957.

Fussell, Paul. *Wartime: Understanding and Behavior in the Second World War.* New York: Oxford University Press, 1989.

Geva, Ilana. "The Warsaw Ghetto as a Total Institution." M.A. thesis, Bar Ilan University, 1988.

Gilbert, Martin. *Atlas of the Holocaust.* New York: Macmillan, 1982.

———. *The Holocaust: A History of the Jews of Europe during the Second World War.* New York: Holt, Rinehart and Winston, 1985.

———. *The Second World War: A Complete History.* New York: Henry Holt, 1989.

Glazar, Richard. *Trap with a Green Fence: Survival in Treblinka.* Evanston, Ill.: Northwestern University Press, 1995.

Goldhagen, Daniel J. *Hitler's Willing Executioners.* New York: Knopf, 1996.

Goldstein, Bernard. *The Stars Bear Witness.* New York, Viking, 1949.

Gollwitzer, Helmut, Käthe Kuhn, and Reinhard Schneider. *Dying We Live: The Final Messages and Records of the Resistance.* New York: Pantheon, 1956.

Gottlieb, Roger S. "The Concept of Resistance: Jewish Resistance during the Holocaust." *Social Theory and Social Practice* 9, no. 1 (Spring 1983): 31–49.

Green, Gerald. *The Artists of Terezin.* New York: Schocken, 1978.

Gross, Nathan. "Aryan Papers in Poland." *Extermination and Resistance, Historical Sources and Material* 1 (1958): 79–86.

———. "Unlucky Clara." *Yad Vashem Bulletin* 15 (1964): 55–60.

Grossman, Chaika. *The Underground Army: Fighters of the Białystok Ghetto.* New York: Holocaust Library, 1987.

Gruber, Samuel. *I Choose Life.* New York: Shengold, 1978.

Grynberg, Henyk. *Childhood of Shadows.* London: Vallentine, Mitchell, 1969.

Gurdas, Luba Krugman. *The Death Train.* New York: National Council on Art in Jewish Life, 1978.

Gurewitsch, Brana, ed. *Mothers, Sisters, Resisters.* Tuscaloosa: University of Alabama Press, 1998.

Gutman, Israel. *Fighters among the Ruins: The Story of Jewish Heroism during World War II.* Washington, D.C.: B'nai B'rith Books, 1988.

———. *The Jews of Warsaw, 1939–1945: Ghetto, Underground, Revolt.* Bloomington: Indiana University Press, 1982.

———. *Resistance: The Warsaw Ghetto Uprising.* Boston: Houghton Mifflin, 1994.

Gutman, Israel, ed. *Encyclopedia of the Holocaust.* 4 vols. New York: Macmillan, 1990.

Gutman, Yisrael, and Michael Berenbaum, eds. *Anatomy of the Auschwitz Death Camp.* Bloomington: Indiana University Press, 1994.

Gutman, Yisrael, and Cynthia J. Haft, eds. *Patterns of Jewish Leadership in Nazi Europe, 1933–1945: Proceedings of the Third Yad Vashem International Historical Conference, Jerusalem, April 4–7, 1977.* Jerusalem: Yad Vashem, 1979.

Gutman, Yisrael, and Shmuel Krakowski. *Unequal Victims: Poles and Jews during World War II.* New York: Holocaust Library, 1986.

Gutman, Yisrael, and Livia Rothkirchen, eds. *The Catastrophe of European Jewry.* Jerusalem: Yad Vashem, 1976.

Gutman, Yisrael, and Avital Saf, eds. *The Nazi Concentration Camps: Structure and Aims, the Image of the Prisoner, the Jews in the Camps; Proceedings of the Fourth Yad Vashem International Historical Conference, Jerusalem, January 1980.* Jerusalem: Yad Vashem, 1984.

Gutman, Yisrael, and Efraim Zuroff, eds. *Rescue Attempts during the Holocaust: Proceedings of the Second Yad Vashem International Historical Conference, Jerusalem, April 8–11, 1974.* Jerusalem: Yad Vashem, 1977.

Hallie, Philip P. *Lest Innocent Blood Be Shed: The Story of the Village of Le Chambon and How Goodness Happened There.* New York: Harper and Row, 1979.

Halter, Marek. *La Mémoire inquiete, il y a cinquante ans: Le Ghetto de Varsovie.* Paris: Editions Robert Laffont, 1993.

Hart, Kitty. *I Am Alive.* London: Abelard Schuman, 1961.

Heinemann, Marlene E. *Gender and Destiny: Women Writers and the Holocaust.* Westport, Conn.: Greenwood, 1986.

Heller, Celia S. *On the Edge of Destruction.* Detroit: Wayne State University Press, 1994.

Heller, Fanya Gottesfeld. *Strange and Unexpected Love: A Teenage Girl's Holocaust Memoirs.* Hoboken, N.J.: KTAV, 1993.

Henry, Frances. *Victims and Neighbors: A Small Town in North Germany Remembered.* South Hadley, Mass.: Bergin and Gravey, 1984.

Herbert, Ulrich. *Nationalsozialistische Vernichtungspolitik, 1939–1945.* Frankfurt: Fischer Verlag, 1998.

Herzog, Elizabeth. *Life Is with People.* New York: International Universities Press, 1952.

Heschel, Susannah, ed. *On Being a Jewish Woman: A Reader.* New York: Schocken, 1983.

Heyes, Peter, ed. *Lessons and Legacies: The Meaning of the Holocaust in a Changing World.* Evanston, Ill.: Northwestern University Press, 1991.

Heyman, Eva. *The Diary of Eva Heyman.* Jerusalem: Yad Vashem, 1974.

Hilberg, Raul. *The Destruction of the European Jews.* New York: New Viewpoints, 1973.

———. *Perpetrators Victims Bystanders: The Jewish Catastrophe, 1933–1945.* New York: Harper-Collins, 1992.

———. *The Politics of Memory: The Journey of a Holocaust Historian.* Chicago: Ivan R. Dee, 1996.

Hilberg, Raul, Stanisław Staron, and Josef Kermisz, eds. *The Warsaw Diary of Adam Czerniakow: Prelude to Doom.* New York: Stein and Day, 1982.

Hillesum, Etty. *An Interrupted Life.* New York: Pantheon, 1983.

Hirszfeld, Ludwik. *HISTORIA JEDNEGO ŻYCIA* [A life history]. Warsaw: Pax, 1957.

Hoffman, Alice G. "Reliability and Validity in Oral History." *Today's Speech* 22 (Winter 1974): 23–27.

Iranek-Osmecki, Kazimierz. *He Who Saves One Life.* New York: Crown, 1971.

Jackson, Livia E. Bitton. *Elli: Coming of Age in the Holocaust.* New York: Times Books, 1980.

Jaffe, A. J., and Herbert F. Spirer. *Misused Statistics: Straight Talk or Twisted Numbers.* New York: Dekker, 1987.

Jastrow, Robert. *Until the Sun Dies.* New York: Norton, 1977.

Johnson, Eric A. *Nazi Terror: The Gestapo, Jews and Ordinary Germans.* New York: Basic, 1999.

Kaplan, Alice. *The Collaborator.* Chicago: University of Chicago Press, 2000.

Kaplan, Chaim A. *Scroll of Agony: The Warsaw Diary of Chaim A. Kaplan.* Trans. and ed. Abraham I. Katsh. New York: Collier, 1973.

Kaplan, Marion A. *Between Dignity and Despair.* New York: Oxford University Press, 1998.

———. *The Jewish Feminist Movement in Germany.* Westport, Conn.: Greenwood, 1979.

Karas, Joža. *Music in Terezin, 1941–1945.* New York: Beaufort, 1985.

Karay, Felicja. *Death Comes in Yellow: Skarżysko-Kamienna Slave Labor Camp.* Amsterdam: Harwood, 1996.

Karski, Jan. *The Great Powers and Poland, 1919–1945: From Versailles to Yalta.* New York: University Press of America, 1985.

———. *Story of a Secret State.* Boston: Houghton Mifflin, 1944.

Katz, Esther, and Joan Miriam Ringelheim, eds. *Proceedings of the Conference on Women Surviving the Holocaust.* New York: Institute for Research in History, 1983.

Kautsky, Benedict. *Teufel und Verdamte.* Vienna: Verlag Der Wiener Volksbuchhandlung, 1948.

Kazik. *See* Rotem, Simha.

Kermish, Joseph, ed. *To Live with Honor and Die with Honor: Selected Documents from the Warsaw Ghetto Underground Archives "O.S."* Jerusalem: Yad Vashem, 1986.

Kiedrzyńska, Wanda. *Ravensbrück.* Warszawa: Książka i Wiedza, 1965.

Kiełar, Wiesław. *Anus Mundi.* New York: Times Books, 1972.

Kizelstein, Shamay. "Paths of Fate: Auschwitz-Birkenau No. B-1968." Yad Vashem.

Klein, Gerda Weissman. *All But My Life.* New York: Farrar, Straus and Giroux, 1992.

Klibanski, Bronka. "In the Ghetto and in the Resistance." Paper delivered at the International Workshop on Women in the Holocaust at Hebrew University of Jerusalem, June 1995.

Klukowski, Zygmunt. *DZIENNIK Z LAT OKUPACJI ZAMOJSZCZYZNY. 1939–1944* [Zamość: Diary during the occupation, 1939–1944]. Lublin: Lubelska Spółdzielnia Wydawnicza, 1958.

Kogon, Eugen. *The Theory and Practice of Hell.* New York: Berkeley, 1980.

Kohn, Moshe M., ed. *Jewish Resistance during the Holocaust: Proceedings of the Conference on Manifestations of Jewish Resistance, 1968.* Jerusalem: Yad Vashem, 1971.

Kohn, Nahum, and Howard Roiter. *A Voice from the Forest.* New York: Holocaust Library, 1980.

Koonz, Claudia. *Mothers in the Fatherland: Women, the Family and Nazi Politics.* New York: St. Martin's, 1987.

Korboński, Stefan. *The Polish Underground State: A Guide to the Underground.* Boulder, Colo.: East European Quarterly, 1978.

Korczak, Janusz. *Ghetto Diary.* New York: Holocaust Library, 1978.

Kowalski, Isaac, ed. *Anthology of Armed Resistance to the Nazis, 1939–1945.* 3 vols. New York: Jewish Combatants Publishing House, 1986.

Koweńska, Lea Garber. "Dos vos hot sich fargidenkt oyf aibik" [What is remembered forever]. *Żurnol fun Sovietisher Heimland* [Journal of the Soviet Homeland] 4 (1971): 92–102.

Krakowski, Shmuel. *The War of the Doomed: Jewish Resistance in Poland, 1942–1944*. New York: Holmes and Meier, 1985.

Krall, Hanna. *Shielding the Flame*. New York: Henry Holt, 1986.

Kraus, Otto, and Erich Kulka. *The Death Factory: Documents on Auschwitz*. New York: Pergamon, 1966.

Kremer, S. Lillian. *Women's Holocaust Writing: Memory and Imagination*. Lincoln: University of Nebraska Press, 1999.

Kubar, Zofia S. *Double Identity: A Memoir*. New York: Hill and Wang, 1989.

Küchler-Silberman, Lena. *One Hundred Children*. New York: Doubleday, 1961.

Kuper, Jack. *Child of the Holocaust*. New York: Doubleday, 1968.

Laguardia, Gemma Glück. *My Story*. New York: David McKay, 1961.

Landau, Ludwik. *KRONIKA LAT WOJNY I OKUPACJI* [The chronicle of the war and occupation]. 3 vols. Warszawa: Państwowe Wydawnictwo Naukowe, 1962.

Langbein, Hermann. *Against All Hope: Resistance in Nazi Concentration Camps, 1938–1945*. New York: Paragon House. 1994.

———. *Die Stäkeren: Ein Bericht aus Auschwitz und Anderen Konzentrantionslagern*. Cologne: Bund Verlag, 1982.

Langer, Lawrence L. *Holocaust Testimonies: The Ruins of Memory*. New Haven: Yale University Press, 1991.

———. *Preempting the Holocaust*. New Haven: Yale University Press, 1998.

Langer, Lawrence L., ed. *Art from the Ashes: A Holocaust Anthology*. New York: Oxford University Press, 1995.

Laqueur, Walter, ed. *The Holocaust Encyclopedia*. New Haven: Yale University Press, 2001.

Laska, Vera. *Women in the Resistance and in the Holocaust: The Voices of the Eyewitnesses*. Westport, Conn.: Greenwood. 1983.

Latour, Amy. *The Jewish Resistance in France, 1940–1944*. New York: Holocaust Library, 1981.

Lengyel, Olga. *Five Chimneys: The Story of Auschwitz*. New York: Howard Fertig, 1983.

Lestchinsky, Jacob. "Economic Aspects of Jewish Community Organization in Independent Poland." *Jewish Social Studies* 9, nos. 1–4 (1947): 319–338.

———. "The Industrial and Social Structure of the Jewish Population of Interbellum Poland." *YIVO Annual Social Science* 2 (1956–1957): 243–269.

Levi, Primo. *The Drowned and the Saved*. New York: Summit, 1986.

———. *Survival in Auschwitz*. Trans. Stuart Wolf. New York: Collier, 1965.

Levin, Dov. *Fighting Back: Lithuanian Jewry's Armed Resistance to the Nazis, 1941–1945*. New York: Holmes and Meier, 1985.

Levy-Hass, Hannah. *Inside Belsen*. Totowa, N.J.: Barnes and Noble, 1982.

Lewińska, Pelagia. *Twenty Months at Auschwitz*. New York: Lyle Stuart, 1968.

Lifton, Betty Jean. *The King of Children*. New York: Schocken, 1988.

Lifton, Robert Jay. *The Nazi Doctors*. New York: Basic, 1986.

Lingens-Reiner, Ella. *Prisoners of Fear*. London: Victor Gollancz. 1948.

Lomax, Judy. *Women of the Air*. New York: Dodd, Mead, 1987.

Lubetkin, Civia. *In the Days of Destruction and Revolt*. Ghetto Fighters' House, Israel: Ghetto Fighters' House, 1981.

Lummis, T. "Structure and Validity in Oral Evidence." *International Journal of Oral History* 2, no. 2 (1981): 109–119.

Lusky, Irena. *La Traverse de la nuit*. Geneva: Livre Metropolis, 1988.

Mark, B., *RUCH OPORU W GETCIE BIAŁOSTOCKIM* [The underground movement in the Białystok ghetto]. Warszawa: Żydowski Instytut Historyczny, 1952.

Marks, Jane. *The Hidden Children: The Secret Survivors of the Holocaust*. New York: Ballantine, 1993.

Marrus, Michael, ed. *The Nazi Holocaust*. Vol. 17, *Resistance to the Holocaust*. Westport, Conn.: Meckler, 1989.

Marrus, Michael R., and Paxton, Robert O. *Vichy France and the Jews*. New York: Schocken, 1983.

Martin, Elaine, ed. *Gender Patriarchy and Fascism in the Third Reich*. Detroit: Wayne State University Press, 1993.

Maurel, Micheline. *An Ordinary Camp*. New York: Simon and Schuster, 1958.

Mayer, Arno. *Why Did the Heavens Not Darken?* New York: Pantheon, 1989.

Mead, Margaret. *Male and Female*. New York: Dell, 1949.

Meed, Vladka. "Jewish Resistance in the Warsaw Ghetto." *Dimensions* 7, no. 2 (1993).

——— *On Both Sides of the Wall: Memoirs from the Warsaw Ghetto*. Washington, D.C.: Holocaust Library, 1993.

Mendelsohn, Ezra. *The Jews of East Central Europe between the World Wars*. Bloomington: Indiana University Press, 1983.

Merin, Yehuda, and Jack Nusan Porter. "Three Jewish Family Camps in the Forests of Volyń, Ukraine, during the Holocaust." *Jewish Social Science* 156, no. 1 (1984): 83–92.

Meyer, Peter. *The Jews in the Soviet Satellites*. Syracuse, N.Y.: Syracuse University Press, 1953.

Micheels, Louis J. *Doctor 117641*. New Haven: Yale University Press, 1989.

Michel, Henri. *The Shadow War: European Resistance, 1939–1945*. New York: Harper and Row, 1972.

Michelson, Frida. *I Survived Rumbuli*. New York: Holocaust Library, 1979.

Neumann, Margarete Buber. *Milena: The Story of a Remarkable Friendship*. New York: Schocken, 1989.

Noakes, J., and G. Pridham, eds. *Nazism, 1919–1945*. Vol. 3, *Foreign Policy, War and Racial Extermination*. Exeter, Devon: University of Exeter, 1988.

Nomberg-Przytyk, Sara. *Auschwitz: True Tales from a Grotesque Land*. Chapel Hill: University of North Carolina Press, 1985.

Nyiszli, Miklos. *Auschwitz: A Doctor's Eyewitness Account*. New York: Fawcett, 1960.

Oberski, Jona. *LATA DZIECIŃSTWA* [Childhood]. Warszawa: Książka i Wiedza, 1988.

Ofer, Dalia. "Cohesion and Rupture: The Jewish Family in East European Ghettos during the Holocaust." *Studies in Contemporary Jewry* 14 (1998): 143–165.

Ofer, Dalia, and Lenore J. Weitzman, eds. *Women in the Holocaust*. New Haven: Yale University Press, 1998.

Oliner, Samuel P. *Restless Memories: Recollections of the Holocaust Years*. Berkeley: Judah L. Magnes Museum, 1986.

Ostrowski, Shmuel. "Of War and the Holocaust." Unpublished diary (Yiddish). Yad Vashem, 1970.

Owen, Alison. *Frauen: German Women Recall the Third Reich*. New Brunswick, N.J.: Rutgers University Press, 1994.

Pawełczyńska, Anna. *WARTOŚCI A PRZEMOC, ZARYS SOCJOLOGJCZNEJ PROBLEMATYKI OŚWICIMA* [Values and oppression: Outline of sociological problems in Auschwitz]. Warszawa: Państwowe Wydawnictwo Naukowe, 1973.

Pawłowicz, Sala, and Kevin Klose. *I Will Survive*. New York: Norton, 1962.

Perechodnik, Calel. *Am I a Murderer?* Boulder, Colo.: Westview, 1996.

Perl, Gisella. *I Was a Doctor in Auschwitz*. New York: International Universities Press, 1948.

Peukert, Detlev J. K. *Inside Nazi Germany: Conformity, Opposition, and Racism in Everyday Life*. New Haven: Yale University Press, 1987.

Picker, Henry, and Heinrich Hoffman, eds. *Hitler Close Up*. New York: Macmillan 1969.

Pilecki, Witold. *The Auschwitz Volunteer: Beyond Bravery*. Trasl. Jarek Garlinski. Los Angeles: Aquila Polonica Publishing, 2012.

Pisar, Samuel. *Of Blood and Hope*. Boston: Little, Brown, 1979.

Poliakov, Leon. *The History of Anti-Semitism*. New York: Schocken, 1974.

Polonsky, Antony. *Politics in Independent Poland, 1921–1939*. Oxford: Clarendon, 1972.

Porter, Jack Nusan, ed. *Jewish Partisans: A Documentary of Jewish Resistance in the Soviet Union during World War II*. Vol. 1. New York: University Press of America, 1982.

Poznański, Jakub. *PAMIETNIK Z GETTA ŁÓDZKIEGO* [Łódź ghetto memoir]. Łódź: Wydawnictwo Łódzkie, 1960.

Prawdzic-Szlacki, Janusz. *NOWOGRÓDCZYZNA W WALCE, 1940–1945* [Nowógrad is fighting]. London: Oficyna Poetow I Malarzy, 1976.

Presser, J. *The Destruction of the Dutch Jews*. Trans. Arnold Pomerans. New York: Dutton, 1969.

Rashke, Richard. *Escape from Sobibor: The Heroic Story of the Jews Who Escaped from a Nazi Death Camp*. Boston: Houghton Mifflin, 1982.

Ringelblum, Emanuel. *KRONIKA GETTA WARSZAWSKIEGO* [Chronicle of the Warsaw ghetto]. Warszawa: Czytelnik, 1983.

———. *Notes from the Warsaw Ghetto: The Journal of Emanuel Ringelblum*. New York: Schocken, 1975.

———. *Polish-Jewish Relations during the Second World War*. Ed. Józef Kermisz and Shmuel Krakowski. Jerusalem: Yad Vashem, 1974.

Ringelheim, Joan. "The Holocaust: Taking Women into Account." *Jewish Quarterly* 39, no. 3 (1992): 19–23.

Rittner, Carol, and Sandra Myers, eds. *The Courage to Care: Rescuers of Jews during the Holocaust*. New York: New York University Press, 1986.

Rittner, Carol, and John K. Roth, eds. *Different Voices: Women and the Holocaust*. New York: Paragon House, 1993.

Ritvo, Roger A., and Diane M. Plotkin. *Sisters in Sorrow*. College Station: Texas A&M University Press, 1998.

Rohrlich, Ruby, ed. *Resisting the Holocaust*. New York: Berg, 1998.

Roland, Charles G. *Courage under Siege*. New York: Oxford University Press, 1992.

Rosenberg, Blanca. *To Tell at Last*. Urbana: University of Illinois Press, 1993.

Rotem, Simha (Kazik). *Memoirs of a Warsaw Ghetto Fighter: The Past Within Me*. New Haven: Yale University Press, 1994.

Rowbotham, Sheila. *Woman's Consciousness, Man's World*. London: Pelican, 1973.

Rubenstein, Richard L., and John K. Roth. *Approaches to Auschwitz: The Holocaust and Its Legacy*. Atlanta: John Knox Press, 1987.

Rudashevski, Yitskhok. *The Diary of the Vilna Ghetto, June 1941–April 1943*. Ghetto Fighters' House, Israel: Ghetto Fighters' House, 1973.

Rufeisen, Hela Schüpper. *POŻEGNANIE MIŁEJ 18: WSPOMNIENIA ŁUCZNICZKI ŻYDOWSKIEJ ORGANIZACJI BOJOWEJ* [Goodbye to Mila 18]. Kraków: Wydawnictwo "Beseder" S.C., 1996.

Sakowska, Ruta. *DWA ETAPY* [Two phases]. Warszawa: Wydawnictwo Polskiej Akademii Nauk, 1986.

———. *LUDZIE Z DZIELNICY ZAMKNIETEJ* [People in the closed quarters]. Warszawa: Państwowe Wydawnictwo Naukowe, 1975.

Samuel, Vivette. *Sauves les enfants*. Paris: Liana Levi, 1995.

Schoenfeld, Gabriel. "How Much Holocaust Is Too Much? When Hitler Stole the Pink Rabbit." *Journal of the Jewish Theological Seminary* 9, no. 1 (Fall 1999): 8, 9, 20.

Schulman, Faye. *A Partisan's Memoir: Woman of the Holocaust*. Toronto: Second Story Press, 1995.

Schwarz, Leo W., ed. *The Root and the Bough*. New York: Rinehart, 1949.

Sefer Hapartizanim Haihudim [The Jewish partisan book]. Merchavia, Israel: Sifriat Hapoalim, 1958.

Seidel, Rochelle G. "Women's Experiences during the Holocaust—New Books in Print." *Yad Vashem Studies* 28 (2000): 363–378.

Sendlerowa, Irena. "O DZIAŁALNOŚCI KÓŁ MŁODZIEŻY PRZY KOMITETACH DOMOWYCH W GETCIE WARSZAWSKIM."

BIULETYN ŻYDOWSKIEGO INSTYTUTU HISTORYCZNEGO 2, no. 118 (1981): 91–118.

Sereny, Gitta. *Into That Darkness: From Mercy Killing to Mass Murder.* New York: McGraw-Hill, 1974.

Shapiro, Robert Moses, ed. *Holocaust Chronicles: Individualizing the Holocaust through Diaries and Other Contemporaneous Personal Accounts.* Hoboken, N.J.: KTAV, 1999.

Shelley, Lore, ed. *The Union Kommando in Auschwitz.* New York: University Press of America, 1996.

Sierakowiak, Dawid. *The Diary of Dawid Sierakowiak: Five Notebooks from the Łódź Ghetto.* New York: Oxford University Press, 1996.

Silberman, Lena Küchler. *One Hundred Children.* New York, Doubleday, 1961.

Silten, R. Gabriele S. *Between Two Worlds: Autobiography of a Child Survivor of the Holocaust.* Santa Barbara, Calif.: Fithian Press, 1995.

Smolar, Hersh. *The Minsk Ghetto: Soviet Jewish Partisans against the Nazis.* New York: Holocaust Library, 1989.

Sofsky, Wolfgang. *The Order of Terror: The Concentration Camp.* Princeton: Princeton University Press, 1997.

Solomian-Loc, Fanny. *Woman Facing the Gallows.* Amherst, Mass.: Word Pro, 1981.

Steinberg, Lucien. *Not as a Lamb.* Farnborough, Hants: Heath, 1970.

Steinberg, Paul, *Speak You Also.* New York: Henry Holt, 1996.

Stephenson, Jill. *Women in Nazi Society.* New York: Barnes and Noble, 1975.

Stoltzfus, Nathan. *Resistance of the Heart: Intermarriage and the Rosenstrasse Protest in Nazi Germany.* New York: Norton, 1996.

Streit, Christian. *Keine Kameraden Die Wehrmacht und Die Sowietischen Krieggefangenen, 1941–1945.* Stuttgart: Deutsche Verlag Anstalt, 1978.

Strobl, Ingrid. *Das Feld des Vergessens.* Berlin: Edition ID-Archiv, 1994.

Stroop Report, The: A Facsimile Edition and Translation of the Official Nazi Report on the Destruction of the Warsaw Ghetto. New York: Pantheon, 1979.

Suhl, Yuri, ed. *They Fought Back: The Story of the Jewish Resistance in Nazi Europe.* New York: Schocken, 1967.

Świebocka, Teresa, ed. *Auschwitz: A History in Photographs.* Bloomington: Indiana University Press, 1993.

Szmaglewska, Seweryna. *Smoke over Birkenau.* New York: Henry Holt, 1947.

Szmajzner, Stanisław. *Hell in Sobibór: The Tragedy of a Jewish Adolescent.* New York: Edition Bloch, 1968.

Szwajger, Adina Blady. *I Remember Nothing More: The Warsaw Children's Hospital and the Jewish Resistance.* New York: Simon and Schuster, 1990.

Szyfman, Arnold. *Moja Tułaczka Wojenna* [My wartime wanderings]. Warsaw: Wydawnictwo Obrony Naraodowej, 1946.

Szyper, Claire Prowizur. *Conte à rebours.* Brussels: Louis Musin, 1979.

Tec, Nechama. "Between Two Worlds." *Journal of Literature and Belief* 18, no. 1 (1998): 15–26.

———. *Defiance: The Bielski Partisans*. New York: Oxford University Press, 1993.

———. *Dry Tears: The Story of a Lost Childhood*. New York: Oxford University Press, 1982.

———. *In the Lion's Den: The Life of Oswald Rufeisen*. New York: Oxford University Press, 1990.

———. "Jewish Resistance: Facts, Omissions, and Distortions." Occasional Paper, United States Holocaust Memorial Museum, Research Institute. Washington, D.C.: Research Institute of the United States Holocaust Memorial Museum, 1997.

———. "Methodological Considerations: Diaries and Oral History." *Holocaust and the Arts* 4, no. 1 (2000): 87–94.

———. "Sex Distinctions and Passing as Christians during the Holocaust." *Eastern European Quarterly* 18, no. 1 (March 1984): 113–123.

———. *When Light Pierced the Darkness*. New York: Oxford University Press 1986.

Tec, Nechama, and Daniel Weiss. "A Historical Injustice: The Case of Masha Bruskina." *Journal of Holocaust and Genocide Studies* 7, no. 3 (Winter 1997): 366–377.

Tedeschi, Guiliana. *There Is a Place on Earth: A Woman in Birkenau*. New York: Pantheon Books, 1992.

Temchin, Michael. *The Witch Doctor: Memoirs of a Partisan*. New York: Holocaust Library, 1983.

Tenenbaum, Joseph. *Underground: The Story of a People*. New York: Philosophical Society, 1952.

Tillion, Germaine. *Ravensbrück: An Eyewitness Account of a Women's Concentration Camp*. New York: Anchor, 1975.

Todorov, Tzvetan. *Facing the Extreme*. New York: Henry Holt, 1996.

Troller, Norbert. *Theresienstadt: Hitler's Gift to the Jews*. Chapel Hill: University of North Carolina Press, 1991.

Trunk, Isaiah. *Jewish Responses to Nazi Persecution*. New York: Stein and Day, 1979.

———. *Judenrat*. New York: Stein and Day, 1977.

Valkhoff, Ziporah. *Leven in een Niet-Bestaan*. Utrecht: Stiehing ICODO, 1992.

Vrba, Rudolf. *I Cannot Forgive*. New York: Sidgwick and Jackson, 1964.

Waite, Robert G. L. *The Psychopathic God, Adolf Hitler*. New York: New American Library, 1978.

Weinstock, Eugene. *Beyond the Last Path*. New York: Paul and Gaer, 1947.

Wells, Leon. *The Janowska Road*. New York: Macmillan, 1963.

Wiesel, Elie. *Night*. New York: Avon, 1969.

Wiesenthal, Simon. *The Sunflower*. New York: Schocken, 1997.

Wołozhiński-Rubin, Sulia. *Against the Tide: The Story of an Unknown Partisan*. Jerusalem: Posner and Sons, 1980.

Wood, Thomas, and Stanisław M. Jankowski. *Karski: How One Man Tried to Stop the Holocaust*. New York: Wiley, 1994.

Wróński, Stanisław, and Maria Zwolakowa. *POLACY I ŻYDZI, 1939–1945* [Poles and Jews, 1939–1945]. Warszawa: Książka I Wiedza, 1971.

Wyman, David S. *The Abandonment of the Jews.* New York: Pantheon, 1984.

Yahil, Leni. *The Holocaust: The Fate of European Jewry.* New York: Oxford University Press, 1990.

Yehudei Yaar [Forest Jews, as told to Y. Ben Dor by Tuvia and Zus Bielski, Sonia and Lilka Bielski, and Abraham Viner]. Tel Aviv: Am Oved, 1946.

Zassenhaus, Hiltgunt. *Walls.* Boston: Beacon, 1974.

Zawodny, Janusz K. *Death in the Forest: The Story of the Katyn Forest Massacre.* New York: Hippocrene, 1988.

Ziemian, Joseph. *The Cigarette Sellers of Three Crosses Square.* Minneapolis: Lerner, 1975.

Ziemiński, Stanisław. "KARTKI DZIENNIKA NAUCZYCIELA W ŁUKOWIE Z OKRESU OKUPACJI HITLEROWSKIEJ" [Pages from the diary of a teacher from Łuków during the Hitlerite occupation]. *BIULETYN ŻYDOWSKIEGO INSTYTUTU HISTORYCZNEGO* 27 (1958): 105–112.

Zuccotti, Susan. *The Holocaust, the French, and the Jews.* New York: Basic, 1993.

———. *The Italians and the Holocaust.* New York: Basic, 1987.

Zuckerman, Yitzhak. *A Surplus of Memory.* Los Angeles: University of California Press, 1993.

Zyskind, Sara. *Stolen Years.* Minneapolis: Lerner, 1981.

Zywulska, Krystyna. *I Came Back.* New York: Roy, 1951.

Index

abortion, 60

Abramovicz, Dina, 191–192

active vs. passive fighting, 20–21

Adrejcwskie forests, 97

Ainsztein, Ruben
  Jewish Resistance in Nazi-Occupied Eastern Europe, 14
  They Fought Back, 14

AK. *See* Home Army

Akiva organization, 72, 172

Alexandrowicz, Julian
  bravery of, 102–103
  escape from Krakow ghetto, 103
  satisfaction in helping others, 106
  transfer to forest post, 105–106
  work with AK, 104, 105
  work with Żegota, 104

Allies
  disregard for Jewish condition, 4, 186
  promises to preserve Poland, 181
  support of underground movement, 5

Altman, Tosia
  escape from Mila 18 bunker, 177
  interrogation/death of, 179
  letter to Leah Silverstein, 166
  photo of, 179

work as courier, 178–179

work with ŻOB, 163, 179

American Jewish Joint Distribution Committee (JDC), 62, 177

Anielewicz, Mordechai
  comments on Warsaw ghetto uprising, 81
  dislike of Mila 18 suicides, 176–177
  as head of ŻOB, 72, 73–77, 163
  photo of, 74
  request of Hela Schupper, 174

anti-Jewish Aktions
  "Bloody Thursday," 206n11
  mass murders during, 86–87
  resistance efforts during, 79
  response of survivors, 87
  in Slonim ghetto, 88

anti-Semitism
  of AK, 104, 117–118
  among Soviet partisans, 107
  Antoni Zieleniewski's views of, 31
  of Nationalist Party, 42, 184
  in occupied territories, 27
  of Polish people, 52, 80
  of Polish prisoners, 124
  of Soviet partisans, 93, 98

anti-Semitism (*Cond.*)
    at Warsaw University, 23
    of Yasha Gusev, 99
    Zygmunt Rytel's comments on, 21
Arendt, Hannah
    "banality of evil," 11, 200n17
    Eichman in Jerusalem, 8
    interpretation of Jewish complicity,
        8–9, 11
    and Louis de Jong, 9
    omission of facts in research, 11
Armia Krajowa (AK). *See* Home Army
Armia Ludowa (AL), 45
arms
    accumulation as resistance, 13
    Allies rejection of requests for, 4
    an army without, 15
    difficulty in obtaining, 8, 13, 38,
        77, 84
    German attempts to collect, 91–92
    inadequate supply of, 11
    provided to Jewish partisans, 45
    underground obtains, 5, 169–170
    value placed on by partisans, 90–91
    in Warsaw uprising, 80
Artenstein, Zacharia, 82
Asch, Nathan, escape from deportation,
    68
Atlas, Icheskel, commitment to fighting
    Germans, 120–121
Auerswald, Heinz, food allocation
    orders, 64–65
Auschwitz
    Bela Chazan Yaari's imprisonment
        at, 123
    Birkenau *Bekleidungskammer*, 131–132
    brutal response to rebellion plans,
        133–135
    crematorium IV uprising, 135–138
    failure of rebellion plans, 132–133
    general rebellion plans at, 128–129
    initial inmates of, 17, 125
    investigation of Kommando uprising
        at, 137–142

    Jewish resistance in, 127–128,
        131–132
    Josef Mengele's visits to, 124
    lack of resistance cooperation in, 126
    Polish anti-Semites in, 124
    political prisoners in, 126
    subcamps at, 124
    underground movement, 14–15, 125
    willingness of new arrivals to
        cooperate, 130–131
Austrian resistance group, in
    Auschwitz, 126
autonomy
    connection with survival, 191–192
    search for through resistance, 10, 147

"banality of evil," Hannah Arendt's
    concept of, 11, 200n17
Baum, Bruno, support of Auschwitz
    rebellion plans, 131
Beatus, Frania, 179–180
Bekleidungskammer, 131–132
Belarus forests
    challenges of life in, 40
    flight of Russian soldiers into, 84
    women's lives in, 94–96, 207n17
Belorussia. *See* Belarus forests
Belzec death camp, 185
Bergen-Belsen concentration
    camp, 178
Berlinski, Hirsch, description of
    uprising, 77
Bernson and Bauman Hospital, 194–195
Bettelheim, Bruno, as promoter of
    Jewish complicity, 7–8, 11
Beutelager munitions center, 92, 96, 102
Bialystok ghetto, 123, 180
Bielanowicz, Mordechai, transfer to
    Auschwitz, 127
Bielski, Tuvia
    ethos of resistance by saving, 121
    extraordinary achievements of, 110
    meets Hersh Smolar, 113
    photo of, 111

Bielski Jewish partisan group, cooperative
    efforts of, 112–116
Birkenau
    See also Auschwitz
"blame the victim" accusations, 2
Blatt, Thomas "Tovi," 153
Bleichman, Ephraim (Frank)
    early life of, 32–34
    hides in Bratnik forest bunkers,
        37–39
    kills Polish collaborators, 39
    opposition to AK, 43
    Rather Die Fighting: A Memoir of
        World War II, 46
    refusal to be transferred, 34–36
Bloch, Zelo, resistance efforts of, 147
"Bloody Thursday," 206n11
Bobkov, Nikolai, 99
Borkomorowski, Tadeusz, 117–118, 184
Brande-Heller, Anna, 194–195
Bratnik forest bunkers, 37–38
Breslaw, Shmuel, work with ŻOB, 72, 163
Buchenwald, 7
Bukowska, Leokadia. See Silverstein,
    Leah
burials, availability in ghettos, 165

Central Committee of the Soviet
    Communist Party, 39
Central Welfare Council (RGO), 160
Chapajev brigade, 97–98
Chelmno, Poland, 153
Chernishev, Vassily. See Platon (General)
Chorazycki, Julian, work with
    underground, 149–150
Christian Labor Party, 25, 42, 183
Ciechanow, Poland, 127
Ciechanow Jewish resistance group,
    127–131
collaboration/collaborators
    attack on Ephraim (Frank)
        Bleichman, 38–39
    fear of reprisals, 3–4
    frequency of, 3

identification of Jews by, 27
Lithuanian collaborators, 90
reveal location of Bratnik forest
    bunkers, 38
sources of, 4
in Treblinka, 148
ŻOB elimination of, 72–73
compassion, providing balance with, 194
contagious diseases, penalty of death
    for, 58
cooperation
    acts of kindness as, 191
    of Jewish partisans and AK, 43
    as key to facilitating resistance, 4, 15,
        46, 130, 147
    in kibbutzim, 164
    preventing in ghettos, 54
    Zygmunt Rytel's reference to, 19–20
Council for Aid to Jews. See Żegota
couriers
    challenges of life as, 188
    Emanuel Ringelblum's praise of, 158
    Jan Karski as, 183
    lack of local support for, 5
    women as, 158, 163–164, 167–168,
        172, 178–179
crematorium IV
    resistance groups at, 128, 132–133
    uprising in, 135–138, 143
cultural activities, effect on Jewish
    morale, 58–59
Cylenski, Boris, 154
Cyrankiewicz, Jozef
    as Prime Minister of Poland, 130
    rebellion plans and, 129, 131, 133
    transfer to Auschwitz, 126
Czech resistance group, in Auschwitz,
    126
Czerniakow, Adam
    death by suicide, 67
    petition to halt ghetto construction,
        52
    photo of, 53
    wartime diary of, 8–9

Czestochowa, Poland, 165
Czuperska, Anna, 123

Dachau concentration camp, 7, 160
Davies, Norman, 106
day-to-day survival
    connection to autonomy, 191–192
    importance of solidarity to, 146–148,
        149, 196
    as resistance effort, 13, 191
    women's contribution to, 55–57, 63
Defiance: The Bielski Partisans (Tec), 110
de Jong, Louis, 9
Denmark, acceptance of Jewish
        immigrants, 22
deportation
    escape from, 68
    exemption from, 194–195
    from ghettos, 67–71
    of orphanages to Treblinka, 69–70
    physical resistance to, 68
    refusal of, 68
    response to, 72
    from Slonim ghetto, 74
    submission to, 68
    suicide as response, 67–68
    survivor shame in, 71–72, 76
Destruction of European Jews, The
        (Hilberg), 8–9
Detachment 51 unit, 93
disobedience, as resistance, 10
Dobroszycki, Lucjan, 15
document forging
    as resistance effort, 13
    Zygmunt Rytel's work in, 18–19
Dror organization, response to
        deportations, 72
Dubov, (Soviet General), 114
Dworzecki, Mark, 57–58

Eck, Nathan, attack on notion of
        passivity, 12, 200n19
Edelman, Mark, 195
education

admission quotas, 15
    in ghettos, 59
    prohibitions to, 58
    respect for, 56
    Warsaw University, 22–23
Eichman in Jerusalem (Arendt), 8
Eichman trial, Hannah Arendt's coverage
        of, 11
Einhorn, Ahron, refusal of deportation,
        68
Einsatzgruppen, cruelty of, 26
Eisenbach, Artur, view of Emanuel
        Ringelblum, 48
Eitani, Arieh, description of German
        kindness, 192–193
Endecja, anti-Semitism in, 23
Engel, David, on values of Jews in Polish
        ghettos, 49
Epstein, Thea, on work as a courier,
        158–159
European Jews, 1943 status of, 4

Feldhendler, Leon, 154–157
Ferstenberg, Lusia, 131
"Final Solution," origins of plan for, 26
Fiodorowicz, Yefim, 94, 107
food
    allocation amounts, 58, 64, 161–162,
        203n37
    denial of for "misdeeds," 87
    inadequate supply of, 51–52, 59–60
    for "missing Jews" of Skarzyn, 29–30
    sale of to Jewish, 33–34
    smuggling/sharing in ghettos, 65, 164
    women's role in providing, 55
forest life
    Adrejewskie forests, 97
    Belarus forests, 40, 84, 94–96, 207n17
    Bratnik forest, 37–39
    encirclement of forest partisans,
        114–117
    Katyn Forest mass graves, 181
    Lipiczanska forest, 120
    Nalibocka forest, 113, 114–115

Polish forests, 41–42, 43–44
Pruszkov forest, 90
Frank, Anne, 7–8
Frank, Martina, 144
Frank, Vincent, 144
Franz, Kurt, 151
Freiburg work camp, 193
Frenzel, Karl August, apology of, 153
Freund-Waldhorn, Dobka, 60–61
Friedman, Philip, research of, 13–14, 53
Frohlich, Julek, 60–61
Fryman, Chaim, assistance to ghetto
    escapees, 175
Fuchs, Herta (Ligeti), 138

Gaertner, Alla, 137, 138–139, 142
Galewski, Bernard, 152
Gancwajch, Abraham, 178
German Army
    acts of kindness by soldiers, 192–194
    attempts to collect arms, 91–92
    encirclement of forest partisans,
        114–117
    executions of POWs, 84
German occupation/oppression
    1943 increase in persecution, 28
    as cause of Polish migration, 25
    developing view of, 44
    discussion at World Zionist Congress
        (1939), 47
    elimination of Jewish leaders, 5
    goal of humiliation, 27
    inability of Jews to undermine, 10
    initial Jewish view of, 32
    lives of Jewish women under, 50
    persecution of Jewish men under,
        26, 50
    purpose of, 4, 6
    responses to, 3, 17, 28
German POW exchange scheme,
    177–178
Gestapo
    arrest of Bela Chazan Yaari, 123
    arrest of Jan Karski, 185

arrest of Jurek Wilner, 166
cruelty of, 187
discovery of Grojecka Street
    bunker, 83
Giterman, Itzchak, death in Warsaw
    ghetto, 66
GL. See Gwardia Ludowa
Glazar, Richard
    escape from Treblinka, 151–152
    experience at Treblinka, 146–147
    hesitation to be interviewed,
        144–145
    plans for Treblinka uprising,
        150–151
    time in Teresianstadt, 149
    on Treblinka culture, 149
Goebbels, Joseph, view of Polish, 26
Gomerski, Hubert, 155–156
Gradowski, Henryk, assistance to Jurek
    Wilner, 166
Graf, Judith, in Soviet partisan
    movement, 94–95
Grodno, Poland, Bela Chazan Yaari's
    visits to, 123
Grojecka Street bunker, 68, 83
guerrilla fighters, 205n1, 206n2
Gusev, Yasha, anti-Semitism of, 99
Gutman, Israel
    arrival in Auschwitz/Birkenau, 130
    fear of torture, 139
    publications on Warsaw Ghetto
        revolt, 14–15
    suspicion of Euen Koch, 138
    view of AK, 184
    view of crematorium IV uprising, 136
    view of Kommando revolt,
        143–144
    work in underground, 130–132
Guzik, David, 177
Gwardia Ludowa (GL)
    acceptance of Jewish fighters, 80
    development of Armia Ludowa, 45
    in Southeastern Poland, 44
    Zygmunt Rytel's work with, 22

Halperin, Ada, 137
Hashomer Hatzair
    Aba Kovner and, 6
    Ciechanow Jewish resistance group
        and, 127
    Israel Gutman as member, 130–131
    Leah Silverstein as member, 161, 162
    Mordechai Anielewicz and, 73
    response to deportations, 72
    Roza Robota as member, 134
    Tosia Altman as member, 178–179
    Yosef Kaplan as member, 165
Hehalutz organization, 122
Heinsolor, Miriam, work with ŻOB, 163
Henryk "Shmendryk." See Smolar, Hersh
Heydrich, Reinhard, order for
        Judenrat, 49
hiding places, in ghettos, 66–67, 76, 88, 90
Hilberg, Raoul
    The Destruction of European Jews, 8–9
    omission of facts in research, 10
    as promoter of Jewish complicity,
        11–12
Himmler, Heinrich, destruction of
        ghettos, 77–79
Hitler, Adolf, view of Polish, 26, 206n7
Holocaust scholars, moderate approach
        of, 15
Holocaust survivors, self-reported
        reasons for survival, 191
Holocaust trials, Richard Glazar's
        testimony at, 152–153
Holuj, Tadcuszkj, transfer to Auschwitz,
        126
Home Army (AK)
    anti-Semitic policies of, 42–43, 104,
        117–118
    Antoni Zieleniewski's work with, 30
    claim of Jewish assistance, 184
    cooperation with Jewish partisans, 43
    Jan Karski's work with, 183
    role in occupied Poland, 42
    support of Auschwitz rebellion plans,
        129, 131

view of ghetto uprising, 78–79
    Zygmunt Rytel's work with, 22
honorable death, 75, 81
Hotel Polski, 177
House Committees (Warsaw ghetto),
        mutual aid activities by, 62–63
humanitarian activities
    effect on Jewish morale, 58–59
    in Jewish ghettos, 57, 58, 62
    as resistance effort, 13

infanticide, 60–61, 207n17
International Military Tribunal (1945–46),
        lack of discussion of Jews, 2
Iser, Shmuel, 173
Izbica Lubelska, 185

Jagiellonian University, persecution of
        Polish elites at, 160
January Aktion, 79
JDC. See American Jewish Joint
        Distribution Committee
Jewish annihilation
    disbelief of, 6
    distinct stages of, 34–35, 47
    for German economic benefit, 21
    ghettos as first step, 52
    origins of plan for, 26
    renewed concentration on, 60
    world leaders' knowledge of, 186,
        187, 188
Jewish children, efforts to protect,
        60–62
Jewish civilians, routine murder by
        Germans, 26
Jewish complicity
    assertions of, 2
    assumption of, 15
    Hannah Arendt's interpretation of,
        8–9, 11
    New Year's Manifesto (1942) and, 7
Jewish concentration camp inmates, dire
        conditions faced by, 126–127
Jewish Councils. See Judenrat

Jewish Fighting Organization (ŻOB)
elimination of collaborators, 72–73
Mila 18 headquarters, 173
turning point for, 78
Warsaw headquarters, 172–173
in Warsaw uprising, 80
work in ghettos, 76–77
Jewish Fighting Union, in Warsaw
uprising, 80
Jewish ghettos
1947 death sentence mandate, 57
burials in, 165
conditions in, 52–53, 54, 58, 66,
161–162
deportations from, 54–55, 67–71
deportation survivor shame in,
71–72, 76
early rumors about, 52
effect on cooperation, 5
efforts to protect children in, 62–63
escape from, 175
as first step to Jewish annihilation, 52
food allocation in, 59–60, 64, 161
hiding places in, 66–67, 76
instability of, 54
labor system in, 59
manipulation of inmates in, 57–58
murder of "useless" Jews in, 60, 67
mutual aid activities in, 57, 58, 62
preventing food smuggling in, 65
prohibition against procreation, 60
survival in, 53–54
underground movement in, 62
women's contribution to survival in,
55–56
See also Warsaw ghetto
Jewish Historical Institute (Warsaw), 22
Jewish laborers, maltreatment/
disappearance of, 32–33
Jewish men
as chief enemies of Third Reich, 26, 50
effect of ghettos on, 55
Jewish Military Union (ŻZW), 72, 73, 77
Jewish passivity

arguments for, 11–12
assumption of, 1–2, 15
Isaiah Trunk's research on, 14
mythology of, 6
Nathan Eck's views on, 12
Jewish people
inattention to post-war fates of, 3
lack of post-war recognition as
victims, 2
as Nazi collaborators, 3, 4
Jewish refugees, in Soviet-occupied
Polish territories, 48–49, 50, 184
Jewish resistance
as armed struggle, 15, 148 149
in Auschwitz, 127
day-to-day survival as, 13
differing chronology of, 4
effect of topography on, 5
German retaliation to, 3
ingenious strategies of, 10, 15,
155–156
Israel Gutman's research on, 14–15
lack of post-war recognition of, 2
multiplicity of forms, 12–13
Raoul Hilberg, 9–10, 11–12
readiness of, 81
reality of, 190
Ruben Ainsztein's writings on, 14
search for cooperative parties, 4
Soviet aid to, 40
view of Jewish youth, 75
Jewish Resistance in Nazi Occupied Eastern
Europe (Ainsztein), 14
Jewish Scout organization, 160
Jewish "self-hatred," 200n19
Jewish underground
AK claim of assistance to, 184
disbelief in extermination, 6
leadership of, 5–6
organization of, 75–76
Jewish youth organizations, supply
of underground leadership,
5–6
Jodla detachment (AK), 105

Judenrat
    corruption among members, 53
    diverse reactions of, 14
    executions of, 50
    female members of, 50
    inmates' view of, 53
    Isaiah Trunk's research on, 14
    lack of support for underground, 5
    as Nazi instrument, 9
    order for establishment of, 49
    Phillip Friedman's research on, 13–14
    Raoul Hilberg and, 8–9
    refusal to accept ghetto conditions,
        58
    requirement to supply laborers,
        32–33, 59, 87
    role in ghettos, 62
July Aktion
    "Bloody Thursday," 206n11
    mass murders during, 86–87
    response of survivors, 87

Kahn, Eliahu, work in House
        Committee, 63
Kaminski, Yakov, 127, 128–129, 132
Kamionka, Poland, 32, 34
Kampel, Mania, 210n52
Kampfgruppe (Struggle Group), 128–129,
        131, 132–135
Kanal, Israel, attempted assassination by,
        72–73
Kaplan, Chaim, description of anti-
        Semitism, 27
Kaplan, Yosef, 72, 163, 165
Karski, Jan
    on assistance from non-Jews, 189–
        190
    call for common alliance, 184–185
    call to honor attempts to save Jews,
        186–187
    collection of evidence by, 185
    compassion for underground
        workers, 188
    death of, 190

denouncement of anti-Semitism, 185
    early life of, 182, 183
    informs world leaders of Jewish
        annihilation, 186, 187, 188
    insistence of world-wide Holocaust
        knowledge, 190
    photo of, 189
    as professor at Georgetown
        University, 188–189
    recognition by Yad Vashem, 183
    torture by Gestapo, 185
    work as courier, 163
    work in Washington, D.C., 188–189
Katyn Forest, mass graves in, 181
Kerski, Jan. See Karski, Jan
kibbutzim, in Warsaw ghetto, 162, 163
Kielar, Wieslaw
    description of Kommando uprising,
        142–143
    memoirs of, 210n50
    removal from Auschwitz, 143
Kielce, Poland, 105
Klener, Yankel, election as Commander,
        37
Klooga concentration camp, Julek
        Frohlich's death in, 61
Koch, Eugen, 138
Kolo, Poland, 22–23
Kommando revolt, 135–138, 142–144
Kommandos
    duties at Auschwitz, 127–128
    eagerness to fight, 132–134
    interrogation over rebellion plans, 137
    murder of, 133–134
    work with underground, 131–132
Kosovo, 93, 97
Kovner, Aba, 6
Kozibrodzka, Lea, 178
Kozilbrodzka, Lonka, 123
Krakow, Poland, persecution of Polish
        elites in, 160
Krakow ghetto, 102
Krakowski, Shmuel, on AK claim of
        assistance, 184

Krasnaja Gorka, 115–116
Kronika (historical text), 82
Krzemienice, Poland, 15
Kulka, Moshe, transfer to Auschwitz, 130
Kurland, Zvi, 152

Langbein, Hermann, 126, 133
Laniewska, Katarzyna, transfer to
    Auschwitz, 123
Lanzmann, Claude, 189
Latvia, Nazi collaboration in, 3
Laufer, Yehuda, 130–132
Lazower, Henryka, submission to
    deportation, 68
leadership, role in resistance, 5
Leczynski, Lolek, 22–24
Lejkin, Yakov, 65, 73
Lejtman, Shlomo, 154
Levi, Primo, opposition to "banality of
    evil," 11
Lida ghetto, 74, 110
Ligeti, Herta. *See* Fuchs, Herta
"like sheep to the slaughter," origin of
    phrase, 6
Lipiczanska forest, 120
Lithuania, Nazi collaboration in, 3, 90
Lodz ghetto
    construction of, 52
    liquidation of, 193
    "Mrs. Mokrska" House Committee
        work, 63–64
    Sara Zyskind's experience in, 56–57
Lubartow ghetto, transfer of Kamionka
    Jews to, 34–35
Lubetkin, Cywia, assistance to ghetto
    escapees, 175
Lubetkin, Zivia, work with ŻOB, 72, 163
Lublin ghetto, 74

Madejsker, Sonia, work as courier, 178
Mafia organizations, 149–150
Marchwinski, Jozef, 119
Margolis, Ala, 196
Margolis, Anna, 194–195

Markow, Fiodor, betrayal by, 119–120
Masarek, Rudi, resistance efforts of, 147
Mechlis, Michal, plan to save Bielski
    partisans, 115–116
Meed, Shlomo, 52, 56
Meed, Vladka
    chronic hunger of, 57
    identification card of, 168
    photo of, 51
    recollection of ghetto lecture, 58–59
    view of women's roles in ghettos,
        55–56
"menashke," 131
Mengele, Josef, 124
Miete, Kütner, 151
Mila 18
    collective suicide at, 81, 176–177
    German discovery of, 176
    relocation of ŻOB headquarters to,
        173
Milaszewski, Kasper, 115
Miller, Stefan, death by suicide, 68
Minsk ghetto, 109
Mir ghetto, 89
"missing Jews" of Skarzyn, 29–30
money-for-passports exchange scheme,
    177–178
Monowitz. *See* Auschwitz
moral effects, of Jewish resistance, 10
Morczak, Wladyslaw, 68, 83
Moscow University, 24

Nalibocka forest, 113, 114–115
Narodowe Sily Zbrojne. *See* National
    Armed Forces
National Armed Forces (NSZ), 42, 115,
    157
Nationalist Party
    anti-Semitism of, 42, 184
    and Polish government-in-exile, 183
    and Polish underground, 25
Nazi General Government, Polish
    government-in-exile and, 183
New Year's Manifesto (1942), 6

Nirenska, Pola, 189
Nossig, Alfred, assassination of, 73
Novogrodek ghetto, 74
Nowolipki Street, Oneg Shabbat
    archives at, 71
NSZ. *See* National Armed Forces
Nuremberg Trials (1947–48), 2

Okinowo, 93
Oneg Shabbat, 49, 62, 66, 68, 70–71
orphanages, deportation to Treblinka,
    69–70
Oswiencin concentration camp. *See*
    Auschwitz

Pajewski, Theodor, 69
Pankiewicz, Tadeusz, 102, 207n20
Paris revolt (1944), 13
partisan movement
    effect on Jewish morale, 40
    formation of, 39
    inclusion of Jews in, 40
    Jewish partisans, 43–46
    value placed on professionals, 91,
        100, 206n12
    See also Bielski Jewish partisan group;
        Soviet partisans; Vilna Partisan
        Organization
passing (as non-Jews), 20
passive vs. active fighting, 20–21
Pawiak prison, 83, 123
Peasant Party, 25, 183
physicians
    need for, 96
    in partisan groups, 91, 100, 206n12
Pieczorski, Alexander, 155–156, 157
Pilecki, Witold, 125, 129, 130
Platon (Soviet General), 113–114, 118
"the pleasure of the Sabbath." *See* Oneg
    Shabbat
Poalei Zion Left party, 47, 107–108
Podgorze ghetto, 102
Podlesie, Poland, 28
Polesie, Poland, 107

Polish army, support of Polish
    underground, 25
Polish elites
    hiding in Jewish ghettos, 88–89
    Hitler's determination to destroy, 181
    imprisonment in Auschwitz, 124, 125
    as most threatened population, 17
    persecution by Einsatzgruppen, 26
    persecution in Krakow, 160
    refusal to heed warnings, 89
    removal during Aktions, 86–87
Polish Foreign Service, 183
Polish forests, 41–44
Polish government-in-exile
    basic principles of, 42, 183
    Jan Karski's view of, 183–184
    lack of concern for Jewish people, 184
    political movements included in,
        42, 183
    Stalin's abandonment of, 181
    use of former army officers, 25
Polish Jews, school admission quotas, 15
Polish officers
    murder by USSR, 181
    saved by underground, 160
    work with AK, 125
Polish Peasant Party, 42
Polish Socialist Party (PPS)
    Antoni Zieleniewski as member, 22
    response to deportations, 72
    support of Żegota, 20
    Zygmunt Rytel as member of, 16–19
Polish underground
    protection of former Polish officers, 25
    summer of 1943 success of, 27
    varied political ties of, 126
    work of Jan Karski in, 182–183
Polish Workers Party (PPR), cooperation
    with Jewish partisans, 44–45
Polska Partia Robotnicza. *See* Polish
    Workers Party
Polska Partia Socjalistyczna. *See* Polish
    Socialist Party
Ponary, mass shootings at, 166

Ponmarenko, Pantileimon, 39
Porat, Dina, on Kovner statement, 6–7
PPR. *See* Polish Workers Party
PPS. *See* Polish Socialist Party
prisoners of war (POWs), execution by
    German Army, 84
procreation prohibition, 60–61
Pruszkov forest, 90

Rabinowicz, Hannah, 110–112
Rada Główna Opiekużcza. *See* Central
    Welfare Council
Radom, 105
*Rather Die Fighting: A Memoir of World
    War II* (Bleichman), 46
Raysko, Poland, 136
religious observances, prohibitions to, 58
Remba, Nachum, 69–70
Resilience and Courage (Tec), 194
resilience vs. resistance, 4, 15
resistance
    conditions necessary for, 4
    definition of, 4, 13
    importance of strategic base to, 5
    multiplicity of forms, 12–13, 196
    need for cooperation in, 4, 130
resistance groups. *See* Jewish resistance
Reuerstin, Regina, 175
RGO. *See* Central Welfare Council
Ribbentrop-Molotov Agreement, Stalin's
    pressure to honor, 41
Ringelblum, Emanuel
    anguish over fate of Jewish children,
        61–62
    arrest/execution of, 83
    contribution to history by, 49, 70–71,
        72, 82–83, 83
    dedication/self-sacrifice of, 48
    description of women's lives, 50–51
    disappearance of, 68
    on food allocation/smuggling, 64–65
    photo of, 48
    praise of couriers, 158
    refusal to flee German invasion, 47–49

return to Grojecka Street bunker, 69
study of Jewish women, 62–63
on tragic deaths in ghetto, 65–66
tribute to ghetto activists, 63
view of Adam Czerniakow, 68
view of Jewish history, 14
Ringelblum, Judyta, 68, 83
Ringelblum, Uri, 68, 83
Rizyszczyce, Poland, 122
Robota, Roza
    execution of, 142
    photos of, 127, 134
    refusal to divulge information, 138,
        139, 140–141
    speaks to Zippi Spitzer-Tichauer,
        140–141
    work with underground, 131–132,
        134–135, 140–141
Roniker, Jerzy, 160
Rosblat, Lutek, assistance to ghetto
    escapees, 175
Rotkopf, Tonia, description of German
    kindness, 193–194
Rotman, Lutek, 172, 174
Rotman, Maria, 172, 175
Rozycka, Marylka, work as courier, 180
Rudashevski, Yitskhok, 54–55, 59
Rufeisen, Oswald, 89
Russian casualties, in German
    captivity, 39
Rytel, Zygmunt
    on anti-Semitism, 21–22
    determination to fight suffering, 18
    early life of, 15–17
    imprisonment in Auschwitz, 17–18
    on motivation of youth, 21
    murder of brother by German
        officer, 17–18
    photo of (1966), 19
    recognition by Yad Vashem, 17
    view of Jews he helped, 18
    work in films, 20
    work with underground, 18–19,
        20, 22

schools. *See* education

Schupper, Hela
    early life of, 171–172
    escape from Warsaw ghetto, 174–176
    photo of, 171
    reaction to Mila 18 suicides, 177
    relationship with Lutek Rotman, 172
    survival of, 178
    work as courier, 172

Schutzstaffel (SS)
    July 1942 Aktion, 86
    removal of Polish elites by, 89, 181
    routine murder of Jewish civilians
      by, 26

Secret Arms Organization (TOB), 154

self-reliance, role in resilience, 4

Serafinski, Tomasz. *See* Pilecki, Witold

Sereny, Gitta, 145

"service givers," 95

Shefet, Zvi
    acceptance of father's work
      assignments, 87
    anti-Semitism endured by, 107
    break-up of family unit, 92–93
    description of Slonim takeover,
      85–86
    and partisan groups, 91–92, 93, 107
    refusal to leave family, 87–88

Shefet family
    attempts to join partisan group, 91–92
    division in, 92–93
    escape from Slonim ghetto, 90–91
    losses in Aktions, 88

Shoah (film), Jan Karski's view of, 189

Sicherheitsdienst (SD), murder of Jewish
    civilians by, 26

Sikorski , Wladyslaw, 100–102, 104,
    207n18

Silverstein, Leah
    description of starvation, 161–162,
      164–165
    description of Warsaw ghetto, 161
    early life of, 159
    life on the Aryan side, 167–168

    obtains guns for underground,
      169–170
    photo of, 161
    relationship with Jurek Wilner,
      165–166
    watches Warsaw ghetto burning, 167
    work as courier, 170–171

Skarzyn, Poland, "missing Jews" of, 28–29

Skarzysko Kamienna, Poland, 170

Slapak, Cecylia, study of Jewish women,
    62–63

Slonim, Poland, 85–87

Slonim ghetto
    burning of, 90
    deportations from, 74
    hiding places in, 88, 90
    Mina Volkowisky in, 95–97
    SS Aktion in, 88

Smolar, Hersh
    aids other escapees, 110
    assists Bielski partisans, 113–114
    as devout communist, 107–108
    discusses partisan duties, 118–119
    escape from Minsk ghetto, 109–110
    establishes Minsk underground, 109
    imprisonment in Poland, 108
    meets Tuvia Bielski, 113
    move to Kiev, 108
    refusal to leave Poland, 109
    saved by General Platon, 113
    view of Atlas Icheskel, 121
    view of Tuvia Bielski, 121

Sobibor concentration camp
    number of deaths at, 153
    solidarity in, 153–154
    Soviet POWs at, 154–155
    underground movement at, 154

Socialist Party, 25, 42, 183

Soldatenheimat, 168

solidarity
    importance in survival, 146–148,
      149, 196
    in Sobibor camp, 153–154

Sonderkommandos. *See* Kommandos

Soviet Army
    approach to Auschwitz, 133
    collapse of divisions in, 39
    ethnic makeup of, 84
    failure to hold Slonim, 85–86
Soviet-German friendship treaty, 39
Soviet-German war
    collapse of Red Army divisions, 39, 84
    German defeat at Stalingrad, 41
Soviet-occupied Polish territories, as
        haven for Jews, 48–49, 50, 184
Soviet partisan movement
    anti-Semitism in, 93, 98, 107
    cruelty of, 99–100
    ethnic tolerance of, 41
    infanticide in, 207n17
    lack of attacks upon Germans by, 85
    motivation of, 84–85
    Stalin's politicizing of, 41
    view of ghetto escapees, 85
    women's participation in, 94–95
Soviet-Polish cooperation, 106, 117
Soviet Union
    attempts to organize partisans, 85
    denial of Polish officers murders, 181
    refusal of Zionist entry, 122
Spitzer-Tichauer, Helen (Zippi), work
        with underground, 139–141
SS. See Schutzstaffel
Stalin, political agenda of, 41, 181–182
Stangl, Franz, 145
Starachowice, Poland, 171
Star of David, wearing of, 27, 87
starvation, Leah Silverstein's description
        of, 161–162, 164–165. see also food
Story of a Secret State (Karski), 188
Stroop, Jurgen, 81, 205n86
Sudouwicz, Israel, 152
suicide
    as alternative to capture, 173
    euthanasia of Warsaw orphans, 195
    as honorable death, 81
    as response to deportation, 67–68
survivors, attitude of "rich" vs. "poor," 18

Swietokrzycka Street, Oneg Shabbat
        archives at, 71
Szafirstein, Regina, 137, 138–139, 142
Szczara River, 85
Szengut, Tuwia (Tadek), 168–169
Szerynski, Jozef, 72–73, 73
Szternfeld, 70
Szwajger, Adina, 194–196

Tarnow underground, 169
Tec, Nechama
    Defiance: The Bielski Partisans, 110
    meeting with Antoni Zieleniewski,
        22–31
    meeting with Ephraim Bleichman,
        32–46
    meeting with Richard Glazar, 144–145
    meeting with Tuvia Bielski, 110
    meeting with Zygmunt Rytel, 16–22
    Resilience and Courage, 194
Tennenbaum, Mordechai, 123
Teresianstadt ghetto, 149
They Fought Back (Ainsztein), 14
TOB. See Secret Arms Organization
Tolman-Zlotnicki, Hadassah, 131
topography, effect on resistance efforts, 5
Trap with a Green Fence, The (Glazar), 145
Trawinki concentration camp, 68–69
Treblinka
    deportations from Warsaw ghetto to,
        67–69
    Julian Chorazycki's work in, 150
    prisoner escape from, 156–157
    rebellion at, 144–145, 147, 151–152,
        155–157
    Richard Glazar's memories of,
        145–149
Trunk, Isaiah, research on the Judenrat,
        14

Umschlag Platz, 68
underground movement
    in ghettos, 62
    inexperience of commanders, 5–6

underground movement (*Cond.*)
Julian Chorazycki's work in, 150
leadership in, 5
new definition of, 12–13
Zygmunt Rytel's work in, 20
Under the Eagle pharmacy, 102
Unger, Karl
escape from Treblinka, 151–152
life at Treblinka, 146
work with underground, 150
Union factory, 131
Union of Armed Struggle (ZWZ), 125
United States
power shift created by, 181
pressure to honor Ribbentrop-
Moltov Agreement, 41
See also Allies
uprisings, as suicidal gestures, 13
urban national resistance, focus of, 12–13

Vassia, Dziadzia, 107
Vilna ghetto
1942 New Year's Manifesto, 6
fighters join Markow brigade,
119–120
final liquidation of, 191–192
manipulation of inmates in, 57–58
murder of inmates, 74
prohibition against procreation in,
60–61
Sonia Madejsker's work in, 178
Tosia Altman's work in, 178
Yitskhok Rudashevski's transfer to,
54–55
Vilna Partisan Organization (FPO), 6,
76–77
Volkowisky, Mina
attempts to leave ghetto, 96–97
befriended by Nikolai Bobkov, 99
betrayal by "friend," 98–99, 100
invitation from General Sikorski,
100–102
joins Soviet partisans, 98
relocation to Slonim ghetto, 96

reunites with husband, 100
separated from husband, 97–98
Voroshilov, Marshal Clement
Efremovich, 39

Wachalska, Stanislawa. *See* Meed,
Vladka
Wagner, Gustav, 155–156
Wajcblum, Ester, 137, 138–139, 142
Warsaw, Poland
food shortages in, 51–52
Jewish Historical Institute, 22
refugees' arrival in, 47
Warsaw ghetto
Bernson and Bauman Hospital,
194–195
conditions in, 65, 161–163
construction of, 52
converted Jews in, 72–73
deportations to Treblinka, 67–69
escape from, 175
Frania Beatus' work in, 179–180
Itzchak Giterman's death in, 66
orphan euthanasia at, 195
planned destruction of, 79
sealing of, 160–161
Warsaw ghetto uprising
April 1943, 78, 79–80
August 1944, 13, 106
Himmler's destruction command,
77–78, 79
Israel Gutman's research on, 14–15
Yitzhak Zuckerman's view of, 10–11
Warsaw University, attacks on Jewish
students at, 23
Wehrmacht
Hitler's view of, 181
and Slonim ghetto Aktion, 88
Wengrover, Jehuda, 177
White Rose, 118
Wieliczka, Poland, 50
Wilczynska, Stefania, 70
Wilner, Jurek (Arieh)
arrest and torture of, 166

relationship with Leah Silverstein,
165–166, 167
suicide of, 176
work with Jewish underground, 72, 76
Wirths, Eduard, 133
Wlodawa, Poland, 151, 153
Wolski, Mieczyslaw, arrest/execution of, 83
women
in Auschwitz munitions factory, 131
carrying arms, 94
conditions endured by, 50–51, 62–63,
95–96, 207n17
contribution to ghetto survival,
55–57, 63
physical resistance to deportation, 68
prohibition against procreation, 60
serving on Judenrat, 50
in Soviet partisan movement, 41, 94
work as couriers, 158, 163–164,
167–168, 172, 178–179
work in German factories, 193–194
work in kibbutz, 164
World Zionist Congress (1939), 47

Yaari, Bela Chazan, 122–124
Yad Vashem
historian at, 6
recognition of Jan Karski, 183
recognition of Zygmut Rytel, 17

Zabludowicz, Noah
resistance work of, 132
transfer to Auschwitz, 127
visits Roza Robota's cell, 141–142
Zamenhof Street, 77
Zarki farm (Zionist experiment), 165
Żegota
Julian Alexandrowicz's work with, 104

Zygmunt Rytel's work in, 20
Zieleniewski, Antoni
commissioned as Polish officer, 24
decision to help "missing Jews,"
29–30
delay in revealing wartime activities,
31
early life of, 22
escape to Podlesie, 28
joins PPS, 22
relationship with Lolek Leczynski,
22–24
views on anti-Semitism, 31
witnesses anti-Semitism as Warsaw
University, 23–24
work with Home Army, 30
ŻOB. See Jewish Fighting Organization
Zoliborz neighborhood (Warsaw), 18–19
Zuckerman, Antek, 72, 174, 176
Zuckerman, Yitzhak
armed confrontation by, 77
description of armed confrontation,
82
photo of, 78
Warsaw ghetto uprising
commemoration, 10–11
work with Frania Beatus, 186
Zwiazek Walki Zbrojncj. See Union of
Armed Struggle
ZWZ. See Union of Armed Struggle
Żydowska Organizacja Bojowa. See
Jewish Fighting Organization
Żydowski Zwiᵃzek Wojskowy. See Jewish
Military Union
Zygielbojm, Szmuel, 186
Zyskind, Sara, experience in Lodz
ghetto, 56–57
ŻZW. See Jewish Military Union